Praise for *Walking the Invisible*

'Stewart's passion and enthusiasm for the Brontës' lives
and work and the landscape that shaped them is palpable
and infectious. If you weren't struck […] with "Brontë
Fever" before, after reading this you may well be.'
Yorkshire Post

'An essential co[…]
Lancashire[…]

'A terrific tribute to the B[…]
landscapes that shaped […]
Guardian

'[An] imaginative and elegant trek through
the landscape of the Brontës.'
Grazia

'An authoritative, inspirational and often humorous
companion to a great Yorkshire family and the landscape that
shaped them – and many others – throughout history.'
Yorkshire Life

'Literary but unpretentious.'
My Weekly

Michael Stewart is Head of Creative Writing at the University of Huddersfield, and author of *Ill Will*, as well as three other novels and a selection of poetry. His debut novel, *King Crow*, won the Not the Booker Prize in 2011.

Michael is also the creator of the Brontë Stones project – four monumental stones situated in the landscapes between the birthplace of the Brontës in Thornton and the Parsonage in Haworth – inscribed with poems by Kate Bush, Carol Ann Duffy, Jeannette Winterson and Jackie Kay.

MICHAEL STEWART
with maps by Christopher Goddard

WALKING
THE
INVISIBLE

Following in
the Brontës' Footsteps

ONE PLACE. MANY STORIES

HQ
An imprint of HarperCollins*Publishers* Ltd
1 London Bridge Street
London SE1 9GF

www.harpercollins.co.uk

HarperCollins*Publishers*
1st Floor, Watermarque Building, Ringsend Road
Dublin 4, Ireland

This edition 2022

1
First published in Great Britain by
HQ, an imprint of HarperCollins*Publishers* Ltd 2021

ISBN: 9780008430221

MIX
Paper from
responsible sources
FSC™ C007454

This book is produced from independently certified FSC™ paper
to ensure responsible forest management.

For more information visit: www.harpercollins.co.uk/green

This book is set in 11/15.5 pt. Adobe Garamond Pro by Type-it AS, Norway

Printed and Bound in the UK using 100% Renewable Electricity at
CPI Group (UK) Ltd, Croydon, CR0 4YY

For Kate

CONTENTS

'I'll walk where my own nature would be leading: it vexes me to choose another guide.'

EMILY BRONTË

INTRODUCTION

BRONTË FEVER

I wasn't born with a Brontë obsession. As far as I know, it is not a congenital condition. But these past few years I've been struck with Brontë Fever. I'm not the only one. Over the course of my fanaticism, I've met others. Some of them appear quite normal. There are no flags or bells. They walk amongst us.

I was born and brought up in Salford, a city within a city, and went to a failing comprehensive that also 'educated' most of The Happy Mondays. It was a school built on a marsh and made of plasterboard. There were head- and boot-shaped holes in the walls, where the pupils had found an outlet for their ardour. It was sinking. Actually sinking. The science labs were on the same level as the all-weather pitch. I was in the bottom class for English and was not allowed to study the 'classics'. Instead, we were given books that were written in a simple style, avoiding big words and grammatical complexity. They often had a glossary at the back. So, I never encountered the work of the Brontës. We were told we weren't bright enough.

Shortly after I left school, the building was demolished and the site flattened. At sixteen, I started work in a factory in an area of Manchester called Newton Heath. Thousands of people worked there, mostly men, though few of them lived to see retirement. I used to visit my local library every Saturday morning and take out three books: two fiction and one non-fiction. During the bus journey to and from work, I'd read them. One of those books was *Wuthering Heights*. I already knew some of the story. I'd watched the 1939 MGM adaptation with my mother when I was a kid, and I'd come across the characters of Cathy and Heathcliff even earlier, in Kate Bush's debut single. But the novel was very different. At first, I wasn't even sure if I liked it. I found it a bit of a slog to begin with, but I persisted. Slowly the story and characters drew me in. Somehow, they took hold of me and wouldn't let go.

Gradually, over the years, my obsession grew. I learnt that Emily was part of a family that had published some of the best-known works in Victorian literature. After reading Emily Brontë's *Wuthering Heights*, her only published novel, I then went on to read the work of her sisters. Charlotte's first published novel *Jane Eyre*, then her second *Shirley* and then her final book *Villette*. I read Anne's *Agnes Grey* and *The Tenant of Wildfell Hall*. I read their poems and their letters, everything they had written, including the things that weren't published in their own lifetimes. I read the work of their brother Branwell and their father Patrick. I moved to Thornton, a village in West Yorkshire and the birthplace of the Brontës. My interest in their literary work began to extend to their lives. I wanted to discover them for myself. I started to hunt them down. Beginning in Thornton, I imagined Patrick Brontë pacing the same streets as me. A curate in his late thirties, he moved here with his family from Hartshead in 1815. He would have walked right past my door every day. I wondered what life was like for him and his family then. I read the stories he wrote during his time in the village.

I read what others had written about them. I was curious to find out myself to what extent Emily was the wild one, Branwell the drunk, Anne overlooked and Charlotte the ambitious one, driving the rest of them on. I soon found that these myths, although based on some truth, were far from the reality, which was just as compelling to me. I joined the Brontë Society and started to pore over the essays in their journal, *Brontë Studies*. But the one book I returned to again and again was *Wuthering Heights*. I became fixated on the two gaping holes in the narrative: where had Heathcliff come from? And where did he go during the missing years? And I started to write a novel that would fill in the gaps. That novel became *Ill Will: The Untold Story of Heathcliff*, and during my research I recreated the walk that Cathy's father, Mr Earnshaw, takes on foot, from Yorkshire to Liverpool. I also spent many hours walking the moors around Haworth, writing the book as I tromped across the landscape, talking into a Dictaphone that I always carried in my pocket.

My quest to find the landscapes that inspired the Brontës had begun. I went to Broughton-in-Furness, where it was claimed Branwell Brontë sired an illegitimate child, and from there to Thorpe Green, where he was dismissed from his role as a tutor for having an affair with his employer's wife. I went to Dentdale and Law Hill in search of the origin myths behind Emily Brontë's only published novel. I visited North Lees Hall in Hathersage to discover the inspiration for Charlotte Brontë's *Jane Eyre*. I retraced Anne Brontë's last days in Scarborough and became captivated by the story of the Luddites in Charlotte's *Shirley* and how this contrasted with what the movement was like in real life. In short, I travelled all over the north of England in search of their lives and landscapes. In doing so, I realised how important it was to encourage other people to visit these places too. I wanted people to engage not just with their lives and literary works, but with the places that had inspired them.

Up on the moors, I had a profound understanding of the texts. I started to connect with their writings in a visceral way. It was like I had discovered another layer, and I sank further in. The words and the moors were one.

This led to my Brontë Stones project. I realised their birthplace was overlooked in contrast to the parsonage in Haworth where they moved in 1820, and I wanted to bring it to people's attention and connect it to Haworth. I came up with the idea of a literary trail, with stones along the way, to mark the bicentenaries of the siblings' births and encourage more people to experience the landscape that had inspired them. This was a landscape that had surrounded them and offered them a place of solace, but also at times must have felt like divine punishment, when the winds were wuthering and rain ripped through the sky like lead shot, with only shawls and hobnail boots to protect them from the relentless elements.

But the Brontë Stones wasn't conceived as a heritage enterprise. The project was also about celebrating female writers now. Alongside the Bradford Literature Festival, I commissioned the then Poet Laureate Carol Ann Duffy, the singer–songwriter Kate Bush, the Scottish Makar Jackie Kay and the award-winning novelist Jeanette Winterson to write poems that would be carved on each of the four stones. These four writers have pushed forward contemporary literature in the same ways the Brontë sisters opened up the possibilities of the Victorian novel and Victorian poetry. Bold, experimental, playful and dark, the four poems are a recognition of what is alive about our language today.

Pip Hall, the fine letter carver I worked with on the project, emphasised the power of the poems by taking her stylistic cue from the plentiful surrounding inscriptions, dating from the Brontës' era, in local streets and churchyards. 'In drawing the lettering and devising layout,' she said, 'I wanted the poems to look as if they belonged in their settings. The letter shapes at that time were typically broad, bold and serifed, with a distinct contrast between the vertical and horizontal strokes.' At other times, Pip responded to the encompassing landscape, drawing on curves to follow the gentle contours of meadow and moor.

Alongside this project, I devised four walks: one from Thornton to Haworth, and three circular walks for each of the sisters. Maps of these walks are available and included in this publication. They are drawn and designed by the cartographer Christopher Goddard, who makes beautiful bespoke illustrations, very much in the Wainwright tradition.

The 'Brontë Stones Walk' is a characterful nine-mile route over the hills from Thornton to Haworth that takes in all four of the Brontë Stones. It is a linear trek over the moors that also includes Ogden Kirk, Denholme Beck, Nan Scar and Oxenhope, following the Brontë Way in places but elsewhere offering interesting alternatives. The 'Charlotte Brontë Walk' is a simple four-mile walk around Thornton. It follows a short loop across the hills around Thornton, starting at St James's Church, opposite the Old Bell Chapel, where Patrick Brontë worked. It also takes in Thornton Hall, Hanging Fall, Thornton Viaduct and the Brontës' birthplace, and has some great views over the valley. The 'Anne Brontë Walk' is a varied seven-mile ramble around the lush valleys north of Haworth, taking in Newsholme Dean, the Worth Valley and Holden Park. It follows the 'Railway Children Walk' to begin with, before climbing through

Oakworth and Holden Park to the charming hamlet of Newsholme and Pickles Hill, then dropping down to follow the River Worth back towards Haworth and Parson's Field, where the Anne Stone is placed. The 'Emily Brontë Walk' is, as you would expect, a strenuous and remote fifteen-mile yomp across the moors high above Oxenhope and Haworth, traversing the landscape that inspired *Wuthering Heights*. This is a hearty hike over the wild moorland Emily loved to roam. The route takes in Top Withins, Alcomden Stones and Ponden Hall, as well as various other beautiful sites.

I don't believe that anyone can really connect, can really understand, the Brontës' literary oeuvre without experiencing this uniquely bleak countryside, without experiencing the force of the hat-stealing winds, the earthy smell of the peat bogs, the haunting call of the curlew in the summer and the warning rattle of red grouse all year round. And the aim of this book is to link landscape with literature by emphasising the relationship of wandering with the writing of fiction. Both allow the mind a creative freedom. As Charlotte herself said, 'The idea of being authors was as natural to us as walking.'

This book immerses the reader in the lives and landscapes of the Brontë family. It is a walking book, but it is also a social and literary history of the North. I want you to walk with me but see through their eyes as I compare the times they lived in with the times we live in now. Let's start in the village where they were born.

1

'MY HAPPIEST DAYS' - PATRICK'S THORNTON

This story begins at the Old Bell Chapel on Thornton Road. Once the walls were strangled by green snakes of ivy, but a volunteer group ripped the limbs and sinews of vegetation, revealing these eerie remains: a broken bell tower, crumbling walls and medieval tombstones. This is where Patrick Brontë came to preach when he moved his family from Hartshead, West Yorkshire, in 1815. He brought his wife Maria and their two daughters, both still babies: Maria junior and Elizabeth. The younger daughter was named after Elizabeth Branwell, her mother's younger sister. The parish Patrick had just left was a similar size to that of Thornton, with about 5,000 parishioners. It was a promotion of sorts, as it was the first time he'd not been staying in paid lodgings. He had his own parsonage, purpose built a few years before. And he also had free time. It was during his stay in Thornton that he wrote his two most literary works, *The Cottage in the Woods* and *The Maid of Killarney*, so perhaps he was considering a life as a man of letters at this point.

In his new position, he had half the number of baptisms but the same number of funerals. The reason for this is something of a mystery, but I think the answer lies in the character of the village at that time. Thornton was a crucible of nonconformism: Congregationalists, Methodists, Baptists, English Presbyterians and others. Look around Thornton now and you will see that it is still full of illicit burial grounds that go back to this time: the sinners, the suicides and the unbaptised.

He came to a church that was in a state of disrepair. Commissioned by Sir Richard Tempest, who was knighted by King Henry VIII, it had over the years decayed, so that when Patrick took over, the floor of the church was gaping, and gaps in the stone flags allowed the putrid fumes of the dead, buried beneath, to seep into the main hall. The physical corruption of the chapel followed the example of Tempest's moral corruption. Despite holding the position of justice of the peace for the West Riding of Yorkshire, and later high sheriff of the entire county, allegations mounted of vice and violent behaviour, including murder. He died in jail in 1538.

Thornton Hall, where Richard Tempest lived, is the building behind the chapel, although it is hard to get a good view, as trees, high hedges and walls now obscure it. It's privately owned and something of a fortress, festooned with razor wire. The village stocks are now located in the grounds. But these trees were not there during the time of the Brontës, and it isn't hard to imagine a four-year-old Charlotte, peering out of the front bedroom window of the parsonage, which was on the edge of the village, to see the chapel where her father worked, and also the grand hall behind it, as there were no buildings between their home and the chapel.

There are many contenders for the halls that influenced Thornfield Hall, the home of Mr Rochester in *Jane Eyre*: Haddon Hall near Bakewell, North Lees Hall in Hathersage and High Sunderland Hall near Halifax (also an influence on Emily's *Wuthering Heights*), but I like to look closer to home. Surely the similarity of 'Thornton' and 'Thornfield' is no coincidence? Thornton Hall would have been Charlotte's first encounter with a three-storey medieval estate home, and a formative memory.

I want to get up above Thornton and see how the view has changed from Patrick's day, so I squeeze through a wrought-iron gate to the left of the hall, beneath overgrown hawthorn, and follow a downhill path that meanders south-east across a farmer's field to Pinch Beck. My dog, Wolfie, runs ahead of me. He's a border–springer cross but shares traits with neither breed. Not the OCD of the sheep dog or the ADHD of the spaniel. He's a blue merle, with a black-grey coat. He has one brown eye and one blue, a characteristic of the blue-merle genetic pattern. The view is green fields and drystone walls, with plenty of lush wooded areas. I join a walled lane by the site of the old corn mill, where the milling wheel has been set into the bridge over the beck, and follow Corn Mill Lane to its end. It's a dice with death as I cross Cockin Lane. Cars careen round a blind corner at sixty miles an hour, and there is no pavement. I join Low Lane, where the pavement leads past the site of Low Lane Pit (now Hole Bottom Beck Yard), turning right at an unsigned footpath beyond, where a path leads along the edge of the field from a rough stile. I reach a stone stoop and, as I do, see a flash of white, blue and pink – a jay, the most colourful of the corvids, as it dives for cover, making its rasping screech as it dips into the canopy of an oak tree. It's a good spot for birds here, and I regularly see a little owl perching on a bare branch further up. It's also worth looking upwards, where buzzards often rise on a gyre of warm air, and it is common to see a pair being mobbed by local crows, who find their presence alarming.

From the stone stoop the path climbs up Hanging Fall hill along the line of an old wall on the right. I stop at the top to take in the panoramic view across Thornton. With all this free time on his hands, as well as writing poems and stories, Patrick did a lot of walking. And not just for leisure. His parish spread from Thornton to encompass Allerton, Denholme, Wilsden, and Clayton, and he would have headed along this route as he made his way to his Clayton parishioners. He would have walked this area extensively, as he never owned a horse. The distance from Denholme to the centre of Clayton is more than five miles.

At the top of Hanging Fall, I turn right along a wall then skirt round the foot of Rabbit Hill, which is peppered with myriad rabbit holes. It looks like an upturned colander. Wolfie sniffs at the entrance to the burrows. He has caught a few in the past, usually the sick or the lame, but there is nothing for him today. I walk along the top of a judd wall, a type of retaining wall that is built from a quarry's waste material then backfilled to form a level field. The gorse is on fire with yellow flowers. It's early September and the air is crisp. The earth is firm underfoot.

In 1816, Patrick and Maria's family expanded with the arrival of Charlotte. Branwell followed in 1817, then Emily in 1818 and finally Anne in 1820. I think we can conclude from this that Patrick and Maria were fond of each other – Maria's nickname for her husband was 'Saucy Pat'. Patrick wrote that their five years in Thornton were the happiest of their lives. And you can see why. In April 1820, having outgrown the Thornton parsonage, Patrick moved the family to Haworth, and very soon things took a turn for the worst. Maria became very ill and died of uterine cancer in 1821. A few years later, the two eldest daughters died of consumption. Their time in

Thornton was the only sustained period that they were all together as a family. When they loaded their possessions onto those flat waggons and made the journey to Haworth, they must have thought they were travelling to a better future, not to one of tragedy.

Charlotte was four years old when they moved and would have had a living memory of the village. But that's not to say that the other children wouldn't have been familiar with Thornton's streets and the surrounding countryside. When Maria died, the family spent some time at the Firths' on Lower Kipping Lane. Dr John Scholefield Firth was the local physician who befriended the Brontës when they first moved to the village.

The heather is blooming and the bilberry bushes are flecked with blue berries. At the end of the judd wall, I follow the path to a fine viewpoint which overlooks The Towers observatory and the chimney of the adjacent fireclay works. A kestrel hovers over Hanging Fall, and it is here that I often see a falconer, training his hawks: the strong, sneaky winds are a good test for any juvenile raptor. During the summer months, it is a place where a local bagpiper stands, blasting out his discordant tunes.

From here you can see all the village clearly – the viaduct to the left and the remains of Prospect Mills in front, which burnt down so spectacularly in 2016. The fire reached up high above the horizon, and the ensuing conflagration resembled the gates of hell in a Hieronymus Bosch painting. But today the view is peaceful, and the air is still, and I imagine Patrick standing here, the view of the village less extensive, and the surrounding countryside more dominant, composing one of his sermons, or working on a literary endeavour. Perhaps this view inspired *The Cottage in the Woods*? At over thirty pages long, it is one of his most ambitious narratives and starts with a strange statement about the 'sensual novelist and his admirer' being creatures of 'depraved appetites and sickly imaginations'.

The story itself is a didactic work about a young girl called Mary and her pious parents, devout Christians who lead a simple life of prayer and labour, and a classic rake by the name of William Bower, who falls for Mary and eventually finds God. There are clearly parallels with the Book of Job, and it is a rather dreary read. Nevertheless, there are some fine phrases with an ear for poetry, such as 'their hearts were sweetly tuned to every note of nature's music' and 'a pure spring of water, which issuing in a crystal rill, tinkled down to a rivulet in the vale'.

His next literary endeavour was even more ambitious. *The Maid of Killarney* is also a work of religious didacticism, but it is a more accomplished text. Over seventy pages, it is his most sustained piece of writing. It is episodic and uses some novelistic techniques, such as detailed description, character development and dialogue.

Two characters, Albion and Mr Mac Fursin, are discussing the beauty of the Irish countryside compared to England and Scotland when they come across a cabin and a fair maid nursing an old dying woman. The men want to know what the old lady has done to prepare for death. It becomes clear that she is a Catholic. They ask her what she thinks of the Pope – can he open heaven's gate? No, she replies, only Christ can do this. And what of the priest, the men want to know – can he forgive sins? Once again, the woman answers that only Christ can do this. But when they ask her if she wishes to die as a Roman Catholic, she answers yes. They are perplexed. The old lady dies, and Albion attends the wake, where he meets the father of the maid, who he learns is called Flora. Albion is seduced by Flora's harp playing, and the subsequent chapters are a series of ordeals that prove that Albion is pious enough to marry Flora, and Flora is pious enough to be his bride.

It is formulaic, and the moral is too obviously forced: that if you read your Bible and follow its instruction, and live a pious life, you will be rewarded with a fair maid. But it is also possible to see Patrick stretching his narrative abilities here, trying to go further than he had before. Had the family stayed in Thornton, perhaps he would have gone on to write a full-length novel. I wonder to what extent Patrick's writing inspired his children?

I bear right down some steps to reach Brow Lane on the edge of Clayton, turning right briefly down Brow Lane only as far as a narrow gate on the left opposite the drive to Fox Brow. A path leads down the fields and then along the wall beside the former railway line, before crossing it at a broad stone bridge. I head straight across the rough track beyond to reach a stile in the wall behind Station House. I follow a narrow track to the end then turn right on a path that soon becomes the Great Northern Railway Trail by the site of the former Queensbury Station, linking Bradford, Halifax and Keighley. The station was one of only a few in the country with platforms on each side of a triangular junction and was known as the Queensbury Triangle. The construction of the line began in 1874 and was completed in 1878. Ten men died building it. There is no memorial to mark their deaths. Passenger services were withdrawn in 1955, goods in 1961. It seems like a lot of blood, sweat and toil for such a short-lived service. If it were still in use, the village would be a very different place, another middle-class commuter town.

On the left is where the railway line went under a tunnel beneath Queensbury, coming out in Holmesfield. At one and a half miles, it is one of the longest tunnels in England. When Sustrans first opened the tunnel to examine it with a view to building a cycle- and footpath, they found the remains of a mighty cannabis farm. The tunnel was full of abandoned growing equipment, hydroponic systems and withered plants, stripped of their psychotropic buds. It was a canny spot, so deep beneath Queensbury that even heat-detecting helicopters couldn't find it, and the sounds of the petrol generators were muffled by tonnes of earth and rock. Despite talk of reopening the tunnel, it still remains boarded up, and pitch-black anti-vandalism paint festoons the entrance.

Further along the path is the gravestone of John Dalby. The headstone is sited here for rather obscure reasons. John Dalby worked for the rival Midland Railway for more than fifty years, first as a clerk and later as a canvasser espousing the virtues of his company over the Great Northern. So, its location here is more the product of accident than intent. Dalby was born in Clayton in 1817 (he was the same age as Branwell, who also worked for some time in the railway industry, although his stint was to be brief and disastrous) and was working as a porter when he married a local farmer's daughter, Ann Greenwood, in 1848 (the year of Emily and Branwell's deaths). He died three years after her in 1893 and was buried in St John's Church in Clayton, but some of the gravestones were subsequently dumped here. Most were disposed of, but perhaps John's lay hidden under the brambles until it was rescued and resurrected. In any case, situated by a leafy glade and moss-covered stones, it is a magical place to sit and rest a while.

Beyond Ashby House, I head straight across Cockin Lane and along the trail as it continues above High Birk Beck. I come to Headley Lane, with Upper Headley Hall to the left. A grade I listed building from the reign of Elizabeth I, it is now a working farm-house. Built by the Midgley family, who were Lords of the manor of Headley, it remains remarkably unaltered. The porch is dated 1604. From here, I could continue to follow the Great Northern Trail over Thornton Viaduct, but instead I bear right along an ancient stone-flagged packhorse route that connects Headley Hall to Kipping House, where the Firths lived. This is the route that Patrick would have taken between these two esteemed establishments. Next to Kipping House was Kipping Barn, which was a meeting place for nonconformists. Like Patrick, John Scholefield Firth was an evangelical, so both men would no doubt have been sympathetic to the nonconformist cause.

Maria and Patrick became good friends with Elizabeth Firth, John Firth's only daughter, who was eighteen at the time, just a few years younger than Maria. Elizabeth had just lost her mother, who had been thrown into the road when her gig was overturned. The women would regularly meet for afternoon tea, and Elizabeth, who kept a diary of these meetings, became godmother to Elizabeth Brontë in 1815 and to Anne in 1820, and was also proxy godmother to Charlotte. When Maria died in 1821, the children stayed with the Firths, and Patrick later proposed marriage to Elizabeth. She turned him down, but they remained friends throughout their lives. She records in her diary a picnic with Patrick at local beauty spot Ogden Kirk in 1818 (the year Emily was born), where the Emily Stone is now carved.

Kipping House is now privately owned. I was invited to view it a few years ago, when the then owner had restored much of the original features. Regency carved-mahogany furniture and authentic wall decorations made it possible to get a sense of how it would have been in the early nineteenth century, with a large, light-filled main room facing south over an extensive garden that rolled down to the beck.

As I re-enter the village and make my way along Thornton Road up across the small area of parkland known locally as Ebor, I arrive at the Black Horse pub. It's late afternoon and the sun is way past the yardarm. The Black Horse is the only extant tavern from the time of the Brontës. When the family moved to the village in 1815, there were six drinking establishments. Now there are only three. Public houses are closing at an alarming rate across the country.

Inside the pub it is dark and cool. I pay for a drink and sit in a corner. I remember my first visit, after my wife Lisa and I had viewed the house we were buying. The pub had been much busier then. I'd got chatting with a bloke at the bar and had bought him a lager. I found out later that he'd just got out of Armley Prison. Done six months for shooting up the village taxi rank after a night out. He'd got a taxi home and then realised that his wallet was missing, so he'd gone back to the rank and argued that it must be in the cab. He was told there was no wallet. Not satisfied with this answer, and feeling cheated, he had gone home, dug up his father's gun, which was buried in the back garden, returned once more to the taxi rank and shot the place up. Afterwards, sitting on his sofa, reflecting on the incident as he waited for the police to come and arrest him, he had discovered his wallet down the back of the seat. It had been there all along.

This is a pub where anything can happen. It's always been welcoming, a friendly place, but not without incident. I've often wondered what specific qualities it has that have made it last the test of time, when all the other pubs are long gone? It can't be the bricks and mortar, which are unremarkable. I look around at the clientele – hard lives and hard livers, faces like unmade beds – and wonder how different they are from the drinkers who came here in the early nineteenth century, the labourers and tradesmen, still in their work clobber. Hewn from the same rock, drawn from the same waters, they know how to enjoy themselves in the here and now. The clothes have changed but not the lines on their faces or their attitudes. Perhaps it is just its location, positioned centrally in the village so that everything else seems to spoke outwards from it. It was here where the village stocks were originally positioned, and Patrick must have seen thieves, drunks, the blasphemers and adulterers, fastened to the boards, receiving their rough punishment. He was a life-long opponent of alcohol.

I finish my drink. Outside the air is heavy with the pungent stench of heat-treated animal waste from the fat refinery up the hill. I think about the maggot farms that were around in the nineteenth century and played an important part in the local economy here. Perhaps the air that Patrick and his family breathed was just as foul. The local mills and factories, belching out toxic smoke, were newly built. Now they have been bulldozed, blazed or stand derelict. I walk past Kipping School, built by Congregationalists in 1819, and eventually arrive at my destination: the birthplace of the Brontës. It was here that Charlotte, Branwell, Emily and Anne were all born.

When I first moved to the village, the birthplace was a museum owned by the crime writer Barbara Whitehead. On sunny days, I used to play chess with her in our garden. After her death, it was sold to a landlord who covered up a lot of the original features and partitioned the building, turning it into flats. Then, in 2013, Mark and Michelle De Luca bought the property, restored a lot of its original features, including the fireplace downstairs, close to where the literary siblings were born. Sitting by the hearth, it is possible to imagine them playing on the rug. It is now a café.

When I first had the idea for the Brontë Stones project, I approached Mark and asked him if I could put a stone near his property to commemorate Charlotte's bicentenary. He said, 'I can do better than that,' and suggested I apply to Historic England to have a stone mounted in the outside wall of the building. I supervised the cutting of the hole in the wall and the instalment of the four-hundred-kilogram stone, with the help of a friend and my son. I watched Pip carve the letters of Carol Ann Duffy's poem in situ. It took her weeks to complete. Looking at it now, just a few months after all the work has finished, it already seems like it has always been here. It is part of the fabric of the building, and to remove it would be to destroy the outside wall.

I look at the stone, tall and narrow, stretching up like a door or a coffin lid. At this time of day, the sun draws deep shadows in the carved letters and an optical illusion makes them stand out as though they are embossed rather than engraved. To the left of the stone is the family plaque, and above the door the date stone. I think about what Patrick said, in a letter written in 1835: 'I've never quite been well since I left Thornton. My happiest days were spent there.' Sadly, things were about to take a turn for the worse for the family.

2

'ARE YOU A PAGAN?' - ON THE TRAIL OF THE BRONTË STONES

Out of the blue, I receive an email from a Hungarian woman called Alina. She has booked a hotel, she has booked a flight and she has booked a tour guide to give her a tour of my Brontë Stones trail. Only the tour guide, whose name is Johnny Briggs, is in hospital and can't now do it. He has contacted her to say that, in any case, it is my project and that I will be glad to do it. I've never spoken to Johnny Briggs. I've never heard of Johnny Briggs (only the actor of the same name who played Mike Baldwin in Coronation Street), and I don't really fancy the gig. I try to wriggle out of it.

'But I have booked a flight. I have booked hotel. I cannot cancel. I lose money.'

'The thing is—'

'Please. I will pay you anything. I have to do this.'

I try and think of an excuse. It isn't a question of money. The forecast is rain, and after a few months of tours of the various walks and stones, I'm a bit Brontëd out.

'It's not about the money,' I say.

'Then you will do it?'

I agree to meet her at 1 p.m. on Saturday outside the Old Bell Chapel. Three days before, I look at the weather forecast. Saturday is heavy rain, and the Met Office have issued weather warnings. But Sunday is sunny. I contact her and ask her if she can do Sunday instead. She tells me that her flight gets her in to Yorkshire on Friday evening and she flies back Sunday morning. Saturday is the only day. 'OK,' I say, 'but bring waterproofs.'

When I arrive at the gates, she is already there. She is wearing spray-on jeans, thin canvas pumps and a quilted bolero jacket, the sort you'd wear for a shopping trip in Covent Garden. It's not yomping gear, and certainly not waterproof. She also has a large, white-leather handbag over one shoulder, with gold chains and gold trimmings. It has an open top.

'Hello, my name is Alina.' She holds her hand out for me to shake. 'Are you a pagan?'

'Err … well … erm … a bit … I suppose.'

'I knew it. I knew you were a pagan. I am also pagan. I hate Christians. I hate Muslims. And I hate Romanians.'

Great start, I think. I change the subject: 'Have you brought waterproofs?'

'No.'

'The forecast is heavy rain.'

She shrugs. We look at the sky. It is bruised with dark-grey clouds that hang low like a threat. 'Are you walking in them?' I ask, pointing to her canvas pumps.

'Yes.'

The walk is fairly easy going, but it does take us over moorland with some boggy patches. 'I thought we'd start here,' I say. 'Patrick brought his family here in eighteen—'

'I know all that,' she says, interrupting. 'Let's go.'

We cross Thornton Road and squeeze through the snicket that runs between St James's Church and the rectory. We walk along Market Street past the Baptist Chapel, until we get to the Brontë birthplace. We stand near the steps and stare at the Charlotte Stone:

The vice of this place clamps you;
daughter; father
who will not see thee wed,
traipsing your cold circles
between needlework,
bed, sleep's double-lock.
Mother and siblings,
vile knot under the flagstones, biding.
But the prose seethes,
will not let you be, be thus;
bog-burst of pain, fame, love, unluck.
True; enough.
So your still doll-steps
in the dollshouse parsonage.
So your writer's hand
the hand of a god rending the roof.

Duffy's poem does not sidestep the dark reality of much of Charlotte's life. In May 1849, Anne Brontë died, leaving Charlotte motherless, brotherless and sisterless. The poem is full of oppressive imagery: 'the vice ... clamps you'; 'cold circles'; 'vile knot'. But it also offers salvation in verse form. Writing was Charlotte's escape, and though she was only four feet eleven inches in height, she became a literary giant.

'This is where they were all born,' I say. 'And this is the Charlotte Sto—

'I know this,' she says. 'Come on, I want to see moor. This is why I come.'

We head up West Lane and straight across the open ground to the left of the Black Horse. Kipping House is below us. I think about stopping here and explaining the Firth connection but then think better of it. We make our way past the Great Northern and turn up Royd Street. At the top, we turn left along a grassy bank below a small playground that the locals call 'the mugger'. We climb up the hill along a narrow-walled track and turn left at the top through a gap, joining the Brontë Way as it crosses several small fields that enclose young bulls that are fearful of my dog, who is running ahead of us.

'What is your dog called?' Alina asks.

'Wolf. Or Wolfie. He answers to both.'

'The wolf is my symbol. I am the wolf.'

She pulls up her jacket and blouse and shows me a tattoo on her back. The ink is mostly black and depicts a snarling wolf emerging from a forest.

The now-fenced path soon enters Thornton Cemetery. We stop by the Brontë Stone, carved with Jeanette Winterson's poem:

BRONTESAURUS
Fossil record of a miracle
Bone by Bone
Word for Word
Three Women writing the Past into the Future
Line by Line

Listen to the Wildfell of your heart
Do not betray what you love
The earth opens like a book
You are come back to me then?
BRONTISSIMO

It's a sort of tribute to the legacy of all the family and what they achieved. It is the most playful of the four pieces and alludes to how literary reputations become fossilised over time. It links the 'now' of the poem with the 'then' of the literary work. Ultimately, though, it asks us to reappraise their writing, to find what is still fresh and original.

The poem directly references Anne Brontë's second novel *The Tenant of Wildfell Hall*, which was condemned by Charlotte following Anne's death and subsequently fell into obscurity. One could argue that the subject of this novel was far ahead of its time; now is a good time to reappraise its value and see it as the radical text that it was. Not only does the novel's protagonist, Helen Graham, leave her husband, taking her son with her (a then illegal action), she goes unpunished for it. The novel also shows Helen to have had an independent income as an artist – a profession that was dominated by men throughout the nineteenth century – and tackles the subject of marital rape, which wasn't outlawed in the United Kingdom until 1991. Today, it is considered a landmark in feminist literature.

The stone lies beneath the shade of sycamore trees, staring out over Pinchbeck Valley. The cemetery feels like a fitting place for the tribute, referencing, as it does, bones and words. That's what we are surrounded by: bones and words. And the words will outlive the bones.

Jeanette was nervous about being included with three other writers known for their poetry rather than their prose, but she needn't have been. The poem stands up well. When Pip and I selected the stone, we wanted something that had a rough back and top, to fit the idea in the poem of the earth opening up like a book. But some of the residents of the village thought it was broken. 'What have they put it in like that for?' one woman said. 'The bleedin' top has snapped off.' It does look, in contrast to the black marble tombstones close by, with their gold lettering, to be unfinished. But that was the intention.

'You take photo,' Alina says and passes me her phone.

Next, we make our way back to the main path and through the gate at the far end. We follow a path above Close Head and climb to a bend, where we bear left through another gate. We follow the edge of the fields through a series of gates till we reach Close Head House, where a track leads up to the road near the White Horse pub. We follow the road left for a short while through Well Heads then turn right, taking a path that bends left to cut a defined line across a series of fields towards Morton Farm. To our right, we can see the remains of Doe Park, a medieval deer park, commissioned by the same Richard Tempest who built the Old Bell Chapel and lived at Thornton Hall.

There are still deer to be found in these parts, but not the large red deer Tempest and his men would have hunted. The roe deer that now roam the wooded parts of the valley are much smaller. I often see their white skuts as they retreat into the undergrowth. They are sprites of the forest. Back in the time of the Tempests, this area would have been surrounded by an earth bank and a wooden palisade fence. It covered most of the area around Denholme Beck between Denholme and Cullingworth. The name Denholme Gate refers to one of the entrances to the deer park. Eventually, deer hunting fell out of fashion, and the land was divided up when the Tempest family fortune was gambled away in the early seventeenth century.

'It is beautiful,' Alina says. 'I take picture.'

I look at the darkening clouds above us. The air fizzes with water particles. Rain is heading our way.

We keep left of the farm building at Morton, which is guarded by a dog the size and temper of Cerberus, and head straight across the track and through a field gate. There's a good view of Denholme Beck here and Doe Park Reservoir, with strange outcrops of rock and moss that make the fell look lumpy. We then follow a wall across the hillside towards the building at Denholme Clough. We cut left through a gate just before the stream and soon after join the drive leading up to the road.

Next, we turn up Cragg Lane and follow a path behind the houses that leads to a busy road. We cross this and follow Black Edge Lane up onto the cusp of the moors. There are rough fields on either side and some wild meadow. A curlew cries out its warning: 'music as desolate, as beautiful / as your loved places', according to Norman MacCaig's poem 'Curlew'. We watch it fly above us. The curlew is named after a sliver of moon, the shape of its bill. A little further on, lapwings dance and flap. The collective noun for a flock of lapwings is a 'deceit'. The birds are known to feign injury in order to lead their predators away from their chicks. Wolfie has caught the scent of something, and he runs off across a quarried area of wasteland. He returns with a rabbit in his mouth. Alina gasps, 'What is this?'

'I think it's a rabbit,' I say.

'But we must take it to the vet.'

'It's too late for that. It's dead.'

'We must do something.'

I think she is going to cry, so I wrack my brains to find words to comfort her. 'It had mixy,' I say. 'It was in a lot of pain. He was doing it a favour.'

'What is mixy?'

'Myxomatosis,' I say. 'It's a disease that affects rabbits. It's horrible. They get tumours and go blind. Eventually they die, but it takes weeks. It's a slow and agonising death. So, you see, it's better this way.'

'I see. But your dog, will he catch it?'

'No, it's OK. Only rabbits get it. It's not contagious for other animals.'

'No?'

'I think hares can get it. But that's it.'

'Your dog is a good dog. He saved this rabbit from pain.'

We turn left through a gate and drop down to join Foreside Lane, which leads past the ruins of Ash Tree Farm. The path crosses bleak and dramatic moorland, and despite the clouds the view is clear for many miles around. The moor undulates with dark tracts of peat bog, green ridges of fern and patches of purple heather. Behind us looms the large ridge of land that encompasses Bingley, Ilkley and Rombalds Moor. In front of us looms the less elevated Ovenden Moor.

'These are the moors that inspired Emily,' I say.

'Ah, yes, the moors. I take picture.'

We soon reach Ogden Kirk and the Emily Stone. 'Kirk' is a local word for rock. It rises up from Hebble Brook at the cusp of Thornton Moor. This jagged hump stands sentinel over Skirden Edge. When the sun shines on its face, it sparkles with spots of quartz, tiny diamonds embedded in the skin of the stone. It's the most remote spot along the nine-mile Brontë Stones walk from Thornton to Haworth, from where the Brontës were born to where they matured into adulthood.

The face of the kirk is mottled with ochreous orange and murky black patches. Freckled with green lichen. It brings to mind fire and iron. Where Pip has cut into the kirk's skin with tungsten chisels, the rock beneath is exposed and has a bright-yellow colour that shines gold in some lights. The words are framed by cragged ridges of stone and fretted with verdant ferns:

> She stands outside
> A book in her hands
> 'Her name is Cathy,' she says
> 'I have carried her so far, so far
> Along the unmarked road from our graves
> I cannot reach this window
> Open it, I pray.'
> But his window is a door to a lonely world
> That longs to play.
> Ah Emily. Come in, come in and stay.

Kate Bush's poem is something of a mystery. The first line, 'she stands outside', is perhaps a reference to the first lines of her song 'This Woman's Work'. Emily has carried her character 'Cathy' to her grave and now she stands outside a window. The window, which she cannot reach, is perhaps a reference both to the scene in *Wuthering Heights* when Cathy's ghost appears outside the sleeping Lockwood's bed chamber and also to the lyrics of Bush's 1978 debut, with the refrain, 'let me in at your window'. It is in any case a porthole to another world.

Alina and I stop to read the poem. As we do, the sun appears from behind the clouds and illuminates the rock face so that the letters glow gold and the tiny diamonds of quartz sparkle in the light like stars.

'It is destiny,' Alina says.

We read the poem. Alina takes pictures. I extract my lunch from my rucksack, a sandwich and broth from my flask.

'Do you want some?'

'I had a big breakfast. English breakfast. Very big.'

'They share the same birthday,' I say.

'Who?'

'Emily and Kate. The thirtieth of July. Kate Bush was sixty this year, the same year as Emily's bicentenary. It's also forty years since Kate's debut single "Wuthering Heights" reached number one in the charts here.'

'Ah, yes, I read about this in magazine. This is where your love of Emily Brontë starts? You were a child and you listened to the song.'

She's done her homework. 'I'd just turned seven,' I say. 'I got a tape machine for my birthday. I taped the song off the radio. I was obsessed by it. I filled a C60 cassette with it. I think my mum was worried about me. She took me to one side and told me the story of *Wuthering Heights*.'

'And this is where you began?'

'I suppose.'

'What is it about this song?'

'I don't know. I think it was the lyrics. This woman asking to be let in at the window. I couldn't work out why she didn't use the door.'

'You were a strange child.'

'My mother thought so.'

We sit in the sunlight and absorb the surroundings. It's a secluded beauty spot that was well known to the Victorians. Surely Patrick would have talked to Emily about his picnic here with Elizabeth Firth, and perhaps Emily would even have come to find the spot herself. On the edge of Thornton and Ovenden moors, which are cut in two by the sharp incline of Ogden Clough, the air is peaceful with the pleasant trickling sound of the beck below. In front is Round Hill, to our right Skirden Edge and to our left the wooded tops of Spice Cake Hills. Above us the clouds have dispersed. It looks like the forecast was wrong, or Alina has cast a pagan spell.

I think back to early June when Pip was here carving the letters into the stone. It was the hottest week of the year – in fact, the hottest on record for many years – and Pip had to submerge herself fully clothed up to her neck in the peaty waters of Hebble Beck every half hour or so, just to stop herself from overheating. It was so hot she also had to bury her diamond-encrusted sharpening block. I watched her chip into the rock with my heart in the roof of my mouth. One mistake and the whole thing would have been spoilt.

'It is lovely here,' Alina says. 'Has Kate been to see it?'

'Yes, I think so. She was spotted by a walker. Someone emailed me.'

I put my flask away and fasten my rucksack. We leave the dramatic crest of Ogden Kirk and take the main path to the shoulder of Thornton Moor. Beneath our feet, newts scurry. The earth is soft with peaty soil and spongy with sphagnum. As we reach the brow of the moor, the view opens up again and Rombalds Moor reappears. We continue down Hambleton Lane, soon joining a fence line, descending steeply to join Thornton Moor conduit. To our left, we can just make out a dark shape close to the horizon: Top Withens, the main inspiration for the location of Wuthering Heights. We head straight on past the gate, then fork left at a sign to descend past the remains of a metal hut. The fells here are populated with a breed of sheep known as Lonk, hardy enough to tackle the braying winter winds and musket balls of ice-cold rain. The wool is too tough for clothing and is used instead in carpet manufacturing.

To our right is a lonesome sycamore tree that marks the abandoned farm of the Hays. Here the 'Book Stones' lie, two huge slabs that cover an open cellar, or what is left of it. They now contain a bonus carving – this was going to be the original site of the Emily Stone, and I'd wanted Pip to mark the spot. I point out the carving to Alina.

'What is "E.B."?'

'It's just Emily's initials. Pip carved them for me.'

'Why did she do this?'

'I asked her to.'

After telling Anita Rani, one of the programme's presenters, on BBC *Countryfile*, along with millions of viewers, that this was where Pip was going to carve Kate's poem, I'd thought I had better do something. It was only after the programme had aired that I'd discovered Ogden Kirk and changed my mind about where the poem should go.

Beneath the slabs, in shadow of the cellar, we can just make out the remains of a sheep, the fleece stained with peat soil and the bones picked clean, first by corvids then by tiny insect life. The skull peers out at us, as though it has been placed here as part of a Satanic ceremony. We sit on the slabs and take in the stunning vista of Oxenhope.

After a stone stoop, the path bears down to reach a bridge over Stubden Conduit. We follow this conduit as it meanders and snakes a line around several steep cloughs. One such clough is a wooded hollow called Nan Scar. In the 1880s, there was a rifle range here. The name comes from the Welsh word '*nant*' for a small river. There is said to be a twite reserve around here, but I have never been fortunate enough to see these small, shy brown finches.

'Where is the Anne Stone?'

'Well, the thing is … it's in Dent.'

'Dent? Where is Dent?'

'About a two-hour drive away. It's in a field near Pip's studio. It was the first stone she carved. It's supposed to be in the meadow behind the parsonage in Haworth.'

'Why is it not there?'

'There have been problems with the contract.'

'What problems?'

'It's complicated … we can go and have a look at the hole the stone mason has dug if you like. I can read you the poem off my phone. It's a very good poem.'

'Why would we want to look in hole?'

We eventually arrive at Leeming Reservoir, with its ornate valve tower, and follow the track behind until we reach the village of Oxenhope and the steam railway station. The Reverend Donne in Charlotte Brontë's novel *Shirley* was inspired by Joseph Brett Grant, who was Patrick Brontë's assistant curate. He became the first vicar of Oxenhope in 1851, when the fine Norman-style church was built here. Its name means 'valley of the oxen'. Though there are no oxen now, just comfortably well-off commuters with 4x4 vehicles and topiary hedges.

We take a path that follows the river into Haworth and walk past a row of pretty cottages. 'This is not safe,' Alina says.

'What's not safe?'

'This door. This window. I wouldn't sleep if I lived here.'

'It's not so bad.'

'But there are no bars. And not enough locks. Where I live, Romanians would easily get through this.'

We walk up the main street of Haworth past the Black Bull

pub, a favourite drinking hole of Branwell Brontë. Branwell was the secretary of the Freemasons Lodge of the Three Graces which met at this inn. He was also a leading member of the Haworth Temperance Society, which might seem odd, but it appears that Branwell only took to drink towards the end of his short life. Why he did will become clearer later.

According to Elizabeth Gaskell, who we now know, due to the work done by Juliet Barker and others, was not a very reliable source, Branwell's conversational talents were a bit of a pull. She claims that he was known to make his escape through the back door or by jumping through the kitchen window when his family came to seek him at the front of the inn, or when fleeing from debtors who came to settle his bar bills. Today, it is in the hands of a voracious pub company whose punitive contract ties in the tenant to an exclusive buying deal. I've seen a succession of young hopefuls take on the place, filled with foolish optimism and go-getting spirit, only to find it is hardly possible to make a living when the profit margins are so thin. It should be the best pub in the village, instead of the last-chance saloon.

A group of big-bellied, bald-headed lager drinkers huddle round the entrance, smoking and vaping.

'The English, they drink too much. They drink and drink.'

'They do. They used to blame it on the water,' I say. 'The water here was particularly unclean. The streams ran through the graveyard.'

'But why do they drink so much now?'

'I don't know. Maybe it's just habit,' I say as I bid Alina farewell, pocket my guide fee and make my way to the Old Hall Inn for a much-needed beer.

Post Scriptum

The Anne Stone is now in its proper place in the top-right-hand corner of Parson's Field, a wild meadow behind Haworth Parsonage Museum. It was a spot that Rebecca Yorke and I chose. Rebecca is the head of communications and marketing at the museum. We sat on a bench lower down and discussed how we might place the stone. At nearly a tonne in weight, it wasn't an easy task. Anne Brontë was the only Brontë sibling who was not buried in the family vault beneath the floor of St Michael and All Angels' Church in Haworth. Instead, she was buried in Scarborough, where she died. It was a place she had visited several times when she holidayed there with the Robinsons, as we will discover later in the book, and somewhere that she held in great affection. Her grave is in St Mary's churchyard, beneath the castle walls, overlooking the bay. Jackie Kay's poem acknowledges this separation and acts as a sort of homecoming:

> These dark, sober clothes
> are my disguise. No, I was not preparing
> for an early death, yours or mine.
> You got me all wrong, all the time.
> But sisters, I'll have the last word,
> write the last line. I am still at sea –
> but if I can do some good in this world,
> I will right the wrong. I am still young,
> and the moor's winds lift my light-dark hair.
> I am still here when the sun goes up,
> and here when the moon drops down.
> I do not now stand alone.

Carved into a stone that sits at the top of the wild meadow behind the parsonage and looks out at the graveyard, the family vaults and the surrounding moorland, triangulating these points of biographical significance, it is the largest of the moveable stones, and contains a poem within a poem. Kay emphasised certain words, and Pip Hall has carved them flat instead of her usual V cut, so that the words sometimes jump out and at others diminish, depending on the light. It is a startling effect. One such word is 'wrong', which stands out twice, making us think of the wrong that was done to Anne's work when Charlotte expurgated it following her death, and also of the errors on her original gravestone. There were five of them apparently. They didn't even get her age right.

One of the commonest questions I get asked, after 'Why is the Brontë Stone broken?' (it isn't; it's meant to be like that) and 'Why is the Emily Stone so hard to find?' (it's not that hard), is 'Why is the Anne Stone facing the wall?' The answer is because I want people to read the poem while overlooking the parsonage and the vault under the church where the rest of the family are buried. But you can also see the moors that surround the parsonage from that spot. In short, standing at the stone, looking over the parsonage and the moors, I want you to experience a lump in your throat.

I took a group of walkers to see the stone shortly after it was fitted. We disturbed a woman in her late twenties who was standing close by, beneath a hawthorn, quietly sobbing. We waited in silence for her to compose herself. She explained that she had been to see Anne's grave in Scarborough but that this stone and this poem had moved her more.

3

JAW JHILL AND THE ORIGINS OF WUTHERING JHEIGHTS

I'm standing in front of the gates of the former Law Hill School on Law Lane in Bank Top above Southowram, near Halifax. It is now a family home, but fastened to the outside wall is a newly sited blue plaque, which states that Emily Brontë, the author of *Wuthering Heights*, lived here from September 1838 to April 1839 and taught at Elizabeth Patchett's school for girls, as it was then. These sixth months of work were the only paid employment Emily ever undertook. The work could be, by Emily's own account, long and unpleasant. She wrote to Charlotte that it was 'hard labour from six in the morning to near eleven at night … this is slavery'. Despite this, Emily managed to write a sequence of poems here that showed a new direction in her writing.

I'm here to explore the story of these poems and her time at Law Hill, to find out more about Emily's inner life. I want to familiarise myself with the key places that inspired her only novel, which was to scandalise Victorian society. And I want to explore the story of Law Hill itself, but also the surrounding Walter Clough Hall, Shibden

Hall, High Sunderland Hall and the dramatic ground they cast their shadows over.

Although teaching at Law Hill was Emily's only paid work, her sister Charlotte never referred to it by name, preferring instead to call it the 'Halifax School'. This is odd, given that the school was a good few miles from Halifax. For some reason, Charlotte attributed the writing of the Law Hill poems to Emily's time at Roe Head, when she was a seventeen-year-old pupil of the school. Why did Charlotte change the dates so that it looked like Emily had written the poems three years previously? And why was she so keen to avoid naming the school? Some biographers have put the change down to a memory lapse, but the poems are clearly dated in the manuscript Charlotte used.

We know that after the death of her siblings Charlotte changed quite a few details to make her family seem more respectable and orthodox; for instance, taking the reference to rape out of Anne's *The Tenant of Wildfell Hall*. She also doctored both Anne and Emily's poems, including those that Emily wrote as a teacher here in Southowram. Did something happen to Emily at Law Hill that Charlotte wanted to conceal? Charlotte wrote to her friend Ellen Nussey to explain that Emily had given up her teaching job at the 'Halifax School' due to 'ill health', explaining that she could only regain her health by being 're-established by the bracing moorland air and free life of home'. But Law Hill is in a remote spot, surrounded by splendid countryside not dissimilar to that of Haworth. And there is no evidence, other than Charlotte's letter, that Emily was unwell. On the contrary, she appears to have been the most physically robust of all the sisters, traipsing over mire and moor, through rain and hail. Could it be possible that Charlotte was covering something up?

Law Hill was built by Jack Sharp, who is often cited as the main inspiration for the infernal character of Heathcliff. In the first half of the eighteenth century, Jack Sharp was adopted by John Walker of Walter Clough Hall, also in Southowram, about a mile from Law Hill. He was said to be an unscrupulous character who abused his uncle's kindness. John Walker was a prosperous wool manufacturer and father to four children (Richard, John, Grace and Mary). But he most favoured his adopted son, who, through his deviousness, eventually managed to acquire much of Walker's business. On John Walker's death in 1771 (the year that Mr Earnshaw makes his trip to Liverpool in *Wuthering Heights*), Jack Sharp had full possession of the estate. But this wasn't a legal status, and John's eldest son, the rightful heir, mounted a challenge that he eventually won, ousting Jack in the process. Jack Sharp left, promising revenge. But not before stealing the family silver, as well as many other prized objects. He built Law Hill just one mile away so that it looked down on Walter Clough Hall. He then enticed the easy-going son into gambling and ruin. He also managed to systematically degrade a young cousin of the heir, as Hareton Earnshaw was degraded by Heathcliff. Jack Sharp's manservant was called Joseph, the same name as Heathcliff's manservant, and the surname of one of Miss Patchett's servants was Earnshaw.

Close by was High Sunderland Hall, the carvings above the door of which were similar to those of Wuthering Heights farmhouse. They included two griffins on the inside of the gateway and two misshapen nude men. A grotesque head formed the keystone to the arch of the gateway on the outside, while other heads with lewd faces peered from the cornices of the stonework. The hall was built on the edge of the moor in an exposed spot, similar to that of Wuthering Heights.

In other words, there is much of Law Hill and its surroundings that influenced Emily's writing at this time. On 7 December 1838, halfway through her time at Law Hill, Emily wrote a poem quite different to the others she had been working on up to this point, which were poems relating to the fantasy world of Gondal that she and her sister Anne had immersed themselves in from childhood:

How still, how happy! These are words
That once would scarce agree together
I loved the plashing of the surge –
The changing heaven the breezy weather,
More than smooth seas and cloudless skies
And solemn, soothing, softened airs
That in the forest woke no sighs
And from the green spray shook no tears.
How still, how happy! now I feel
Where silence dwells is sweeter far
Than laughing mirth with joyous swell
However pure its raptures are
Come sit down on this sunny stone
'Tis wintry light o'er flowerless moors –
But sit – for we are all alone
And clear expand heaven's breathless shores
I could think in the withered grass
Spring's budding wreaths we might discern
The violet's eye might shyly flash
And young leaves shoot among the fern
It is but thought – full many a night
The snow shall clothe those hills afar

And storms shall add a drearier blight
And winds shall wage a wilder war
Before the lark may herald in
Fresh foliage twined with blossoms fair
And summer days again begin
Their glory-haloed crown to wear
Yet my heart loves December's smile
As much as July's golden beam
Then let us sit and watch the while
The blue ice curdling on the stream.

This is uncharacteristic of Emily's poems and expresses joy and happiness in a way that many of her others do not. The mood of the poem certainly doesn't fit the sentiment she expresses in her letter to Charlotte. But who does the poem address? Who does she want to sit down beside her to share her love of the 'flowerless moors'? As Brontë scholar Edward Chitham makes clear in his essay 'Law Hill and Emily Brontë: Behind Charlotte's Evasion' in *Brontë Studies*, it is unlikely to have been a pupil, as the 'alone' implies that they are together for the first time without their pupils. It is, as Chitham again points out, more likely to be another teacher. One of Emily's fellow teachers was a woman called Jane Aspden. By coincidence, Emily had visited Jane Aspden's home when she was a girl. 'Aspden', also spelt 'Aspen' and 'Aspin', is the only English surname Emily ever uses in a Gondal poem, one called 'Written in Aspin Castle'. I don't want to jump to any undue conclusions, but it is not unreasonable to assume two things: one, that the two women were colleagues; and two, that they had things in common that would bond them in some way.

This isn't the only theory concerned with Emily's personal relationships. For example, Sarah Fermi, in *Emily's Journal*, maintains that Emily had a relationship with Robert Clayton, who died in 1836. And many readers and academics have been curious about how Emily is able to describe the love between Heathcliff and Catherine with such authentic passion. Of course, it's not necessary to experience something to be able to write about it convincingly. Many authors write about murder, for example, without, we assume and hope, having first-hand knowledge. Shakespeare didn't go to Denmark or Venice or North Africa. H.G. Wells never travelled in a time machine. Jules Verne never took a journey to the centre of the Earth. They made these things up. The imagination is a powerful tool. But that isn't to say that Emily didn't fall in love while she was at Law Hill. As I stand by the gate, so close to the moors that inspired Emily to write one of the most powerful accounts of obsessive and destructive love in English literature, it is tempting to wonder what really went on beneath its sturdy Georgian brickwork.

Law Hill is situated in Bank Top, a small village above Southowram. There is a pub, the Cock and Bottle, and Sam's minimarket, but not much else. I want to get a feel for the landscape around the school, a landscape that I'm sure, despite the long hours of work, Emily would have explored herself. My walk will take me anticlockwise along the ridge where the school is situated. I'm walking in September, the same month Emily came to Law Hill. The branches of the oaks are heavy with green acorns, the rowans ripe with bright-red berries. The sky is ominous with clouds that could disperse in the wind or empty their load over my head. I've got my waterproofs in my rucksack – I'm taking no chances.

I walk up Dog Kennel Lane, an ancient pathway that is now an overgrown snicket between newly built houses, where washing lines sag with wet laundry. The view soon opens out to a huge TV mast, and the dirt track I've been following joins a road that sweeps around the ridge of Siddal Top. The view here is expansive, and you can see the whole of Halifax, surrounded by green and purple moor. Sometimes it is shrouded in mist. Today, the view is so clear that it seems to stretch out indefinitely. The Calder Valley has no end.

This is the valley that hid the work of the Cragvale Coiners in the late eighteenth century as they clipped coins at an almost industrial rate, to the point where they destabilised the British economy. And it is the valley where Ted Hughes was born and Sylvia Plath was buried. It is a valley with many secrets. Surely Emily, in the little free time she was given, would have taken this short walk and been struck by the dramatic beauty of the landscape, and also by its mystery.

Dean Clough is on my right, an impressive cluster of mill buildings and a thin chimney, first leased by the Crossleys to manufacture carpet. The mill would have been much smaller during Emily's time. It was built up after 1841 to become the massive site that it is today. The mill was closed in 1983 and redeveloped by Ernest Hall. It is now home to art galleries, restaurants and bars, and this seat of industry has become a bed of leisure activities. Another mill stands out, close to the railway station, and its slim chimney reaches up improbably tall so that it seems to teeter and almost topple over.

I turn left along a path and across a field. I see the wind farm above Todmorden and hear an ice-cream van in the valley below: 'Teddy Bear's Picnic'. A peculiar effect of the shape of the place amplifies the acoustics. I remember how excited I would get hearing that sound as a kid. I'd run down the street chasing the van. *If you go down to the woods today, you're sure of a big surprise.* The song is clearly humorous and playful, but I've always found the idea of encountering a group of bears gaily playing in the depths of the forest to be deeply disconcerting.

There are characteristic landmarks around these parts that you invariably encounter once you reach a certain height, above the glacial scars that sweep and curve: Stoodley Pike high over Hebden; Emley Mast, a tapered concrete tower to the south, more than one thousand feet tall; and the wind farms over Ogden and Todmorden. I'm struck by the raw beauty of this landscape. By the rugged, scarred juts of fell and heath. What occurs to me about the Calder Valley, above industry and below 'flowerless moors', is just how rich and green it is, with dense deciduous forest. It is a great hiding place for criminals and outlaws – coiners, clippers, cutpurses and highway robbers. I stop at Siddal Top, perch on a bench and wonder if this is the spot where Emily wrote the line 'come sit down beside me' in one of the poems she wrote at Law Hill.

Once on the move again, I drop down to a little hamlet called Park Nook, a cluster of weavers' cottages with mullion windows, largely unchanged from Emily's day. Only a man outside puffing on his vaping device spoils the illusion. In my mind, I replace the vaping machine for a clay pipe and his baseball cap for an eight-panelled cloth one. The path continues down through Elland Park Wood, which sits just above the River Calder. Soft green light dapples through the canopies of oak, ash, sycamore and beech. But above all, there are lots of old holly trees. It is a verdant space, with moss and lichen lining every bark and branch, so that in a certain light, at a certain time of day, everything glows green. Here the trees are not merely alive, they seem sentient. I think about the rhizome network beneath my feet, busy with conversation between each life form. A nuthatch, resembling a small woodpecker, with a black robber's mask, hunts for grubs in the nook of a trunk.

Along a red-brick path, I stop to examine a fly-tipping spot. A piss-stained mattress is leaning against a piss-stained bed base. Near to this is a different type of hoard, a large heap of more than fifty black bin bags that have been dumped by the side of the path, containing rapid-grow compost and clay aeration balls, and what is left of the harvest: withered cannabis plants denuded of their budding flowers – another form of criminality so different to that of Emily's day.

I walk through an overgrown orchard that opens out into a crematorium. There are no graves, just little plastic-looking plaques and benches in honour of the dead, along with rotting flowers in concrete pots. Next to gold lettering, photos of the deceased are glued to black marble. This gaudy ceremony of remembrance would have been alien to Emily. The first official cremation in England wasn't carried out until 1885. And it was much later, in 1902, that the Cremation Act allowed burial authorities to establish crematoria. Just as well, or the ending of *Wuthering Heights*, where Mr Lockwood searches for the graves of Edgar, Cathy and Heathcliff, would have been very different.

I enter the darkness of the wood once again, past a kid on a scrambler motorbike, churning up the track, eventually making my way up a steep incline and out along a walled path. I pass a solitary wind turbine, a symbol of clean energy to some, an eyesore to others. They lie somewhere between fossil fuel and solar in my mind. I'll not pretend that they are a welcome sight, but they are no more off-putting than a pylon. Perhaps time will soften the shock of the new and they will be seen by all with affection, in the way we now view industrial chimneys that once belched out toxic fumes.

The path here passes Southowram Cricket Club, and I hear the familiar smack of willow on leather, followed by 'played!' and 'let it go!' Next is a sharp right down School Lane, before the village stocks, which stand outside Papa Jew's village sandwich shop. The stocks were probably last used in the 1860s so would certainly have been active during Emily's stay. Did she see these large wooden boards and hinges restraining some poor soul's feet? Were they being insulted or spat on? Punched or kicked? Or something even worse? She certainly didn't balk at depicting violence in her work. The scene where Nelly discovers Isabella's dog hanging from a bridle hook still has the power to shock modern readers.

I climb up on to Milking Hill past a row of cottages called Jerusalem Mount and cross over a road with St Anne's Church to the right. I then follow a farm track next to Pasture House to a quarry. On the Ordnance Survey (OS) map, a path seems to cut right through the middle, but there is no sign of it in the flesh. I ask a mechanic who is working beneath a huge Volvo excavator, 'Does the path come through here, mate?'

He stops what he is doing and looks over to me briefly: 'Don't think so, no.'

Instead, the path drops down onto a field that leads to Walter Clough Hall, where John Walker made his disastrous decision to adopt Jack Sharp. Very little remains of the original Walter Clough Hall, and what is left is now a working farm, with milch cows, hens and a few rustic mares. Like many modern farms, it also seems to be a store for bricks, stones and scrap metal.

I then make my way past Marsh Farm, an old building much unchanged from Emily's time here. Perhaps she would have walked past, as she wandered from Law Hill to Walter Clough Hall, thinking about John Walker and Jack Sharp. Thinking about the cuckoo in the nest that kicks the others out. About foundling infants and acts of revenge. It has also been said that Jack was in love with one of John's daughters. Was Emily already putting together the story of *Wuthering Heights*?

The path takes me down past a high-sided drystone wall, black with industry and oxidisation. If you want to see through Emily's eyes, you have to airbrush out the pylons and the wind farms, the burnt-out cars and piss-stained mattresses. But what you are left with is not quite a rural idyll. This space would have been functional: quarries, farmed land, coal mines and brick factories.

When I get to Shibden Hall, the lawn outside the entrance is overgrown with grass and weeds. I think at first that it is closed, but then I see a sign: 'Filming *Gentleman Jack*'. This is Sally Wainwright's new project for the BBC and HBO. Written and directed by her, as was *To Walk Invisible*, her story of the relationship between the three youngest Brontë sisters and Branwell, the year before. Sally's new film tells the story of Anne Lister, a landowner, mountaineer and traveller, but best remembered today for her personal life. Her diaries, hidden in the walls of the hall and written in a secret code, contain intimate details about her many lesbian relationships. She has been called the first 'modern lesbian', and she was known by the residents of Halifax as 'Gentleman Jack', because she dressed in male attire.

Shibden Hall is also one of the possible sources for Thrushcross Grange (along with Ponden Hall) in *Wuthering Heights*. It is probably the only stately home Emily encountered that had a garden as vast as the one she describes at Thrushcross. It has also been said that the character of Shirley, in Charlotte Brontë's second novel of the same name, could be loosely based on Anne Lister, in combination with some of Emily's traits. Several novelists have created fictional encounters between Emily Brontë and Anne Lister, including Maureen Peters (in *Child of Fire*) and Glyn Hughes (in *Brontë*), although in real life they are unlikely to have met. And even if they did, Anne was a snob and would not have associated with a woman beneath her class, although it isn't easy to say what class the Brontës or, in fact, any clerical family were. Patrick would have been paid little more than a humble labourer, yet he mixed with people of all classes and backgrounds. Most of his parishioners would have been farmers, labourers, artisans and mill workers. But his social circle was comprised of the middle and upper classes. Patrick himself was the eldest of ten, and his father was a farm labourer. There wouldn't have been much opulence in his childhood. We do know, however, that Miss Patchett did meet Anne Lister, as it is recorded in Anne's diary.

The lawn has been left to mimic how it would have been when Anne Lister returned home from overseas travels in 1836. The film set is very impressive, and it is hard to know where Shibden Hall ends and the set begins. It is only when I knock on it with my fist that I can tell if it is stone, wood or MDF. I test out a huge kennel at the back of the hall, which looks like it's constructed from brick and timber, only to find it rings hollow.

I ask a volunteer if she knows where the High Sunderland Hall carvings are? She leads me to a yard out back, and I'm surprised to see that what remains of the carvings are heaped in a corner, without even a sign or plaque to explain what they are: a carving of a man's arse, thrusting obscenely; a date stone; a beastly face; a sinister, impish creature; a naked male figure with no head and prominent cock and balls; part of the outside columns. The volunteer explains that they were acquired by accident, and no one knows where the rest of the carvings went. This is all that is left of High Sunderland Hall. The museum acquired these oddments some time in the sixties, several years after the hall was destroyed.

It is not hard to imagine Emily's reaction to these, standing beneath them in their original location, as it is highly probable that she visited High Sunderland Hall. The hall was positioned on Pepper Hill above Hag Lane, overlooking Shibden Dale and peering down on Shibden Hall. It must have been an austere and foreboding presence. But I imagine that while the carvings might have sent a shiver down Emily's spine, she would have also chuckled at them. Either way, they must surely have been placed there as a provocation, albeit a grotesquely humorous one, and the opposite of a welcome mat, by someone who shared Heathcliff's view of visitors.

Some people miss Emily's black humour when reading *Wuthering Heights*, but it's clear to me that she delighted in the macabre, as Lockwood does when first encountering the entrance of Heathcliff's home: 'I paused to admire a quantity of grotesque carving lavished over the front ... a wilderness of crumbling griffins and shameless little boys'.

The sculptures are surrounded by a basket-weaving shop, a tannery, a stable and a reconstruction of Crispin Inn. The original tavern once stood close to Halifax parish church and was a meeting place for Luddites. I leave the yard and make my way through the gardens, heading north-west, under a tunnel, climbing up to Beacon Hill, where an iron basket on a long pole is the only remaining indication of the millennium celebrations that took place across the country on New Year's Eve 1999. I imagine the torch burning bright, connecting up with all the other fires in prominent high places across the land, forming a pattern of light that mimicked the constellations above. Lisa and I were living in Otley at the time, and I remember walking up the Chevin, a brooding hill behind our house, to watch the torch there being lit.

The view opens out to show the whole of Halifax, and I'm reacquainted with Square Chapel, the railway, the library and Dean Clough, as well as Piece Hall, a unique architectural centre for the cloth trade. Dating from 1779, it would have been a thriving statement of wealth and ambition in 1838. Now it is repurposed and contains a theatre, a cinema, a bookshop and a deli, as well as lots of other artisanal shops. The other prominent landmark is Wainhouse Tower. This is perhaps the most recognisable feature over the town. It began as a mill chimney, but a neighbouring mill owner objected, and it was instead finished with a decorated top and a spiral staircase.

It is really apparent from this angle why the basin of Halifax, surrounded as it is by steep moorland and therefore acting like a bucket to collect the water so necessary for the manufacture of cloth, became such a big player in the trade of handwoven textiles. The chimneys that point to the heavens are now just follies, relics of a former time. But Emily would have sat on this hill and watched the smoke billow out of them. She would have peered through a view that was thick with sooty effluence, which makes it even more remarkable that there is so little of the outside world in Emily's novel. The north of England was at the cusp of a revolution: an industrial one, yes, but also a cultural and social one. She forgoes this upheaval to focus on the claustrophobia of Wuthering Heights itself.

❧

As I've mentioned, my fascination with the novel *Wuthering Heights* began forty years ago when Kate Bush's debut single reached number one in the pop charts in February 1978. I'm not sure I really understood much about it. But it was everywhere that month: on Radio One, on Piccadilly Radio (my local radio station), on *Top of the Pops*. It sounded like nothing else in the charts, a million miles from Abba, Darts and The Bee Gees.

My mother watched on, perhaps a little worried by her son's strange, compulsive behaviour. By coincidence, she was reading the novel for the first time. Part of a large Irish Catholic family, she had left school at fifteen to support her siblings, so she never got to complete her education. She was studying an English literature O level at night school. She told me what the story was about. She told me about how, one summer night, after three days of travel on foot, Mr Earnshaw brought a dark-skinned orphan back from the streets of Liverpool to his farm in Yorkshire. She told me about how his daughter Cathy spat at the boy and his son Hindley booted him. And how Mrs Earnshaw had disapproved of the scruffy ragamuffin.

There is something of the folk tale about *Wuthering Heights*, and this must have grabbed my young mind. And there was something fitting about *hearing* this story, as Mr Lockwood does from the housekeeper Nelly Dean. But it wasn't until my late teens that I read the book for myself and could talk to my mother at length about the characters and the plot. Why had Mr Earnshaw brought the boy back, I wanted to know. It didn't make sense. My mother couldn't tell me. Instead, she just shrugged.

❧

I am thinking about this as I climb into bed that night. I redo the walk in my mind. When Daniel Defoe visited Halifax in the early eighteenth century, he saw a pre-industrial town engaged in the business of the clothing trade, confined to the terraced cottages that were stacked up together along every street and lane. He found in every house 'a tenter, and almost on every tenter a piece of cloth, or kersie, or shalloon!' Every domestic dwelling was also a 'manufactory or work-house', with a river running through each one. He found a town surrounded by hills that were full of springs and coal pits, just as Emily would have done. But by 1838, the landscape would have also contained the behemoths of a new form of industry.

Historians are split about whether this social upheaval was to the benefit or detriment of the working people. But John Fielden writes in his 1836 pamphlet about the curse of the factory system that the factory labourer ages prematurely. And political economists were already blaming 'foreign competition' for the poor treatment of workers, a long time before Brexit. Richard Oastler, in his evidence presented to the House of Commons Committee on Child Labour in 1832, talked about how children worked thirteen hours a day or more. He then quoted a West Indian slave master: 'Well, I have always thought myself disgraced by being the owner of black slaves, but we never, in the West Indies, thought it was possible for any human being to be so cruel as to require a child of nine years old to work twelve and a half hours a day.'

I close my eyes and see the landscape in my mind. The moors, the forests, the terraced houses and factories, and, above all, the spires and chimneys, reaching up above the people, stretching to the heavens. I was born at the other end of the Industrial Revolution, at the cusp of post-industry. I grew up on the edge of an industrial estate. My bedroom, a small box room, was the coldest in the house and was cast in a perpetual shadow from the mill chimney across the road. Courtaulds was at one time the world's leading man-made-fibre production company, employing thousands of people. I used to sit on my bed, staring out of the window, watching workers in the morning pouring into the main entrance, then, later on in the evening, pouring out, making their way to the pub up the road or catching a bus home.

I used to stare at that chimney. It was so tall that I couldn't see its top from my window – it loomed over me like an exclamation mark, daring me to climb it. One day, when I was nine or ten years old, Andy Garret and I dared each other. We'd been on the roof of the mill many times, pretending to kick our ball up there by accident, so that we had an excuse in case we were caught. We'd climbed over the roofs of all the surrounding factories, too: Petersgate Paper Works, Truman Steel, and so on. But the chimney was a different kind of challenge. We shinnied up the drainpipe at the side of the factory and made our way across the slate roof towards the base of the chimney, avoiding glass sky lights. I thought at some point that Andy would turn around, grin at me and say, 'Only joking.' But he didn't.

We got to the chimney. The metal ladder that went all the way to the top didn't start at the bottom, but about seven or eight feet up. Andy went first. He stood on my shoulders and had to stretch as far as he could to reach the first rung. Somehow, he managed to pull himself up. Then he dangled down with his legs wrapped around the lowest rung while I jumped and jumped until his hand clasped mine. There was no going back now.

Andy took the lead, and when he got to the top, he shouted for me to hurry up. I was about halfway. I remember looking over to my mum and dad's house. I could just about make out that the television was on in the front room. It was Saturday afternoon, and my dad had returned from the pub and was now watching the football results. My mum was in the kitchen peeling potatoes, ready to make chips for tea. How small they looked. I felt like a god. Then I looked down, and the ladder became a length of elastic. It telescoped, and I clung onto the rungs for my life. I waited for the dizziness to fade away. Then I climbed to the top, where Andy was waiting, and I looked over the city of Salford. I could see everything. I could see in every direction. I could see the red-bricked houses and factories. I could see the River Irwell snake its way along. And in the distance I could see Winter Hill, at the edge of the Pennines that separate Lancashire from Yorkshire, not knowing that one day I would move permanently to the other side of this ridge.

This cotton factory was where my Grandma Fanny worked as a girl. She told me that her and her mates had lured apprentice lads into the storeroom where the bobbins were kept. They'd strip the lads, put an empty milk bottle over their cocks and show them a bit of tit until they rose to the occasion and the bottle got stuck.

The mill was at the centre of my part of Salford, providing work and camaraderie for many, but by 1987 it had closed down, the work outsourced overseas. And in 1989, Fred Dibnah, a local steeplejack who drove around in a steam engine and was often on the television, came along and knocked the chimney down. The site was flattened.

That night, I dream about chimneys and factories, villainous orphans and open moorland. In my head, it's all jumbled up. The next day, I return to Law Hill. I want to ask whoever lives there if I can have a look round. It's a massive imposition, and I've been putting it off, but it's important for me to be able to see the interior. It seems significant somehow to be in the same room where Emily slept and dreamt about errant orphans. But when I pull up outside, I have a change of heart. I can't just knock on someone's door out of the blue. It's not what you do. I hang around for a bit, unable to decide where to go next.

Law Hill is one of a number of origin myths that all stake a claim to being the inspiration for Emily's novel. Another is that of the story of Hugh Brunty, Emily's grandfather. Hugh's grandfather had a farm by the banks of the Boyne. He was a cattle dealer, and on one of his voyages he returned with a strange child: a dark, dirty, very young boy. The family adopted him and called him 'Welsh' because of his gypsy complexion. The boy grew in his adopted father's favours, pushing out his birth children to the point where he took over the business. Juliet Barker in her book about the Brontës offers the story of *Rob Roy*, written by Walter Scott, a favourite author of the siblings, as another source. And there are precedents in the sisters' own juvenilia and in Branwell's unfinished novel.

I sit in my car and stare at the stark exterior of Law Hill. Its stout walls are surrounded by a wounded sky. I put the key in the ignition, start the engine and drive home. Whatever secrets lie in the bricks and mortar of the building will remain there. I wonder if the family who now live under its roof ever dream about Emily.

Post Scriptum

I returned to Law Hill almost a year later, and finally got up the courage to knock on the door and ask if it would be OK to look around. The owner of the house, Nicky, gave me a warm welcome and was happy to show me around. She lives there with her husband, and although her children have flown the nest, they were all visiting when I arrived.

Her house contains many of the original features that Emily would have seen, such as the fireplaces and windows, and Regency carvings and coving. She showed me the view Emily would have enjoyed from her bedroom window, with Pepper Hill in the far distance, once home to High Sunderland Hall. The view then would have been fairly bleak, with just a farm or two, and the rest open fields and moorland. Pepper Hill would have dominated the northern horizon with little else to break up the scene. At 303 metres above sea level, it is the highest point in the area. Siddal Top, to the south, is 247 metres. And although the view now is dominated by new-build housing, it wasn't difficult to get the sense of why the hall would have fed so strongly into Emily's imagination.

It was a beautiful, late summer's afternoon, but Nicky stressed how austere and desolate the place can be in midwinter, when Emily perversely wrote her 'happy' poem. The school where Emily taught is next door and is also now a private residence. But I didn't knock. I thought I'd pushed my luck far enough.

4

EMILY'S BOOTS -
WALKING EMILY'S MOORS

There are, as far as I know, no extant examples of Emily's footwear. The Parsonage in Haworth has several examples of Charlotte's, including a pair of fur-lined evening pumps and a natty pair of cloth ankle boots with leather toes, heels and side laces. But we can only guess what Emily might have worn to traipse across the moors. Both upper and sole would almost certainly have been made out of leather and nailed together. They might have included cloth pieces, and she might have worn them with protective overshoes or pattens. I can't imagine her wearing these iron, leather and wood contraptions for too long. They would have seemed woefully inadequate to us today.

Emily was much taller than Charlotte, by almost a foot. She was the tallest of all her siblings, Charlotte was the shortest, and Anne and Branwell were about the same height. Charlotte at four foot eleven, or thereabouts, was self-conscious about her diminutive size. I suppose, at five foot ten, Emily was self-conscious of her height for different reasons. But her long legs would have given her an advantage over the others. I imagine they struggled to keep up with her as she strode over the moors. She was more of a lone walker in any case, preferring her own company to the company of others.

I'm thinking about Emily's boots as I stand outside my van lacing up my all-singing, all-dancing, high-performance Merrell boots, with their bellows tongue to keep debris out, breathable-mesh lining, single-density removable footbed, moulded-nylon arch shank and air-cushion heel absorption.

I decide to start my fifteen-mile hike across the moors that surround Haworth not in Haworth itself but in nearby Oxenhope. I don't think Emily would have liked modern-day Haworth, with its artisan beers, cake and coffee, vintage clothing, and 'I Am Heathcliff' tea towels. It's not quite fair to call her a misanthrope, but she would have shunned the tourist trail up Main Street to the Parsonage. And she would have been bemused by her literary success and the literary success of Charlotte and Anne. She had no interest in seeing her work published – that was Charlotte's doing. If we are to find the ghost of Emily today, it won't be in Haworth.

From Oxenhope station I follow Mill Lane past the overflow car park up to the main road and head straight across into Dark Lane. After the chimney, I take the first right up Jew Lane and fork right to Back Leeming. I then walk past Milton House and up by the side of the dam wall, joining the path around the shore of Leeming Reservoir.

I attempted this walk on the bicentenary of Emily's birth in July 2018 with a group of walkers who had come from all over the world. I remember standing in the Parsonage Museum gift shop with Audience Development Officer Diane Fare and the hikers, watching the rain punch the windows and bounce off the paving stones like maggots leaping from a pan of hot fat. We could postpone it, I said. Until the weather clears a bit. Diane and I shared a look, a hopeful moment passed between us. But there were angry, dissenting voices. A hue and cry. They had travelled over land and ocean to be here. One woman had come from New Zealand, another America. Spain, Australia, France, Canada. I saw the light in Diane's eyes die – there's no getting out of this. It was on their bucket list, and they were going to proceed no matter what the weather. We were kitted up in waterproofs and Gore-Tex boots, but as I looked at the rain again, pelting the panes and exploding like grenades on the stone flags outside, I knew that we'd be soaked through in half an hour.

Are you sure you don't want to put it off till a better day? They looked like they could kill me for merely suggesting it. I glanced over to Diane again. She was putting on her best let's-make-the-most-of-it face and zipping up her Lowe Alpine jacket. I raised my eyebrows. Come on, I thought, it's only a bit of 'watter', as they say around here.

Now I'm leading the walk for a local walking festival, and it's raining again, though this time the rain is soft mizzle. At the end of the reservoir, we cross Stony Hill Clough and up to a narrow gate. A decent path leads us straight up the slope of Thornton Moor, the first of five moors we are going to explore. We cross Stubden Conduit before nearing a lone sycamore tree in the ruins of the Hays, where the Book Stones lie. I show the group the small neat letter carving in one corner and tell them about how I'd stood here the year before as the *Countryfile* camera crew had filmed me and Anita Rani talking about the Emily Stone.

We climb up towards Hambleton Top. A faint path angles up one of the old holloways leading to Deep Arse Delf. There are two significant clefts, labelled Great Clough and Little Clough on modern OS maps, which were originally called Great Arse and Little Arse, and it's easy to see why: the fleshy folds look like ample buttocks. We pass prominent shelter cairns as we climb Nab Hill.

Below us is the Mist Stone, a slab of millstone grit with a poem by Simon Armitage, carved by Pip Hall. It was this stone that gave me the idea for the Brontë Stones project. It's a fine poem, one of his best, and ideally located here, overlooking Oxenhope and Haworth, although it is often shrouded in the 'milky breath' of mist.

There used to be all-night raves up here, Dionysian dances that went on till dawn. As the sun rose, illuminating the windmills at Ovenden Moor, making the blades of the turbines flicker with white light, it was like last orders at the bar, when the landlord switches on the lights and everyone sees how fucked everyone is. I remember watching a farmer with his border collie, standing there one pinking dawn, taking it all in – the repetitive thumping bass, the strobe lights, the Day-Glo sticks, the poi and diabolo jugglers, and the gurning ravers, chewing the inside of their cheeks – scratching his head, wondering what it was all about. Dressed in flat cap, waxed jacket and Hunter wellies, he couldn't have looked more different from the sweaty and dishevelled semi-naked revellers. These moors have always harboured strange and wild happenings.

We make our way down to Thornton Moor Conduit to the whitewashed Waggon and Horses pub. The ragtag gang of hikers I'm walking with includes Melissa Percell, a psychologist from Adelaide in South Australia, Eileen Prunty Hynes, a dairy farmer from Ireland and a descendant of Patrick Brontë, Alan Hoggart from closer to home in Burnley, Andrew Galloway from Manchester, Kevin Thomas from Brighouse, Paul Maurice from New Zealand and John Newing from Bristol.

I chat with Melissa first. As we walk, she tells me about her first encounter with the work of the Brontës: 'I went to a girls' Catholic school. I can't remember if I read *Jane Eyre* first or *Wuthering*

Heights. They were both in the family library. I was about thirteen. With *Wuthering Heights*, I had to write little family trees. All the Catherines. Apparently, Virginia Woolf did that in her copy. I got through it. Then I studied it for English. I always remember being really struck by both the passion and the violence. That toxic love. I wonder what would have happened to them if they had got together. You know, got married, had kids. All that?'

'I was a bit older than you when I came across it. About sixteen or seventeen. And I think at that age you think that's what love is. But the older you get, you realise it's not what you want. You just want to come home from a day at work, build a fire, open a bottle of wine and put your feet up.'

'I've reread it a few times since. I'm thirty-three now.'

'A significant age.'

'Yeah. I was thinking about my teenage relationships. That there was something sexy about someone who was a bit mean. But I don't think that now. It was the same with Mr Rochester in *Jane Eyre*. I remember swooning when he lets on that he's liked her all this time.'

'Rochester's sadism really comes out of his social class. He is aloof. He feels superior. Where Heathcliff is the opposite. He's a peasant. His sadism comes from insecurity. Lack of social status.'

'I think Charlotte writes about class too. But she was more conventional.'

I nod in agreement. We head around Horden Clough, past the old route between Haworth and Hebden Bridge until we reach the edge of Haworth Moor. We turn left at a boundary stone marked 'H' and follow a path up to Oxenhope Stoop Hill across boggy peat moor. A meadow pipit leads the way, by hopping along a series of wooden fence posts, its white tail feathers flashing like semaphore flags.

'Does being out here, walking in Emily's footsteps, walking the same moors she did, does it give you a different understanding of the book?'

'This is my first time.'

'First time on the moors?'

'Yeah, it's thrilling to be here, even though it's raining a bit. How wild the moors are and windswept. To experience that first hand is really amazing. It makes sense of the book.'

We follow a faint dike up to Dick Delf Hill. There's another boundary stone here, and we veer right. It's easy to get lost round these parts. Aside from the boundary stone, the moor is unremittingly bleak and featureless. In the winter months, when the mist gathers like dragon's breath and you can't see your hand in front of your face, you need a decent compass, and even then there's an element of pot luck. People have died out here. Tripped in the ditches. Sunk into the peat bogs. There was a story on the local news just a few weeks ago about a body found on the moors, pronounced dead at the scene. The tannins in the peat embalm human flesh. Melissa is right, Heathcliff's cruelty echoes the moor's indifference.

It's a relief to reach the flagstones of the Pennine Way. They are deep and solid and bear the marks of industry: cuttings for machine legs to slot into; bolt holes to fix them. They have been reclaimed from the surrounding mills that lie in the valleys, now either derelict or repurposed. There's something intriguingly circular about the journey of these flagstones, made from stone that was quarried hereabouts to line the floors of factories and mills. I imagine the sound that hobnail boots and wooden clogs would have made on them. Now they have been brought back to their place of origin to be trod on by different types of footwear: rubber lug, Vibram and Michelin soles; Salomon, Merrell, Lowa and Keen.

We follow the flagged path of the Pennine Way to the prominent ruin of Top Withens, the farmhouse that is said to have inspired Emily Brontë's location of Wuthering Heights. The rain is now a fine fizz. We stop to eat sandwiches and drink hot liquid from flasks. Andrew opens the top of a can of Nourishment. It's an enriched-banana-milkshake energy drink that comes in a tin can, not an aluminium one – it's the kind of receptacle that you'd more typically find baked beans or tomato soup inside. The makers of the drink are saying: this might be a drink, but it's more like food. Look, see, it comes in a food can, not a drinks can. The first tin cans were produced for the Royal Navy in 1813, but it wasn't until a bit later that canned food became available to the public, so the Brontës would have seen tin-plated cans as a novelty.

We talk about Top Withens and to what extent it was the inspiration for the location of Wuthering Heights. I'm fairly certain that this windswept, remote location matches that described in the book. And it was Ellen Nussey, a lifelong friend of Charlotte Brontë, who made the claim to the artist who illustrated the 1872 edition of *Wuthering Heights*. The name 'Top Withens' is close enough to 'Wuthering Heights' to suggest a connection. But as the Brontë Society plaque states on the wall of the ruin, 'the building, even when complete, bore no resemblance to the house she described'. Certainly, the description of the dwelling in the book matches more closely that of High Sunderland Hall. Places and people in books are rarely straightforwardly plucked from real life. They may be based on a real person, a real place, but the writer combines elements, invents others, makes stuff up. Despite this, the public appetite for fixing each person, each place, is a consistent one.

The ruin was inhabited during Emily's lifetime. Then, in 1893, Top Withens was struck by lightning during a thunderstorm. The roof was partially torn off, flags were cracked and about thirty windows were destroyed. In the kitchen, the blade of a knife was fused by the heat. The dog and cat fled the building in fear. The incident was reported in the *Todmorden and District News*. Today, the building is owned by Yorkshire Water, and when the rain brays and the winds howl, it can be a very welcome place to take shelter.

We head up a faint path behind the ruin to reach the trig point on Withins Height. Trig point is an abbreviated form. Its full name is trigonometrical point. They're known as trig pillars in Ireland, which seems more descriptive of these strange white concrete obelisks. The process of placing trig points on top of hills and mountains was instigated by the OS in 1935 in order to accurately triangulate Great Britain. It should be possible, if the weather is clear, to see two other trig points from any one trig point. There is no chance of that today. On top of every trig point is a brass plate with three arms and a hole in the middle to mount a theodolite – an instrument used to make angular measurements. These days, they have been usurped by aerial photography and digital mapping using lasers and GPS, but they are still marked on OS maps with the symbol of a small triangle. Their presence in the landscape now make them remnants of an analogue age.

We make our way across to Alcomden Stones, which stands on the brink of the wilderness. It's a stunning location, made up of an extensive scattering of large and impressively shaped stones. It was once thought that these slabs were placed here by druids. And it's easy to see why, particularly when you contemplate the flat top of what is called the altar stone. But geologists are fairly certain that the stones were placed here by nature. That's not to say that the ancients didn't utilise them for pagan rituals, or simply for solace. Or even for protection from the harsh elements. It was the historian J. Horsfall Turner, in his 1879 history of Haworth, who makes the claim of a druidic altar, and there are other stones marked with deep-cupped indentations. But none of them can be said with any certainty to have been carved by people instead of the elements. It is likely, though, that such a place would have attracted those predisposed to occult pastimes.

For me, this is a likely source for Penistone Crag, where Heathcliff and Cathy go to shelter and be together, although it is often said that it is more likely to be Ponden Kirk, which we're heading towards. But Ponden Kirk is not an obvious place to shelter. It hangs on a dangerous precipice. From where we stand we get a good view of Stanbury Bog beneath Crow Hill. It was here in 1824 where the silence of the moors was shattered by a massive explosion as the bog spewed out rock and earth across the surrounding hillside after a heavy storm. It polluted the River Aire to such an extent that its waters couldn't be used for some time. According to Juliet Barker, the entire wool industry in the area ground to a halt because the water was so dirty. Patrick Brontë witnessed the event and thought it was an earthquake sent by God. I think about *The Great Day of His Wrath*, the painting by 'Mad' John Martin that hung over Patrick's table in his study. It shows the earth folding in on itself, as God takes revenge for human sin.

On the day of the explosion, the children were out playing further down the moor. Patrick managed to reach them in time, and they sheltered at Ponden Hall. They would have watched the seven-foot-high river of peat, rock and earth pass by their window. Patrick was so impressed by the event that he wrote both a poem and a sermon about it. In his sermon, he describes how the moor sank into two wide cavities, the larger being three hundred yards in length and two hundred yards in breadth. It is no wonder that for Emily the moors were a place of awe and fascination. It was a land that was alive with a terrible destructive beauty.

Next, we head down into the heather of Middle Moor Clough and pick up a path that follows a line of grouse butts above the stream. Shooting parties can pay up to £3,000 for a weekend of grouse shooting. Nouveau-riche businessmen get to dress in tweeds and pretend that they are toffs. We follow this path all the way, crossing the clough to reach a sign above Raven Rock.

I chat to Eileen Prunty Hynes, the dairy farmer from Tipperary. Prunty is her maiden name, Patrick's original moniker. He changed his name around the time he entered St John's College, Cambridge, perhaps to mask his humble origins. 'My father came from the north of Ireland from Monaghan,' Eileen says, 'and his father came from near Belfast, and his father came from Banbridge, near Drumballyroney – Patrick's place. I can't really go back much further than that. There aren't any records. My father was always talking about the Brontës. He used to tell us that we were related to them. My father is dead now, since 1993. And I wasn't really that interested at the time. It was in later years that I got interested. But after he died, I got really fascinated. This is my fourth trip to Haworth. He told me that a relation of his had a stick – tis called a shillelagh in Ireland – belonging to Hugh Prunty. It was sort of a long, thin stick with a big top to it. You don't see them any more. When I was young, they were all over the place. In shops, you know.'

'When I was at school, I got the cane a lot. But I think it got outlawed in about 1986, a year before I left school. How about the shillelagh?'

'I don't know much about that. I don't think it was used in that way. In schools, you know. Anyway, my father told me the story of Welsh and how the grandfather brought the child back from Liverpool.'

'It's interesting, isn't it, because the Hugh Prunty–Welsh story is so similar to that of Jack Sharp.'

'Yes, it is. In my mind, she combined the two stories to create *Wuthering Heights*. And if you go into the church in Drumballyroney, there's paintings all over the church, and one of them is a lovely painting of his family all sitting down having great fun. I think that Patrick was passing on all these stories to his daughters.'

'You can see them, the sisters, as almost substitute wives for Patrick. You can imagine them sat round the dining table, and Patrick having the sort of conversations with them that he might have had with Maria if she had been alive. What sort of age would you have been when your father told you these stories?'

'I would have been in my late teens. And I would have told him to shut up, you know. Especially when he had a few jars in him. And then, all of a sudden, I developed this mad interest. Before I came, last July, I went to the hairdresser, and I was telling her I was off to Yorkshire for Emily's bicentenary and all that. And she said, "Oh my God, I would love to meet a Heathcliff."'

'Oh, dear!'

'And she showed me her tattoo. On her back, all the way from her neck to her backside: "He is more myself than I am". This is the day I was travelling to Haworth.'

We head straight down the steep slope to reach the dam in Ponden Clough. We then follow the path around the head of the clough. Further up, we look back to take in the precipice of Ponden Kirk. There is a gap in the rock beneath through which it was said a maiden could crawl if she was to be married before the year was out. Also, according to Bradford-born author Halliwell Sutcliffe, 'this dark kirk of the wilderness' is a place where 'Pagan mothers once worshipped lustily'. Last time I was here, I walked across the top, and standing on the edge of the kirk were two men who were not in walking attire. It was raining hard, but they were dressed for the high street. I knew that there was a film company making a documentary about Lily Cole, and that they were probably hanging around to film her. I saw some large bags behind them that could have contained their photographic equipment. Then I saw a large black Range Rover approach with Lily inside. Lily was the Parsonage Museum's creative partner in 2018. Her project connected the parsonage with the Foundling Museum in Liverpool, culminating in her short film *Balls*, inspired by the story of Heathcliff in *Wuthering Heights*. Not everyone responded favourably to Lily's appointment. Brontë biographer Nick Holland called it a 'rank farce', a comment that was widely criticised, with several writers accusing him of snobbery.

Eventually, we stop outside Ponden Hall, the Elizabethan farmhouse that is usually cited as the model for Thrushcross Grange in *Wuthering Heights*. Though it is certainly more complicated than that, it would have been an influence on Emily. The Heaton family were good friends of the Brontës, and the children visited the hall regularly. The house had an extensive library that included Gothic romances, books about property acquisition and a folio edition of Shakespeare's plays. There are a number of references to Shakespeare in *Wuthering Heights*, including a direct reference to *King Lear*. Although the main house was built in 1634, an extension was added in 1801, and the lintel above the door is inscribed with this date, which is also the first word of *Wuthering Heights*: '1801 – I have just returned from a visit to my landlord – the solitary neighbour that I shall be troubled with.' Mr Lockwood, the narrator of the story at this point, arriving from London, is referring to his first encounter with Heathcliff in a place he refers to as a 'misanthrope's heaven'.

Ponden Hall is now owned by Steve Brown and Julie Akhurst, who have restored many of the original features. Although it has often been associated with the Lintons' home in the book, it is much smaller than that described by Emily. The bedrooms include one with a box-bed built to the specifications of the bed Mr Lockwood slept in, fitted around a window that matches Emily's description in the book.

From here, we head back into Haworth and along the beck to Oxenhope Station. We are a bedraggled caravan of soggy walkers and Brontë enthusiasts. We haven't encountered any ghosts, but, traipsing over the five moors that surround Haworth, we've walked in Emily's wake. Our feet are wet, despite our high-tech footwear, no doubt as wet as Emily's would have been. For all their precision engineering, in a deluge they are no better than hobnailed boots.

I stop on the way home for a bag of chips. I'm served by a tall, thin woman with long, dark hair. There are two lads in front of me, and they say something to her that I don't catch. She says in response, 'Talk to me like that again, and I'll give you a slap.' She wraps the chips in newspaper and hands me the hot parcel. I look at her, and, for a moment, I swear I'm staring at the reincarnation of Emily.

5

MR EARNSHAW'S WALK TO LIVERPOOL

It's June 2016, and I've decided to recreate the walk that Mr Earnshaw took in 1771 when he travelled from Wuthering Heights to Liverpool. I will set off from Top Withens, it being the most likely source of inspiration for the farmhouse location in the novel.

I left school at sixteen. I didn't go to college, and I didn't do A levels. Instead, I worked in factories around the Manchester area. It wasn't until I was twenty-four that a girlfriend at that time suggested that if I wanted to be a writer, I should go to university to study English literature. It seemed like a good idea. Twenty-odd years later, I'm still with her. It was sound advice.

When I came across John Sutherland's essay 'Is Heathcliff a Murderer?' in the university library in 1995, I was struck by the opening sentence: 'When he returns to Wuthering Heights after his mysterious three-year period of exile Heathcliff has become someone very cruel. He left as an uncouth but essentially humane stable-lad. He returns a gentleman psychopath.' 'Psychopath' didn't quite cut it. Heathcliff doesn't suffer from an absence of feeling but of a surfeit. I started to really think about what had happened to him during those three years. I also started to think more about where Heathcliff was from, why Mr Earnshaw had travelled all the way to Liverpool and back in one trip, and why he had named the boy he brought back after his dead son. I became fascinated by the possibilities.

Mr Earnshaw was a farmer. Why would he travel to Liverpool in the middle of summer when his workload would have been at its most intense? And why wouldn't he take one of the horses from his stable? What would draw him to Liverpool? He couldn't be on business. Liverpool wasn't a market town. Why else would he avoid the established coach that went from Yorkshire to Liverpool unless he was travelling covertly? I started to think more about Liverpool and what it was most known for in 1771. At that time, it was the biggest slave port in Europe.

In the book, Mr Earnshaw walks from Wuthering Heights to Liverpool and back in three days. We are told it is a sixty-mile journey each way. My own calculations make it more like seventy – 140 miles in total. I've walked from my home in Thornton, so by the time I get to Top Withens I've already done twelve miles. Wolfie walks thirty feet in front of me, on the lookout for grouse. I take the Pennine Way, over Dean Stones Edge, dropping down to Walshaw Dean Reservoir. The Pennine Way circumscribes these black waters before snaking south-west, but I leave the path before it does this, travelling instead over High Rakes and White Hill, through the hamlet of Walshaw and then along the wooded clough of Hebden Dale and Hardcastle Crags. I drop south up New Greenwood Lee to Knoll Top, taking a series of pathways until I come to the edge of Colden Clough. I feel a wet pat on my neck. Then another on my cheek. I look up and see silver rods falling from the sky: 'boding abundant rain', as Emily puts it in *Wuthering Heights*.

As I join the Pennine Way again up to Pry Hill past Badger

Fields farm, the rain comes down in buckets. It drips off my head, down my neck and down my spine. It drips off the end of my nose. The lip of my hood is a gutter. Eventually, I join the Rochdale Canal just past Charlestown. I walk along the canal path through Todmorden and then towards Littleborough. As soon as I hit the Lancashire–Yorkshire border, the scene changes. The canal waters that have been populated with middle-class hippies in painted barges now turn dirty with debris and discarded shopping trolleys.

I see the market town of Littleborough in the distance. It's past eight o'clock in the evening, and I've been walking for twelve hours with just a ten-minute break. I'm knackered. I must have walked more than thirty miles, and I can't walk any more. My rucksack felt moderately light when I set off this morning. It now feels like I'm carrying a dead body on my back. I decide that Littleborough will be my home for the night.

When I get to Littleborough, I'm soaked to the bone. My clothes cling to my skin. My feet squidge in the swamp of my boots. I go into the first pub, no dogs, then the second, no dogs, then the third, no dogs. Eventually, I persuade the final tavern to let me in. Despite the 'No dogs' sign, I cut such a miserable figure that the landlord takes pity on me. I sit in the corner and nurse a pint. I'm a pathetic spectacle, dripping rainwater onto the carpet. Wolfie sits by my feet, his fur flattened to his skin. He looks like a starving stray. A hulkish bloke with a bald head and finger tattoos approaches my table.

'Nice dog you got there.' I nod. 'He's shivering, poor thing.'

The man pulls his sweatshirt over his head, lifting his T-shirt up momentarily, revealing a scar on the side of his torso and more tattoos. He pulls it back down again, and then, using his sweatshirt as a towel, he dries my dog.

'I told the landlord to let you in,' he says. 'Us lot, we've got to stick together.' He points to my jacket, which is British Army surplus, and I realise he's mistaken me for a veteran soldier.

'Yeah,' I say and hold my glass up. 'Cheers!' We chink glasses.

'You seen a bit of action, then?'

It's too late now to admit the error. He's bought it hook, line and sinker. He's bumped into one of life's familiars, and it's made his night. I don't have the heart to shatter his illusions.

'Yeah,' I say, and nod in such a grim way I hope he will be silenced.

'Me too,' he says. 'The people round here, the folk in this pub, good people, but they don't know. They haven't got a clue. What it does to you. What you have to do. What you see.'

'I know,' I say. I wonder if it's too late to back out. But he's on a roll.

'I was in Iraq. Tell you what, I still have nightmares. When I came out, I couldn't sleep. I was just drinking. Neat vodka. Straight from the bottle. I'd black out. Wake up somewhere. No idea how I got there. It was chronic. My girlfriend gave me an ultimatum. She said I had to get my head sorted out or she was going to leave me.'

'So, what happened?'

'She left me.'

'Sorry about that.'

'Fuck her. Fucking bitch. They don't understand. They haven't got a clue. I'm telling yer. Fuck that.'

That night, I find a bit of scrap land by the edge of the canal. It's far enough away from the town, a quiet spot beneath the shade of a sycamore. It's dark. I erect my one-man tent with great difficulty. In sober daylight, I can put it up in two minutes. But by moonlight, after five pints, it takes me about twenty minutes. As I climb into my sleeping bag, I realise there is no room for Wolfie. The tent is like a coffin – it fits me with no room for anyone else. He will have to sleep on top of me.

I'm settling down when I hear voices. Muffled at first, they get clearer as a gang of lads approach. I can't hear what they are saying. Wolfie is asleep on top of me. I can just make out their silhouettes from an outside light. They wear hoodies and smoke spliffs of pungent skunk. They play grime through their phones. They laugh and joke. Their laughter sounds sinister. They are harmless enough, I tell myself. Nothing to worry about. But what if, in their stoned states, they think it would be fun to chuck me in the canal? Don't be daft, I tell myself. Why would they do that? It's what lads do. When they're together. They do stuff they wouldn't do on their own. They egg each other on. It would be easy for them to pull out the pegs, grab my bivvie, one at each end, lift it up and launch it into the canal. It's deep at this end. Lock end. I'd sink like a stone. I wouldn't be able to get out of the tent, and I'd drown. Wolfie would drown with me. I take hold of the zipper and stay like that, poised. If they are going to chuck me in the canal, I want a fighting chance. I remain in that position for ten minutes, twenty, half an hour. My heart beats hard in my chest. My arm aches, but I don't let go of the zipper.

At some point, sleep must come, because the next thing I know the voices have gone and the shapes have faded. The gang has disappeared. The only movement is from my dog. His leg muscles spasm as he dreams of chasing a rabbit. I try and get back to sleep, but the weight of him, and the movement, make it impossible for me to rest. I think about waking him up, but then there would be two of us deprived of sleep. I let him dream on, while I lie there in discomfort.

Eventually, day breaks, and I manage to stir Wolfie. He is the very definition of a creature who sleeps like a log. He sleeps the untroubled sleep of the innocent. I shake him gently and he wakes. I zip open the entrance, and we both climb out. He stretches, has a sniff around and pisses up a tree, while I pack up my tent and stuff my sleeping bag into its sack. I load my rucksack. I've travelled light. I feed him his breakfast and watch him chase the empty bowl up the towpath. I stretch. I'm sore and ache all over. The sky is bright grey. The ground is still wet, but the rain has stopped. My plan is to walk along the canal path to Manchester, then head over to Lymm and then Liverpool.

As I walk, I creak. It was a poor excuse for a night's sleep. The water to my left is as still as bath water, and as I pass by I disturb a kingfisher from its hunting spot. It flits past, brilliant blue and golden orange, its bill a black stiletto, and I think, as I always do when I see a kingfisher, of the first line of a Gerard Manley Hopkins poem: 'As kingfishers catch fire, dragonflies draw flame'. It's a bit of a tongue-twister.

I travel south-west past Clegg Hall, with Owl Hill in the distance, then through the edgelands of Belfield and Newbold. The canal passes through the town of Kirkholt, which spreads into Castletown. Past Boarshaw, the canal creeps south-east and then east as it intersects with the River Irk, then it drops a plumbline south as it passes through Chadderton. I seem to be on the outskirts of post-industry and urbanisation, and the view is grey and featureless. This canal was conceived in 1776, five years after Mr Earnshaw's journey, when the area would have been a no-man's-land, with highwaymen and cutpurses, vagrants and vagabonds. The canals brought an end to the highwayman's trade. It's hard to hold up a barge on horseback, even with a pistol. The canal opened in stages, in 1798 then fully in 1804.

The view becomes more urban as the canal goes through Failsworth and then Newton Heath. It was here, aged sixteen, just a stone's throw away, that I started as an apprentice winder – a now obsolete trade involving the fitting of electrical coils in motor casings. The factory was Mather and Platts, and it employed thousands of staff, mostly men, with a few women working in the offices upstairs. I was attached to a bloke called Old Tom, and my job was to assist him. What that meant in reality was standing by his workplace while he fitted electrical coils into motor casings. Occasionally, a motor casing would need to be stripped, and I'd get to work with a hammer and chisel, but mostly it was standing around. You weren't allowed to put your hands in your pockets. If the foreman caught you, he'd give you a bollocking. The factory closed shortly after I left. The whole area has undergone a facelift and has been rejuvenated, and as I reach Miles Platting there is an uneasy mix of hipsters living in narrow boats and gangs of lads in hoodies from the estate, smoking reefers.

I leave the canal just off Ancoats and walk into Manchester city centre. I go down Tib Street, which used to be all pet shops and porno shops, but now is full of hipster bars and boutiques. I remember coming here as a kid to watch the brightly coloured Siamese fighting fish. Each pet shop, and there were more than twenty of them, specialised in a different animal. The whole street stunk of lizard piss, snake shit and sawdust. Now it smells of freshly roasted coffee and speciality herbal teas. I find a café with some seats on the terrace and order a drink. I sit outside with Wolfie.

Everyone is sipping coffee. A woman in a black beret hugs the bowl of her cup as though it were a lover. Her lips kiss the rim. Coffee with froth, with whipped cream, chocolate sprinkles, with a flake in it and a raspberry ripple and a cherry on top, the way you get a child to swallow its medicine. This is the fuel of our service economy. No great ideas were conceived drinking coffee.

I walk through town, past Affleck's Palace, where I used to hang out in the late eighties with all the goths and punks, and down Market Street, wending my way between happy shoppers and homeless beggars. It's an odd mix, this cheek-by-jowl poverty and plenty, but I guess not that different from how it was in the late eighteenth century.

The first factory in England was built in 1717. It was a silk factory on the River Derwent that employed three hundred workers. But it was here in the north that the Industrial Revolution really took off, thanks to a combination of soft water, steep hills and cheap labour. In 1750, the population of Manchester was 25,000. By 1800, it had quadrupled to 100,000. In 1750, there were two factories. By 1800, there were more than fifty. I imagine the great wave of immigration from the rural surroundings, and from further afield – the Emerald Isle and further still – a huge influx of workers to fill the labour holes. Some of them would have come here to seek their fortune only to find themselves out of work and unhomed. It is here in the late eighteenth century that the first soup kitchens began to feed the poor – they are still here to this day. And it is here that drink and drug addiction became a visible problem – it still is today.

Past the spice addicts in Piccadilly Square that stand like extras in a George A. Romero film, down Deansgate, I make my way to Castlefield, where I join the Bridgewater Canal. It was opened in 1761, ten years before Mr Earnshaw's walk. Emily would have been aware of this feat of engineering, it being the first canal in England, although it is not a true canal, as it required an aqueduct to cross the River Irwell. The Duke of Bridgewater built it to transport coal from his mines in Worsley to his factories in Manchester. The duke visited Canal du Midi in France and, after being dumped by the Dowager Duchess of Hamilton, decided on this symbol of his virility.

I cross the aqueduct at Barton and join the road as I now need to head south-west again, through Irlam and Cadishead. The walking here is grim. Close to a massive industrial estate, there is a constant caravan of articulated trucks and flatbeds, spitting out toxic effluence. It has started raining again, a fine mist, and the salts, cements and powders that spray off the back of the lorries coat my skin like a mud mask, with the rain acting as a glue gun. My face soon feels stiff and crusty.

A few years after quitting my factory job at Mather and Platt, I got a fundraising job at an animal charity called Animals in Distress, the head office of which is just around the corner. It was an eventful time, and I remember driving back from one of the charity shops in Withington with a cat in a box, to take to the sanctuary, but somehow the cat had escaped and was running around the car in a state of high excitement. I remember trying to steer straight as the cat leapt up my chest and onto my head.

I traipse along the unremittingly dull Cadishead Way, which again skirts the edges of post-industry. By the time I get to Hollins Green, my feet are throbbing, and I'm in pain from a blister underneath my heel bone. The rain is dropping out of the sky like bowling balls. I stop at the Black Swan. I need to rest my feet. I need to eat. I need a strong drink. Inside, the pub is vast. It comprises a dining area, a tap room and a hotel. My plan is to hide out here till the rain stops and refuel. It's late afternoon, and there are a few punters around the bar and a few diners in the dining area. I order a pint of Guinness and a Jameson chaser. I neck half the whiskey then pour the rest into the stout to sweeten it. There isn't much that is vegan friendly on the menu, so I settle for the halloumi and vegetable kebab without the halloumi.

I drink my Guinness and order another as the food arrives. I eat my kebab. The rain is hammering against the window. I finish my Guinness and order another. There is no let up. It's early evening when the rain eventually stops. I'm four pints in and suitably rested. I settle my bill, haul my sack onto my back again and hit the road, dog in tow. I stop at a corner shop to buy a bottle of red wine and a tin of Butcher's Tripe. I plod and toddle, wincing from the blister that has now popped, exposing fresh red skin. I walk down the A57, turning right at Warburton Bridge Road, passing Hollybank Caravan Park. I think about stopping there for the night, but I reckon I've got about another hour's walking left in me before I collapse.

Along Warburton Bridge, I cross over the River Irwell, close to where it merges with the Mersey. It's a toll bridge, and cars queue as their drivers furtle for change. I pass St Werburgh's Church and approach the village of Warburton. I must have hit the thirty-mile mark by now, and I'm done in. I start looking for somewhere to get my head down for the night. Just outside of the village is a large detached property surrounded by nice flat green fields. It looks uninhabited. I climb over the fence and find a sheltered area under some trees and parallel to a hawthorn hedge. I take off my sack and unload my tent. I start to erect it. As I do, a black 4x4 Range Rover approaches and a man in a blue suit gets out.

'What the hell do you think you're doing?'

Thinking on my feet, I say, 'Is this not a campsite?'

'Does it look like a fucking campsite? Do you see any other campers?'

'Sorry, I thought it said on my map that it was a campsite.'

'Well, it's not, so fuck off!'

I try a different tack: 'Look, I'm sorry. It was an honest mistake. I don't suppose you know anywhere close by I can camp, do you?'

He pauses before answering, thinking it through. He's in no mood to give me salient advice, but at the same time I can see he wants me as far away from his land as he can manage. Eventually, he says, 'Listen, there's a campsite up the road. I'm going past that way. Jump in and I'll give you a lift.'

'But I've got my dog.'

'He can go in the back.'

He opens up the back of his 4x4. There are two guitars in there in hard cases, along with some cables and other sound equipment. He shifts them across and makes room for Wolfie, who jumps in. I get in the front, next to the man. He starts the engine.

'Are you in a band, then?'

'Yeah.'

'Do you get any gigs?'

'Just pub gigs. It's just a laugh. Me and my mates. Used to play every day. Then I didn't pick up a guitar for twenty years. Went into estates.

Made a lot of money. But I wasn't happy. One day I was in my garage, and I just picked up a guitar and started playing again. It felt great.'

'Why did you leave it so long? I mean, if you enjoy playing so much.'

'Long story.'

He goes silent.

'Sorry if I've touched a nerve.'

'I used to be in a band in the eighties. We had a bit of chart success. We were going places, do you know what I mean. But we couldn't get on with each other. Then the lead singer walked and that was it. The chance of making it big. We blew it.' We drive in silence for a while. 'We could have been massive.'

'Still, you've done all right. Made a load of money.'

He nods, but I can see he is not convinced. Money is a poor substitute for adulation. He drives us back out of the village and over Warburton Toll Bridge. Bollocks, I think, as he pulls up outside Hollybank Caravan Park. That's three miles I didn't have to walk today, and three miles I'll have to walk again tomorrow, and my heart sinks.

'There you go, mate.'

'Cheers.'

I rescue Wolfie from the back and wave the driver off. The reception to the Caravan Park is in the dark. I try the door. It's locked. There is no one around. It doesn't look like much of a place. I go around the back and pitch my tent in the middle of a field. There are no other tents, and I wonder if perhaps the campsite has gone out of business. Not that it matters to me, really. I'll stay here if I can, move if someone makes me. I open the can of dog food, spoon it into a bowl and chop it into bite-size chunks. I also open the wine and swig out of the bottle. It's sweet and soft.

I'm thinking about the man who gave me a lift. He looked familiar. I think about all the Manchester bands that were big in the eighties but didn't quite make it all the way – Northside, Candyflip, The Bridewell Taxis – but I can't bring any of their faces to mind. The Happy Mondays, The Inspiral Carpets, The Stone Roses. They all made it in the end, so they don't count. I've already mentioned that I went to the same school as The Happy Mondays. They were leaving as I was starting. We used to watch them rehearse in Wardley Community Centre next to the school. I remember Bez hanging around outside the school gates, trying to cop off with a schooley.

The bloke in the Range Rover looked to be about my age, so they couldn't have been a band from the early eighties, as he would have been too young. Of course, he could have been in The Fall. Pretty much every Manchester musician was in The Fall at some point in the eighties. But their lead singer never walked. The Fall start and end with Mark E. Smith.

I'm halfway into the bottle and still racking my brains when it occurs to me that I should have just asked the man. It would have saved me the headache. And he might have welcomed the chance to chat about it with someone who was interested.

'Do you want a glass for that?'

I look up. A big, fat bald man with tattoos everywhere and no top on is standing over me. He points to my bottle.

'Er, yeah, that would be very civilised. Thanks.'

He disappears and returns with a wine glass: 'You staying long?'

'Nah, just the night. How about you?'

'I live here.'

'You live here?'

'Yeah, we all do. I've got a caravan behind that line of trees there.'

He points over. 'There's a dozen of us live here. We're having a bit of a party later. Why don't you join us?'

'Thanks. I'd like that.'

He nods then walks back the way he came. I take off my boot and my sock and examine the wound. The skin is a livid pink-red and stings like hell. I dig out my first-aid kit, rub soothing cream into it and then apply a plaster. I lie back on the grass and watch the gulls gyre and the clouds drift and mutate. Wolfie curls up beside me, and I stroke his belly. I leave it half an hour or so, before making my way over to where the tattooed man disappeared. I don't have much to offer, just half a bottle of warm red wine.

The campsite beyond the trees is comprised of a dozen caravans, mainly with brightly coloured awnings attached. I hear voices coming from the largest one. There's a flagged patio and a barbecue. I smell it before I see it. The bald, tattooed man is stood over it with a pair of easy-grip tongs in one hand and half a spliff in the other. He flips a steak.

'Hey, you made it. Want some grub?'

'I've eaten, thanks.'

'This is Jenny,' he says, pointing to a woman with shaggy blonde hair. I assume it is his wife or girlfriend. 'And this is Tom.' He points to a boy who is playing with an iPad. He's a mini-me, a slimmer, younger version of his dad, I think, as I look from one to the other. I can see his mum in him too. They share the same oversized philtrum. He's probably about twelve years old.

'Hiya,' Jenny says. The boy just grunts and goes back to his tablet. 'Do you want a lager?' She offers me a can of Stella.

'I've got this, thanks,' I say, and wave my half-full bottle at her.

'Have a sit down. The others will be here in a bit.' I sit on a striped deckchair next to where she is sitting. 'Patrick was saying you're just staying the night?' She takes the spliff and has a toke.

'Yeah. Moving on in the morning.'

'Where are you going?'

'Liverpool.'

'What for?'

I think about telling her the reason but then realise that they will probably think it's a bit of a weird thing to do. But maybe not. I can't decide whether to make something up or to let them in on it. Whatever I make up will probably sound just as weird. Besides, what does it matter. I'm unlikely to ever see any of them again.

'Have you heard of *Wuthering Heights*?'

'The book? Oh, yeah, I had to read it at school. I fucking hate that book. All that Yorkshire dialect. I mean, what the fuck's that all about?'

'Right, yeah. Well, do you remember the bit where Mr Earnshaw goes to Liverpool?'

'Who?'

'You know, the dad. He comes back with Heathcliff.'

'Oh, yeah.'

'Well, I wanted to make the same journey.'

'What for?'

Should I tell them I'm writing a book? I'm just going to dig myself deeper. Make them think I'm an even bigger weirdo. 'Just something to do, I suppose. Every summer, I do a big walk. Last year, I did Hadrian's Wall.'

'Oh, right. Whatever. I couldn't be bothered. Want some of this?' She passes me the spliff. 'You ever read it, Patrick?'

'Have I fuck.'

A black man with jazzy dreads appears with a bag of booze.

'Hey, Buff, how you doing?' Jenny introduces us. He's a plasterer. Lived in Irlam with his missus, but they split up, and he moved here. Two years ago.

'It's how I like it,' he says. 'They can't get me here. No one knows my address.'

Another couple arrives. Then another bloke in a bucket hat. He doesn't suit the hat. No one suits a bucket hat. Then two more, another couple. Before I know it, I'm surrounded by people. The wine has gone, and I'm drinking rum. I'm drinking tequila. I'm drinking vodka.

The next thing I remember is waking up, entombed in my tent. I don't know where I am at first. I stare at the green ceiling, my nose almost touching it, and listen to the sound of a rhythmically roaring engine. I wonder, is it an aeroplane? Or what else could it be? And then it dawns on me that it's not an engine. It's the sound of Wolfie snoring. He's lying on top of me. My tongue is stuck to the roof of my mouth, and my eyelids creak. I've got a heavy feeling in my head that I know is going to grow into a full blown headache in a bit. I unzip the tent and crawl out like an imago emerging from a chrysalis, but instead of morphing into something more colourful, more beautiful, I just collapse on the grass and squint in the light of the rising sun. The horizon is golden. White mist laces a line of trees.

Once on the move again, I walk back over Warburton Toll Bridge and yet again through the village of Warburton. I then walk down Townsfield Lane until I hit the Trans Pennine Trail, which is going to take me all the way to Liverpool. I reckon I've got at least twenty miles until I reach my destination: Liverpool docks.

In 1771, Liverpool was a bustling port, including 105 fleets engaged in the African slave trade. These ships went to the west coast of Africa to pick up their human cargo, before transporting them to the West Indies to work mainly on sugar plantations. Many died on this middle passage, and the dead bodies were thrown overboard. In fact, it was legal to throw the living overboard as well, and those showing visible signs of illness or pregnancy were sometimes despatched in this way. Let's give it a name: murder. Those who lived were confined in tiny boxes, like sardines in a tin. The passage took weeks, and during this time they would be sitting in their own shit and piss. The stench must have been overpowering. It was big business: at that time, 80 per cent of England's wealth was a result of the slave trade; eleven million Africans were transported into slavery and 1.4 million died on the voyage. Between 1763 and 1776, Liverpool was Britain's main slave-trading port. Twice as many vessels engaged in the slavery business here than they did in Bristol. By the end of the century, Liverpool merchants were responsible for 84 per cent of the total British transatlantic slave trade.

The many slaves who were brought to Liverpool were bought and sold openly on the streets and in the town square. I think about this when I arrive at Liverpool docks. It is now a place to drink and eat and shop. You can also visit the Tate gallery. The main dock, the Royal Albert, would not have been built in 1771, but there were several large docks back then: King's Dock, Salthouse Dock and George's Dock. There were goods sheds, tobacco warehouses, spirit vaults, breweries, inns and taverns. The air would have been rich and sharp with strong aromas. The stench of things baking, boiling and burning. Mashing, malting and milling. Sweet yeast and bitter hop. There is no trace now of the poor house or the house of correction. There are no cooperages, block-and-spar-makers' shops or boat-building yards.

I see a young family sitting outside a cocktail bar with a designer pram. The mother drinks a glass of prosecco with a strawberry garnish. The father fiddles with a bottle of fruit cider. I, on the other hand, am here to access the public records of Liverpool Central Library and also the slavery archives of the Maritime Museum just around the corner. The shrieking gulls above connect then with now. As I make my way to the museum entrance, I think again about Mr Earnshaw. In my mind, there can be only one reason why he made this journey, as I have just done, on foot. He came here for a slave.

6

BRANWELL'S BASTARD AND BLACK COMBE

It's a bright spring Saturday morning, and I'm driving down the A595 in my campervan towards the town of Broughton-in-Furness, where Branwell Brontë was employed as a private tutor by the Postlethwaites in 1840 after failing to establish himself as a portrait painter in Bradford. He only lasted about six months before he was abruptly dismissed, and there is a mystery around why he was sacked so suddenly. Some say he was drunk on the job, others that he neglected his duties, but the theory that interests me most is the one put forward by Juliet Barker: that Branwell got a local servant girl pregnant and was run out of town.

I stayed in my van last night on the driveway of old friends whom I've known since the late eighties. We used to hang around the same places in Manchester: Affleck's Palace, Dry Bar, Night and Day Café, and The Hacienda. They now live close to Arnside, on the edge of the Lake District. Donna is the recently appointed head teacher of a special school in Ulverston, and Christian is a part-time librarian. They have three daughters, with similar age gaps to the three younger Brontë sisters. We drank a lot of beer and gin and red wine.

There are hardly any other cars, and for a large part of the journey I have the roads to myself. Wolfie, who has been slumped on the bed in the back of my van, sits up sentinel, instinctively sensing that we are arriving somewhere. As I drive off the A595 onto the C5009, I'm thinking about Branwell's journey to Broughton-in-Furness, setting off by coach from Keighley on New Year's Eve 1839. He came the same way as I've done, travelling by coach out of Yorkshire on the Kendal road, passing Cowan Bridge, where all his sisters except Anne had received a rough education. It was where the two eldest sisters contracted TB and died, which is why Patrick immediately removed Charlotte and Emily to home educate them. It was fictionalised in *Jane Eyre* as Lowood School.

It's a remote spot. As I approached it the previous day, I decided to stop outside the building to read the plaque embedded in the wall: 'Maria, Elizabeth, Charlotte & Emily Brontë lived here as pupils of the clergy daughter's school 1824–25'. I wondered if Branwell had stopped to look around. He would almost certainly have dwelt on the memory of his four sisters leaving and only two returning. He would have been six years old when his eldest sister died, and, having only just lost his mother a few years previously, Maria may have been something of a substitute mother.

He stopped that night at the Royal Hotel in Kirby Lonsdale. As I reached the town, I took a right and parked in the centre. Branwell wrote to his friend John Brown about the night, telling him how he drank whisky and joined a party of gentlemen at the Royal Hotel: 'they gave cunt and pillock ... washing it down at the same time as the room spun round and the candles danced in our eyes ... a regular rumpus ensued ... I found myself in bed next morning with a bottle of porter, a glass, and a corkscrew beside me.' Sounds like he had an eventful evening.

I too called into the Royal Hotel, which is located in the market square. It still provides drink, food and accommodation to the weary traveller, but yesterday's clientele appeared to be more sober – mainly young families, preferring to take advantage of the three-course meal deal rather than strong spirits. Juliet Barker wonders to what extent Branwell's account was exaggerated for the entertainment of his friend. It must be hard to be the son of a holy man. As a young man in your late teens and early twenties, you want to prove your manhood, but being the son of a clergyman makes you square. How tempting it must be to play up your wild side. But if his version is accurate, he would have been nursing a hangover as he travelled to Broughton on New Year's Day 1840, as I am, as I travel into Broughton on 4 May 2019. I park up in the square, get out of my van, let Wolfie out and stretch my legs.

In the centre of the square is an obelisk erected in 1810 to commemorate the fiftieth year of King George III's reign, which was also the year that the king, who suffered from recurring mental illness, finally relapsed and a regency was established. All this was brilliantly dramatised in Alan Bennett's play *The Madness of George III*, which was made into a film, retitled as *The Madness of King George*, starring Nigel Hawthorne as the king and Helen Mirren as his long-suffering queen.

Underneath the obelisk are the village stocks, a double device, consisting of wooden boards and hinges, so that two miscreants can have their ankles fastened. They were originally sited beside the entrance to the lane leading down to the church. They would probably have been fully functioning during Branwell's stay. And he may have witnessed unruly artisans fastened there for a few hours, a day, or even longer. Close by are the fish slabs, where trout and salmon from the River Duddon would have once been sold.

The square consists of the Manor Arms, a real-ale pub, and another extant feature, the tourist information centre, and an arts and craft centre that was once the market hall and includes a fine clock tower. The weathervane perched on top consists of a man whipping a fox that is chasing a rabbit. There is also a restaurant and a café. But the houses and buildings that face this square, built with the grey slate characteristic of this area, are all pretty much unchanged from what Branwell would have seen.

This is all very different to the Broughton of my childhood, an area of Salford where I used to play, with its red-brick terraced houses and scrubbed steps, its cobbled 'backings' and washing lines drooping with damp clothes and bedding.

Just beyond the square is Broughton Tower, which is now a school for children with special needs. It has a history going back to the twelfth century, and the tower itself dates from the early fourteenth century. Further on is a park that ascends to a steep raised copse that overlooks the town. I assume this is what Juliet Barker refers to as High Duddon, although it is not marked on the map. The view from here is spectacular, surrounded on all sides by Cumbrian mountains that in this morning light on the day before May Day glow green and orange. Above me, two buzzards rise on a thermal, spiralling upwards. I can imagine Branwell standing here, his spirits lifting as his lungs breathed in the pure Cumbrian air and his eyes feasted on this spectacular view, watching buzzard, kite and osprey soar. The sky is blue all the way to the horizon. There is not a cloud in sight. The gorse close by blazes with bright yellow flowers, and the bluebells beneath the oak trees glow like cobalt crystal. As he stood on this promontory, perhaps he was thinking about the Lakeland poets – in particular William Wordsworth, whom he had written to in 1837, at the age of nineteen, but also Samuel Taylor Coleridge and his son Hartley, whom Branwell wrote to a few months later. Wordsworth composed a lyric sequence called 'The River Duddon: A Series of Sonnets' between 1804 and 1820, celebrating this area of beauty.

I walk around the village. There are three pubs (which were all around in Branwell's time), a post office, an accountant and a solicitor; a handcrafted furniture shop, two petrol stations, one with brightly coloured fairground bumper cars on the roof; a library, a cattle market, a village notice board, advertising yoga classes and a film club; a butcher and a baker, but no candlestick maker. And there are no signs of the hoop makers, saddlers, nail makers and swill makers that were here during Branwell's stay.

Broughton was once the centre of the swill-making industry. A swill is a shallow oval basket, usually about two feet long, made of oak strips woven from a rim formed from a hazel rod. They were sent to Scotland, where they were in demand for use in potato picking.

Walking these bustling streets, Branwell must have felt a huge sense of freedom mingled with one of isolation. Unlike his sisters, he never went to school, and he had no qualifications. He spent his childhood at the parsonage, being educated by his father. And here he was now, a private tutor to two boys, still only in his early twenties.

I'm standing outside Broughton House, the residence of the Postlethwaite family, a three-storey merchant's house opposite the Old King's Head tavern. It is now, not quite ironically, home to an educational publisher. Robert and Agnes had two boys, John and William. Juliet Barker states that at this time Robert Postlethwaite was the second largest landowner in the area, but, as Tim Cockerill has pointed out in *Brontë Studies*, the source of his wealth is something of a mystery.

It perhaps seems odd that Robert Postlethwaite would entrust his sons' education to a failed portrait painter with no qualifications, and despite having at first made a good impression, within six months Branwell was dismissed from his employment. A pattern repeated with every job he took.

Walking out of town up the hill towards Branwell's lodgings, I come to the parish church. It is an odd-looking building, with a chunky bell tower rebuilt somewhat from the sketch Branwell drew of it in 1840, when it was more elegantly proportioned. At the top of the hill is High Syke House, where Branwell stayed. This is the oldest part of Broughton. 'Broughton' is derived from Anglo-Saxon, and it means 'the settlement by the brook'. 'Syke' is Norse, indicating a brook coming from swampy ground. In 1840, the house was home to Edward Fish, a surgeon. It is well positioned, overlooking the village and the church, with the Cumbrian mountains in the background. You can see the mouth of the Duddon estuary from up here and further on the sea. There is wisteria festooned with lilac blooms growing up the side of the building, but as with Broughton House, there is no plaque to mark Branwell's stay. The town seems rather blasé about its Brontë connection, or even indifferent.

I walk to the crossroads and past the huge wooden cross mounted to the left, with High Cross Inn to my right. Next, I head down the hill towards the River Duddon. A footpath cuts through some farm fields and goes towards Duddon Bridge. The first is full of mad cows with their calves that don't seem to take very kindly to Wolfie. They charge at us with all the speed they can muster. It's that time of year when maternal instincts turn previously docile bovines into rural killers. We try and find an alternative route, climbing over a fence into the adjacent field with sheep and lambs that seem less perturbed by our presence. Some lambs gambol while others bleat for the teat. I walk along the banks of the River Duddon, as Branwell did, with a copy of Wordsworth's sonnets in my pocket. We know he did this from the letters he wrote to his friend Joseph Leyland. The Duddon is a shallow, wide river. The water is crystal clear. I see a farmer approach. I'm trying to avoid a confrontation with him, so as he gets closer I get in there first, going on a charm offensive: 'Hello, I'm sorry. I know I'm trespassing, but your cows wouldn't let me past.'

'You didn't have to climb over the fence. You could have used the gate.'

'Yes, I'm sorry.'

In the end, he is perfectly reasonable and shows me an alternative way.

As Branwell walked along these banks, was he looking at the scene with his painterly eye, wondering how he could capture all this beauty on a stretched canvas frame? In the distance, the dark brow of Black Combe looms over the estuary and village. It's pronounced 'Black Koom'. And it was the subject first of Wordsworth's pen and then, in imitation, Branwell's. Wordsworth wrote two poems celebrating the Combe: 'Written with a Slate Pencil on a Stone, on the Side of the Mountain of Black Combe' and 'View from the Top of Black Comb [sic]'. Branwell's poem is called 'On Black Combe'. The mountain from any view is barren and austere – a threat or a dare. I want to walk up it, but I need to psych myself up. There is something sinister about its foreboding bulk.

I head towards Foxfield, a hamlet by the mouth of the

estuary. I cross the rail tracks and walk along the silted banks, treading carefully on the soft sands. The wind ripples the water and the sun silvers the tips of the waves. There are black-headed gulls bobbing on the surface – they look like buoys – and further on waders: snipe, shank and sanderling. I head along the Cumbrian coastal path, past Well Head and Coal Gate. I bear left taking a path that crosses fields to a golf course. The path circumnavigates the course anticlockwise. Despite blue skies and mild weather, there are no signs of golfers. Over the years, I've seen these spaces diminish in popularity. It seems like the sport has had its day. Golf courses are often sizeable areas of land in good spots. What I'd like is for them to rewild and reforest, perhaps flooding the lower areas to create lakes and marshes.

I drop back down into Broughton, past tennis courts and slate-roofed houses clad with solar panels. I've been walking for more than three hours now, and I stop at the Manor Arms for a rest. I get talking to some drinkers, who it turns out are all 'offcomers', the local term for out of towners. No one has heard of Branwell Brontë. 'Not seen him drinking in here. What time does he usually come in?' one of them jokes.

I wonder where to go next. I've got most of the afternoon left. I could do Black Combe, but I still don't feel ready for it. I'm going to save it for the morning. I know that nearby there is a stone circle, and I decide instead to head out to see it.

I walk through a wood full of flowering wild garlic, with white petals like dancing stars. I climb up a steep clough until I emerge out of the woods into a rugged spot where the remains of a stone circle can be found. But there's not much left. Just two standing stones. This isn't the circle I've come to see, though, that's further on, a couple of miles to the east. I watch Wolfie give chase to a hare, but it outruns him easily. Unlike rabbits, hares don't burrow, instead relying on their speed, agility and cunning to escape their pursuers. It's a strategy that doesn't always work. I find a half-eaten hare corpse by the side of the path. Its skeleton is much bigger than a rabbit's. The skull looks to be twice the size of a rabbit skull. It is still attached to the body by a collar of wet fur.

When I get there, I am struck by the location of the circle, cradled as it is between the rounded slopes of Swinside Fell and Knott Hill, with the majestic Coniston Fells providing a dramatic backdrop. There's nothing in the near vicinity of the stones, and it feels like they are in conversation with the natural geology around us. This is Sunkenkirk Stone Circle, one of the three most important stone circles in Cumbria. It is an almost perfect circle with a diameter of ninety-three feet, and fifty-five of the original sixty stones remain. There is something mystical about its symmetry. The inner ground is perfectly level, like a bowling green. The stones are what the locals call 'grey cobbles'. It isn't as grand as Castlerigg, which is sited just outside of Keswick, but it is just as graceful. The tallest stone is only seven feet six inches, and it stands in a spot marking true north. The circle wasn't recorded until 1794, and it wasn't fully excavated until 1901. So, when Branwell was here, there wouldn't have been much to see. It is interesting to wonder, though, what he would have thought of stone circles. Would he have been as underwhelmed by them as Coleridge was when he visited Castlerigg with Wordsworth in 1799?

It's nearly six in the evening when I get here, and with the exception of a few sheep, I have the place to myself. It is still, peaceful. Perhaps stone circles would have been more Emily's thing. The first man-made structures to worship the gods, built to imitate natural forms and pointing up to the stars. The stones function like a church spire. They connect the earth to the heavens.

❦

The next morning, I get up early. I drive over to Whicham at the base of the Combe. I put the kettle on and fry myself a breakfast. As I sit eating mushrooms on toast and drinking tea, I stare up at its vastness. Even from this distance, the path that snakes up its back is visible. Wainwright said that you could walk it in carpet slippers. But I wouldn't like to try.

I take out and read Branwell's poem 'On Black Combe':

Far off, and half revealed, 'mid shade and light,
Black Combe half smiles, half frowns; his mighty form
Scarce bending into Peace – more formed to fight
A thousand years of struggles with a storm
Than bask one hour, subdued by sunshine warm,
To bright and breezeless rest; yet even his height
Towers not o'er this world's sympathies – he smiles –
While many a human heart to pleasure's wiles
Can bear to bend, and still forget to rise –
As though he, huge and heath-clad in our sight,
Again rejoices in his stormy skies.
Man loses vigour in unstable joys.
Thus tempests find Black Combe invincible,
While we one lost, who should know life so well!

The sun is rising over the sea, and the one cloud in the sky casts a shadow over the mountain's shoulder as I think about

Branwell's line 'half smiles, half frowns'. It's a good line. Not just because it describes how often it is half in sunlight and half in shadow, but also the shape of it – the bowed arch of its back and the crenelated crags that furrow vertically. I think it could be one of the best lines he wrote, because it is also addresses me, the walker, who is equally awed and vexed by it.

As I set off, I'm thinking about Wordsworth, and how, when Branwell climbed this mountain, he may have been thinking about Wordsworth too. He was walking in his wake. As I am now walking in Branwell's. Did he blush as he recalled the letter he had written to Wordsworth three years before?

Sir– I most earnestly entreat you to read and pass your judgement upon what I have sent you, because from the day of my birth to this nineteenth year of my life I have lived among secluded hills, where I could neither know what I was or what I could do ... But a change has taken place now, sir; I am arrived at an age wherein I must do something for myself ... Do pardon me, sir, that I have ventured to come before one whose works I have most loved in our literature, and who most has been with me a divinity of the mind ... Surely, in this day, when there is not a writing poet worth a sixpence, the field must be open, if a better man can step forward ... Now, to send you the whole of this would be a mock upon your patience; what you see does not pretend to be more than the description of an imaginative child. But read it, sir; and as you value your own kind-heartedness – return me an answer if but one word, telling me whether I should write on, or write no more. Forgive undue warmth, because my feeling in this matter cannot be cool; and believe me, sir, with deep respect.

He never received a reply to his letter, which was a curious combination of the lickspittle ('a divinity of mind') and the foolhardy ('there is not a writing poet worth a sixpence'). Certainly, he doesn't appear to have written to him again.

Back in 2017, when the parsonage was celebrating Branwell's bicentenary, they commissioned Simon Armitage to write a series of poems in response to Branwell's artefacts. In one, he chose the letter Branwell had written to Wordsworth, and his response was an imagined reply. The poem was called 'William, It Was Really Nothing'. Armitage is a fan of the Manchester music scene of the eighties, and the title of his poem is clearly a reference to The Smiths and their song of the same name. In his poem, he captures that feeling between intention and reception: 'What glittered like charmed finches over Haworth Church, drifts as rain across Scafell Pike'.

Rereading the letter, I cannot help but feel a great sadness. I also reflect on my own efforts to reach great writers in my late teens and early twenties. Again, without reply. Perhaps it is something that all aspiring writers do, although not something that they would confess to.

As he climbed the mountain, was Branwell still angry that Wordsworth hadn't bothered to reply? While living in Broughton, he wrote first to Thomas de Quincy (who was living in Wordsworth's old house, Dove Cottage) and then to Hartley Coleridge, son of Samuel Taylor. The tone in his letter to Hartley was more consistent. And it must have felt like a breakthrough when Hartley wrote back, inviting him to his home, nearby, at Nab Cottage.

The path cuts diagonally through a field full of sheep and lambs, and, nervous of my dog, the flock parts like biblical waves. I watch the lambs buried deep into their mothers' teats. It always amuses me to see them wag their tails, the way dogs do, to show their excitement. Mammalian milk contains casomorphin, an opioid. No one really knows why it's there, but one possible answer is to make the infant young dependent on their mother. So, when we see lambs sucking hard at the teat, or indeed any infant mammal, we are really watching addicts.

Although the sky was clear twenty minutes ago when I started out, there are now dark clouds around the head of the Combe. The climb to the top is an unrelenting slog, but Wainwright was right about carpet slippers. The ground is soft and steady. Grassed on the whole but even where there is exposed soil, it feels easy underfoot. At six hundred metres above sea level, it is a small mountain in comparison to Scafell Pike or Great Gable, but it's a punishing climb. I'm thinking about how the Romantic writers changed our perception of these great peaks. From something to be feared to that which we revere. What was once thought as rough and ugly, lacking classic symmetry, seems to us now naturally beautiful, effortlessly elegant, combining awe with magnitude, grace with power. We appreciate a mountain's great scale but also the minutiae of its ecosystem.

Black Combe, its form and shape and size, dominates the Duddon valley. It's not hard to see why first Wordsworth and then Branwell would want to ascend its heights and view the world from the vantage point of its peak. As I walk the ravine between Seaness and Moor Gill, there is a shelf of rock to my left that looms over me like a black scythe. To my right, a stream trickles as water oozes from the tops. It's May Day weekend, but I am on my own on this mountain. I imagine that the rest of the Lakes will be teeming with walkers and tourists today. The path is fringed with infant bilberry bushes, fern stalks and heather patches. I can hear but not see the noisy rising song of the skylark. As I mount the first brow of the Combe, the sun cuts through the thick cloud and everything is suddenly illuminated. Now the frowning brow of Black Combe is smiling. Everything is verdant green and gold. The fronds of the bilberry are bronzed, and the sand beneath my feet is polished copper. The grey shingle glows pink and blue. But the view in front is the black furrow of the Combe head. It has its own dark cloud situated above it like a fedora hat.

A few hundred yards further on and the weather suddenly changes again. The sky dulls, the wind whips my cheeks and the air is icy. The top now looks cold and sinister. I stop to place a stone on top of a cairn. These traditions die hard, and in weather less clement than today these makeshift waymarkers can be lifesavers. Did Branwell stop here to add to the pile? Did Wordsworth? Although there are bigger mountains, the steepness of Black Combe never lets up.

Eventually, I climb to the top. It's mostly flat, with a scattering of rocks and clumps of grass. In the middle of this level top, there is a white trig point surrounded by a circular drystone wall that offers scant shelter from the gusty winds. You can see for miles around in every direction: to the east, far out to sea, a wind farm on the horizon; to the south-east, the River Duddon as it opens out into the mouth of the estuary, which in turn bleeds into the Irish Sea; to the north, behind the Combe, the great mounds and undulations of the Cumbrian mountains.

I have been accompanied along my entire journey by the soundtrack of the skylark, but it is only here, standing next to the trig point, that I can look up and see the bird above me, singing its heart out. From the west face of the Combe, I can see the Duddon valley in its entirety. This side of the Combe is corrugated with ravines and gills.

I take out Branwell's poem again and this time compare it to Wordsworth's 'View from the top of Black Comb'.

This height a ministering angel might select:
For from the summit of Black Comb (dread name
Derived from clouds and storms!) the amplest range
Of unobstructed prospect may be seen
That British ground commands: — low dusky tracts,
Where Trent is nursed, far southward! Cambrian hills
To the southwest, a multitudinous show;
And, in a line of eyesight linked with these,
The hoary peaks of Scotland that give birth
To Teviot's stream, to Annan, Tweed, and Clyde: —
Crowding the quarter whence the sun comes forth,
Gigantic mountains rough with crags; beneath,
Right at the imperial station's western base,
Main ocean, breaking audibly, and stretched
Far into silent regions blue and pale; —
And visibly engirding Mona's Isle,
That, as we left the plain, before our sight
Stood like a lofty mount, uplifting slowly
(Above the convex of the watery globe)
Into clear view the cultured fields that streak
Her habitable shores, but now appears
A dwindled object, and submits to lie
At the spectator's feet. — Yon azure ridge,
Is it a perishable cloud? or there

Do we behold the line of Erin's coast?
Land sometimes by the roving shepherd-swain
(Like the bright confines of another world)
Not doubtfully perceived. — Look homeward now!
In depth, in height, in circuit, how serene
The spectacle, how pure! — Of Nature's works,
In earth, and air, and earth-embracing sea,
A revelation infinite it seems;
Display august of man's inheritance,
Of Britain's calm felicity and power!

Some may say Wordsworth's is the better poem. It is more sustained, more ambitious, loftier, certainly. But I prefer the simple ruggedness of Branwell's. He only spent six months of his life here, but it seems to have been a creative six months, not only inspiring him to write poetry, but also to paint and draw. And it seems to have been an amorous time. He wrote to John Brown on 13 March 1840, no doubt talking about Robert Postlethwaite's eighteen-year-old daughter Margaret: 'I have one sitting by me just now – fair-faced, blue eyes, dark haired sweet eighteen – she little thinks the devil is so near her!' But despite his carnal sentiments, he is unlikely to have made a move on his employer's daughter (though employers' wives are another thing, as we'll see). Yet Juliet Barker is also convinced that during his stay he fathered an illegitimate child who died. She writes:

In October 1859, a friend of Mrs Gaskell's, Richard Monckton Milnes, then Lord Houghton, visited William Brown, the sexton of Haworth, and was shown a number of letters written by

Branwell to William's brother John. Among them was the letter
addressed to 'Old Knave of Trumps' from Broughton, which
Brown had clearly not censored as Branwell had requested and
which Houghton was therefore able partially to transcribe.
Beneath his transcript, Houghton noted that Branwell 'left Mr
Postlethwaites with a natural child by one of the daughters or
servants – which died'.

Through impressive detective work, she narrows the possibilities
down to three women in the parish who all gave birth to illegitimate
children during the period: Eleanor Nelson, Frances Atkinson and
Agnes Riley. Eleanor Nelson was nineteen and living at Syke House.
She was possibly a Postlethwaite servant. Frances Atkinson was
seventeen, and the records suggest that she could have been a servant
for either Postlethwaite or Fish. But according to Barker, the most
probable is Agnes Riley, who was twenty-one. Her daughter, Mary
Riley, was born on 20 February 1841, meaning she was conceived
in May while Branwell was living in Broughton. Mary was one of
Branwell's favourite names. There is also the poem that he wrote
in 1846 called 'Epistle from a Father on Earth to his Child in her
Grave', which does what it says on the tin. The unnamed narrator
addresses his child who died when 'the day was in its dawn'. And
'I – thy life's source – was a wandering … keen mountain winds'. It
returns to a well-worn theme in Branwell's work: that the dead are
free, and it is the living who are burdened. Is this autobiographical?
Juliet Barker thinks so.

When he returned to Haworth, we do not know what excuse he
used to explain his dismissal, but if he did father an illegitimate child
here in Broughton, then that could well be the reason. And this was

not perhaps the first time he had fathered a child. Descendants of Mary Ann Judson, who was born at Buckley Farms near Stanbury in 1839, believe she was Branwell's illegitimate daughter by Martha Judson, a twenty-six-year-old married woman.

Sitting on top of a mountain is a great place to contemplate and reflect on our lives. From up here, we have a god-like perspective on the world, but at the same time we feel the smallness and the insignificance of our existence. Was Branwell reflecting on fatherhood? Or was he instead thinking of himself as a great Romantic poet in the Wordsworth tradition? He did not know as he stood on this brooding peak that he was not going to achieve any of his lofty ambitions but would instead die an ignominious death at the age of only thirty-one.

7

LUDDENDEN FOOT

Luddenden Foot railway station no longer exists. In its place is Fairlea Industrial Estate, which includes Vocation Brewery, a 4x4 van seller and one of the worst examples of public art I have ever encountered: a statue of Branwell Brontë. A short, squat figure, less than four feet high, that looks like a cross between a hunchbacked gargoyle and a morbidly obese leprechaun with grotesquely oversized hands. The figure bears no resemblance to Branwell Brontë. He bears no resemblance to any human form, to the extent that you wonder whether the sculptor actually ever saw a drawing of Branwell or ever observed a human being.

It is clearly a popular place for fly-tipping, because next to the statue is a handwritten sign that says 'Please take your rubbish home'. The site has been cleared, but there are still remnants of detritus caught in the metal fence. The statue of Branwell stands beneath two trees, close to this fence. He clutches a scroll with his Goliath hands that are about three times the size of mine. On the scroll there is a quote: 'I cannot think as roses blow'. It is a line from a poem he wrote in December 1841 while he was positioned at this station. Except the sculptor has got the line wrong; it should read, 'I cannot think – think roses blow'. The sculptor has given Branwell a boxer's nose and a squished-in mouth. He has carved bog eyes, each one not only facing in a different direction, but rendered in a different style. There is no attempt at symmetry.

There used to be another really bad statue of Branwell on the towpath of the Rochdale Canal in Sowerby Bridge to mark his time working at that railway station – a badly carved wooden totem pole, with Branwell at the top – but it was burnt down by locals with good taste and is now a charred stump. Sally Wainwright wanted to end her film *To Walk Invisible* with a final shot of the statue but had to cut the scene when the figure was torched. I wonder if the locals knew of her intention?

This statue at Luddenden Foot, the only existing one, marks the spot where Branwell worked as clerk-in-charge from April Fool's Day 1841 until he was dismissed for neglecting his duties in March 1842. Under his watch, £11 1s. 7d. went missing, equivalent to about £1,200 today. Although he was employed for less than a year, it was a creative period for him. He spent a lot of his time exploring the Calder Valley, and it was during this time that 'Heaven and Earth' was published in the *Halifax Guardian*, the first of many of his poems, under the pseudonym Northangerland. Although the literary achievements of his sisters would later eclipse his, he was the first to see his words in print and also the first to use a nom de plume.

In 2017, the bicentenary of Branwell's birth, Christopher Goddard was commissioned by the Parsonage Museum to devise a Branwell walk, from the former station to Haworth, a route Branwell himself took on more than one occasion. Christopher called it the 'Wandering Bard Walk'. At nearly eleven miles, it's a decent linear yomp that takes in some interesting features, exploring the Calder Valley, over the tops of the moors to his family home. It includes varied woodlands, open moors and numerous pubs. I did the walk some time ago, but today I'm only doing a small section of it, ending at the Lord Nelson pub, where Branwell drank with local writers and artists, such as the poets William Dearden and William Heaton, and the sculptor Joseph Bentley Leyland.

I'm with Sarah Fanning, a writer and academic who specialises in film and TV adaptations of the Brontës' novels. She's based in Canada at Mount Allison University in New Brunswick. She's written about adaptations of both *Jane Eyre* and *Wuthering Heights*, and is currently working on an essay about Sally Wainwright's film *To Walk Invisible*. She's just come from an interview with Adam Nagaitis, who played Branwell in the film.

We stand and stare at the statue in disbelief. Sarah takes out her phone and photographs it from various angles. 'It's so telling,' Sarah says at last. 'It symbolises the culture of rejection that's built up around Branwell ever since Gaskell's *The Life of Charlotte Brontë* emerged in 1857.'

'Yes, it's amazing how much that still influences people's impressions of Branwell, isn't it? And maybe the Brontës in general.'

'Gaskell really maligned Branwell in the public's imagination as nothing more than a drunkard and failure who terrorised an otherwise peaceful household. The positive attributes of Branwell's character and his own genius are somehow less interesting to the public, or at least are eclipsed, purposefully or not, by his sisters' more remarkable stories. I'm amazed at how this statue quite literally solidifies the longstanding Gaskellian myth. I'm saddened by how small, ugly and moss-ridden it is. It really hits home how marginalised he still is in the Brontë story.'

It seems Sarah's not a fan of the statue either. We walk up Station

Road, past Milner Place. Although the station is no longer here, the train still rattles past. It must irk the good people of Luddenden that they have lost their rail link, a poorly executed statue of a former employee being no substitute. We cross a wrought-iron bridge over the River Calder. It's wide and shallow at this point, and its waters resemble frothy coffee. A dipper skips onto a stone. It bobs its plump body up and down and cocks its tail. Its creamy white chest contrasts with its dark wing feathers, like it's wearing a bib and tuxedo. It just needs a black bowtie to complete the look. There are still marks on the nearby buildings where the river burst its banks on Boxing Day 2016, causing millions of pounds of damage. We pass the park on our right and to our left a pub called the Old Brandy Wine. The road then goes over the Rochdale Canal, which travels to Hebden Bridge in one direction and Sowerby Bridge in the other. We attempt to cross the always busy Burnley Road. On the other side, we immediately hit a left up some old stone steps that lead to Danny Lane.

As we climb the cobbled road, I turn to Sarah and say, 'So what's this fascination of yours with adaptations? When did it start?'

'When I was an undergraduate student living in Halifax, Nova Scotia, I guess. I was beginning to become interested in media studies, and I saw this new interest merging with my love for Victorian literature and the Brontës more generally. I think at first I was simply interested in seeing how filmmakers brought the complexity of Victorian novels to life on screen.'

'It's interesting to see how adaptions reflect their own time, perhaps?'

'Yes, they act as snapshots of what's going on in the world. You know, what kind of a man is Rochester in Hollywood in the 1940s?'

'You're referring to the 1943 Robert Stevenson version starring Orson Welles as Rochester?'

'Yeah. When you watch that film today, you see war propaganda all over it. I was drawn to how texts like the Brontës' can be read against ongoing ideological changes across history, and how they come to mean something different to us depending on what's going on in our own cultures and societies. You see the impervious soldier-type man striding around in a black cape all the time with a thundering voice.'

'I guess adaptations of *Wuthering Heights* are a good way of seeing that occur, because there is at least one for every age. Particularly the character of Heathcliff. We seem to use him as a totem for something redolent in our culture at any particular time.'

'Exactly. Look what happens in the 1960s. The BBC starts adapting *Wuthering Heights*. And it's no surprise Heathcliff fits perfectly into 1960s counterculture. His ostracism, dejection and anger align closely with the kind of issues 1960s youth culture was facing.'

'This is the one with Ian McShane, right?'

'Yes, the 1967 one. His brooding temperament along with his feelings of isolation and dissatisfaction with his lot – not to mention his Beatles haircut! – find a strong parallel with what was going on in Britain at that moment.'

'I've just chaired a panel discussion about the 1992 film adaptation of *Wuthering Heights*. At Holmfirth Film Festival. I think it's the only film adaptation to include the second-generation story.'

'I didn't like Juliette Binoche in that film. She just giggles through the whole thing. And I think Heathcliff is a much more complicated character than they allow him to be in that film. It's Ralph Fiennes, right?'

'Yeah, his film debut.'

'He looks like a Harlequin male model.'

'The whole thing is too stylised. And that includes Ralph Fiennes. He's got make-up on to create a swarthy complexion. He's wearing ridiculously over-the-top clothing. It's filmed in North Yorkshire, so the landscape is very different.'

'It's very rocky, isn't it?'

'Yeah, limestone. And somehow that takes something away from the characterisation. But also the house itself, Wuthering Heights, is this big Gothic castle.'

'It's hyperbole. It's a complete misreading of the subtleties of the characters. The tone, the atmosphere, it's completely over the top and does a disservice to Emily's novel.'

We reach Ripley Terrace at the top of the hill and take some steps down to a dirt track, which leads to Roebuck's Wood. To our left is a new housing estate comprising mainly three-storey town houses with built-in garages. The view darkens as we pass beneath the canopy of the woods. To our right are a series of red-brick bunkers built during the Second World War. The bunkers were constructed to serve the mill that once stood where the housing estate is now. I don't know if the bunkers were ever used, but I imagine be-clogged mill workers crammed into their dank underground rooms. The bunkers are now used as dumping spaces, or else improvised dens for the estate's children. There is something ominous about the dark mouths of their doorways, leading down to infernal caverns. The entrances are overgrown with ferns and brambles. Not Gothic in the way the Brontës' writing can be said to be Gothic, but creepy and uncanny nevertheless.

'I'm thinking about that other statue,' I say. 'The one that used to be on the towpath near Sowerby Bridge. It was you who brought it to my attention, I think. Poor Branwell, he doesn't seem to get a fair deal. That's true of Sally Wainwright's film as well, maybe. By focusing on the latter part of his story, she somehow distorts the bigger picture of his life. Do you agree?'

'Sally's film gives a lot of space to Branwell, but I think in ways that play into the myth of the alcoholic brother who terrorised the household. Like in Gaskell's biography, *To Walk Invisible*'s Branwell is used to present the sisters as – if not angelic – then certainly as victims of their brother's dissipation.'

'Because he only turned to alcohol towards the end. Aren't you and Claire [O'Callaghan] working on something to do with this?'

'Claire and I have just written about Branwell's portrayal in this film, yes. Initially, we thought that Branwell's story had finally come to the fore, but we quickly started to see just how villainised he is in Sally's film. He doesn't ever get a fair deal, as you say, and it's boggling how, even in an age where there's so much information around mental health and addiction, popular culture continues to push for this narrow view that as a brother Branwell was like the dark, destructive Hindley Earnshaw, Cathy's alcoholic brother who is unable to cope with his grief, without offering any understanding that his behaviours, while often troublesome to both himself and his family, were most likely the result of some form of mental illness.'

'Have you seen *The Brontës of Haworth*? The 1970s Christopher Fry five-part series, I think for ITV?'

'Yeah.'

'I mean, it's really clunky. It's not aged very well, but in a way it's a more faithful depiction of their lives. It doesn't demonise Branwell. We see him first as a bright young thing, full of creative potential, before the descent into alcoholism. And the portrayal of Emily in that is more normalised. And I think what Sally is doing is responding to *The Brontës of Haworth*.'

'I spoke to her about *The Brontës of Haworth*, and she said it was too sanitised. She said they didn't have dirty fingernails. They spoke with posh accents. She said it was way too clean.'

'And all of that is true.'

'And she wanted to get away from that BBC thing of, we are here to inform and educate. She wanted to work against that whole tradition. And I really like *To Walk Invisible*.'

I agree with Sarah. *To Walk Invisible* is an accomplished piece of work. Sarah explains that Sally wanted to show what it was like to live with an alcoholic. I think she succeeded in doing this. But the inevitable outcome of her success is to portray Branwell as unstable and mentally disturbed.

'He comes across as a complete nut in *To Walk Invisible*,' Sarah says.

'He does, and this is why I think in some way Michael Kitchen's portrayal [In *The Brontës of Haworth*] is a more dignified depiction. You see him as a witty, socially functioning character first. In Sally's film, we only see him at the end. By focusing on that dissipation, and not seeing Branwell the aspiring artist, or Branwell the aspiring poet, it overemphasises his pathology.'

'It just shows him as a loser. As a failure.'

What does come across is that this is a man with a broken heart. I remember that feeling of being dumped. Your first love. I was twenty-two. We'd been together two years, and when it ended, I was bereft. I felt like my teeth had been kicked in and my guts ripped out. I had nothing left. I turned to drink and drugs. I lay on the floor and stared at the ceiling listening to *Joy Division* records. I took a scalpel and carved her name in my torso. I tell Sarah about this: 'I went a bit crazy.'

'It can do that to you. And, of course, Branwell never really had Lydia. She was never his. And I wonder how well he really read the situation.'

Sarah is talking about Lydia Robinson, who Branwell had an affair with at Thorpe Green. It has been suggested, since Elizabeth Gaskell's biography of Charlotte, that Branwell's feelings for Lydia were not reciprocated with the same intensity. That for her the affair was just a bit of fun.

'He was still so young, wasn't he? I mean this was 1845. He was only in his twenties.'

'I do wonder sometimes just how much he was in touch with reality. Those mad letters he wrote, like the one to Wordsworth.'

We walk in silence for a short time. It seems to me that so many myth-busting exercises simply lead to more myths springing up, Hydra-like.

As we continue along the path, we have to dodge patches of mud. We pass back gardens with trampolines, collecting shallow puddles of rainwater and autumn leaves. The sight of these trampolines saddens me somehow. They were probably only used a few times before becoming the elephant on the lawn. They'll stay put, getting in the way until the families finally relent and either take them to the tip or sell them for tuppence on eBay. It seems perverse to seek exercise in this way, when you are surrounded by the majestic vale of Luddenden Dean, with the expansive Midgley and Warley moors above. Jumping up and down in one spot, going nowhere, cannot compete with the myriad footpaths that crisscross fell and dell. It's no surprise really that Branwell neglected his duties, with all this beautiful countryside surrounding him.

The path takes us further into the woods, rising above Roebuck Beck to our left. The water flows fast here. It is early November, and the leaves are turning red, gold, bronze and yellow. Wolfie chases squirrels that are busy caching nuts for the winter. Alongside our path is a wrought-iron water pipe that must have been laid when the mill was in operation. It's a chunky, solid piece of engineering. Where the path has washed away, the amateur funambulist can tightrope over the ravines, using this pipe. To our right is the exposed face of the reddish rock. It juts out in angular shelves of granite. The leaves are falling, and the path is strewn with a copper-and-green carpet. There's been a lot of rain, and the path is a soft bog in places. We're approached by an anxious-looking border terrier, clearly searching for whomever he has come with. He runs back and forth, panting. We can hear someone call him in the distance.

A waterfall flows into the beck: 'a pure spring of water, which issuing in a crystal rill, tinkles down to a rivulet in the vale', as Patrick Brontë put it. The path is a raised ledge that has been banked up to support the pipe. We break away from it as we pass over a wooden bridge and then tiptoe stepping stones that take us over another tributary stream. Above us, a huge gritstone tor casts the path into shadow. I like to come here in the spring when the floor is covered as far as the eye can see in the verdant green of wild garlic, or bearlick to give it its folk name. I prefer this name, as it evokes a time when our wooded vales were home to large furry mammals. The young tender leaves make great pesto. The scent in the spring is sharp, sweet and spicy. Now it's earthy and musty. This is also a good spot for tree creepers and nuthatches.

We stop by a fallen oak and sit in the nest of its branches. We drink strong black coffee from a flask, sweetened with red rum. 'You've just been interviewing Adam Nagaitis, right? What did Adam say about playing Branwell?'

'It was remarkable talking to Adam about Branwell. And his passion for Branwell as a writer, artist and brother became really obvious through our discussions. In a BBC interview Adam had given shortly after *To Walk Invisible* aired in the UK, he said he had all kinds of ideas about what Branwell suffered from, but that part of the discussion was either cut or the interviewer didn't ask him to expand on his theories. And this was very frustrating for me, so I decided I would try to contact him myself. For Adam, Branwell was likely ADHD or bipolar.'

'Isn't there a danger in retrodiagnoses?'

Sarah agrees that this can be dodgy territory. But she says that there is compelling evidence that Branwell did likely suffer from mental illness, the symptoms of which he tried to alleviate through alcohol and opium. She explains that one of the things Adam said that struck her most of all was what Branwell's biggest problem in life was: 'He continued to fail himself.'

He was certainly aware that he had already failed others and was coping with that in very self-destructive ways, but he couldn't cope with waking up every day knowing that he was continuing to fail himself. Sarah goes on to explain that this is how Adam approached Branwell's character, really working to internalise this sense of disappointing oneself.

We finish our coffee and walk out of the wood towards Luddenden village, making our way through narrow snickets and oddly cobbled roads, past incongruous new-built houses with white PVC windows.

An Amazon Prime delivery man trudges up a driveway clutching an enormous cardboard package. It's Sunday afternoon, and there's no rest for the wicked. We cross Halifax Lane, past the old corn mill. I think about the mill workers who completed twelve- and thirteen-hour shifts but at least had Sundays off. At one time, all corn grown in the manor of Warley was ground here. The lord of the manor owned the 'Grist Soke' – the compulsory right to grind. All that is left of it now is the old grindstone, which is mounted in a frame of stone. A pea-gravel path winds to the left of this grindstone, and then down steep steps, past the river that once fed the mill.

Luddenden village is a picturesque place, crammed with weavers' cottages with big windows to let light into the workplace. The village is dominated by an incongruously large church, and to the side of this the river has been dammed, cascading white froth. The water was taken in through a goit – a small artificial channel – to create the speed needed for grinding.

As we climb up the hill, we approach the white pebble-dashed Lord Nelson pub, the same pub Branwell Brontë drank in when he was clerk-in-charge at Luddenden Foot Station. It's a seventeenth-century tavern, with many of the original features. Branwell lodged a little further up the hill. We stand at the bar and order two White Witch ales. We sit down at an old oak table, scratched and scarred with time. There are books about Branwell on the shelves above us. The pub was built in 1634 and was called the Black Swan until the Battle of Trafalgar. Lord Nelson was a hero of Branwell's. In the autumn of 1841, Branwell wrote a poem about him. It tells the story of Nelson from his childhood to his death at Trafalgar. Juliet Barker makes the point that Nelson too was a parsonage child and had lost his mother at an early age. It is tempting to wonder whether Branwell sat at this table composing it. He would have certainly thought about him under this roof.

'What do you think of Branwell as a poet? How does he compare, say, to the Romantic poets he was so clearly in awe of?'

'Branwell was the most ambitious poet of the four of them. Emily is lauded as the Brontë poet, but I think people need to remember they had different ambitions. Emily seems to have written poetry for herself, with no intention of publishing. Branwell, on the other hand, desperately wanted recognition, and his desire to publish his poetry is strongly linked to his sense of acquiring a public identity. I think Branwell's poetry is brilliant and hugely overlooked – as is Emily's – but he's also a bit of a wannabe. I think he sought recognition in a way that his attempts at writing Byronic and Shelleyan poems are suggestive of his attempts to identify with the figure of the Romantic poet more than anything. I'm not implying he wasn't an accomplished Romantic poet in his own right, but my impressions are he seems equally to have aligned himself with the image of the Romantic poet.'

It's worth emphasising just how young Branwell was when his first poem was published: still in his early twenties. He must have given his sisters the idea that being a published poet was possible. And tangible. He wrote a poem called 'At Luddenden Church'. I point out of the window to the village church that inspired the poem. It looks out of place, too big for such a small settlement, like it's been plucked from a city and plonked down here. I take out the poem and we read it together. In it, he writes about 'the darkly shadowed hour' that he 'must meet at last', and about joining the 'silent dead'.

'He's anticipating his own end,' I say. 'He's obsessed with death.'

'I assume he was wandering round the graveyard. It's so close to where we are now. And the graveyard is in the shadow of this huge edifice. But it is still odd that surrounded by this beauty and majesty, he is thinking about his death. To be so morbidly fixated.'

I think about Branwell sitting here with his friend Joseph Leyland, drinking and talking about how they were going to shake up the world, as every young artist does. Like Branwell, Leyland died an early death, although he achieved some success as a sculptor first. Like Branwell, Leyland was attracted to the dark side. One of his best-known and regarded works is a statue of Lucifer. He was six years older than Branwell and already achieving accolades during this period. His statue of Spartacus was displayed at the Manchester Exhibition of 1832. It gained a great deal of attention, people saying it was the most striking work on display. And yet, like Branwell, his talent was largely squandered, and he died an alcoholic's death three years after Branwell.

Above the pub was the first members' library in the region. Leyland was a member but not Branwell. It was expensive to join. But they would have no doubt talked about the books in the collection.

At this time, Branwell's star seemed to be rising. We look at another poem published in the pages of the *Halifax Guardian*, this one from 14 May 1842: 'On Peaceful Death and Painful Life'. It's typical Branwell. He asks the reader why we feel sorry for the 'happy dead'. And he asks us instead to mourn the 'dead alive'. 'Whose life departs before his death has come'. For it is 'he who feels the worm that never dies, / The real death and darkness of a tomb!'

'It has a similar tone to *Wuthering Heights*. That's what strikes me most,' Sarah says.

'Yes, that fetishisation of the corpse that goes on in *Wuthering Heights* is going on in his poetry.'

Sarah goes to the bar to get some more drinks. My mind flips back to the last time I was here. I was with the poet Gaia Holmes, interviewing her about her new book of poetry *Where the Road Runs Out*. Like Branwell, she was home educated, and like Branwell she lived for some time in this area. In fact, she out-Branwelled Branwell: she didn't just live next to a church; she lived in a church. We were talking about her new book but inevitably the conversation turned to Branwell. She wasn't a massive fan of his work, but she liked 'Heaven and Earth'. She pointed out the painterly qualities, the way he evoked the Calder Valley with its smoke, silent marshes and moorland greys. Her conclusion, though, was that his poems 'linger darkly'. When Sarah comes back, I tell her about this encounter.

'I've been rereading a lot of his poetry. And I've grown to like it. But I think Gaia nails it with that phrase "linger darkly". Do you agree?'

'There is something troublingly dark in his work. And I wonder, even then, in 1841, whether he felt doomed.'

I look around the room. It's busy with Sunday-afternoon drinkers. An odd combination of young trendies and older farmer types. A young woman, dressing down in matching jacket and Ugg boots, stands at the bar with a black pug on a pink leash. An old bloke in a flat cap and waxed jacket sits opposite us. I suppose this reflects the changing face of Luddenden village.

I tell Sarah that I want to return to Sally's portrayal of the Brontës. I'm intrigued by the original inclusion of the last shot of Branwell's statue. I ask her why she thinks Sally wanted to end the film in that way.

'I don't know. It would completely change everything. The film is subtitled "The Brontë Sisters", which I find troubling, because it is equally about him. There would have been something very mournful and regrettable if she would have been able to do that.'

I'm really glad the film doesn't end with that image. And I'm really glad that statue has been burnt down. I think it would have been a mistake. Such a bad statue.

'Do you want to see the script?'

Sarah finds the script on her phone and shows me the final direction:

EXT. ROCHDALE CANAL, SOWERBY BRIDGE. DAY. A badly decayed fifteen-inch-tall wooden statue labelled 'BRANWELL BRONTË 1817–1848' stands at the side of the canal. One of the eyes is hollow, both his hands have rotted away, and down by his crotch the Sowerby Bridge piss-heads have put an empty Budweiser bottle, amongst other modern-day debris around the dank little picnic site.

Sarah leaves to catch a train, and I make my way home. I call into the village off-licence. As I exit, a man in a red cagoul shuffles his feet and tells me he just needs fifty pence to put towards a tin of beer. I don't quite know why I do it, but I double back and return with a four pack of Tennents Super Strength. The man's eyes light up as I hand it to him. None of the 'piss-heads' I know would be seen dead with a bottle of Budweiser.

8

'AND HERE'S TO YOU, MRS ROBINSON'

It's mid November, and I'm here in Great Ouseburn in North Yorkshire. I've just driven through Little Ouseburn, and there doesn't seem that much between them. They are both linear villages built along one prominent road, each with a church and a pub with a boarded-up 'To Let' sign outside. The people of Little Ouseburn must live in a constant state of inferiority to Great Ouseburn. And the people of Great Ouseburn must live in a constant state of superiority over their diminutively named neighbours.

Wolfie and I are walking towards the River Ouse. Everything is flat around here, which must have been a shock to both Anne and Branwell, having been immersed, really from birth, in a rugged landscape, characterised by folds and corrugated undulations, by gorges that tear deep scars into the hills, by rock formations that jut out and spill across the moors, by miles of barren nothingness and empty fells that stretch out as far as the eye can see.

Anne arrived in May 1840 to take up the position of governess with the Robinsons of Thorpe Green Hall, just up the road from here – it was to form the basis of Horton Lodge in *Agnes Grey*, her first novel. She was there for five years, the longest period of paid employment of any of the siblings. Mr Robinson was lord of the manor of Little Ouseburn. He had shooting rights over nearly two thousand acres of land. Anne must have thought she was doing Branwell a favour when she secured a job for him as private tutor to Edmund, the Robinsons' son, in 1843. And initially this was probably the case. He lasted more than two years, longer than he did in any of his other paid posts, before his affair with Mrs Robinson forced his return to Haworth, where he would decline into alcoholism and sketch a premonition of his own death: a shaky drawing of his own corpse being visited by the grim reaper in the form of a cock-snooking skeleton.

Everything round Haworth is up and down. Everything here is flat and green. The leaves are turning gold, and a red kite soars low in the sky looking for carrion, the remnants of a fox kill or a roadside accident: a badger, a hedgehog, a rabbit, spatchcocked by an SUV.

There's not a lot here. It must have seemed a million miles from Haworth, with its bustling main street, busy mills and nonconformist chapels stuffed with sinners praying for salvation; its pubs and drunks and licentiousness; its apothecary and laudanum guzzlers; its middens overspilling with stinking offal and excrement; its overpopulated houses; and its rancid corpse water.

It's a beautiful autumn day with a clear blue sky. The sun is a copper coin levitating over the eastern horizon, and the fields here are ploughed and planted, seeded or reaped, dormant over winter, ready for spring. I'm looking for the hill that Juliet Barker mentions in her book, but everything is so flat it's really hard to imagine a thing like a hill. It's difficult to know what would be classed as one here – maybe just a slightly raised area constitutes a hill?

An eviscerated pigeon lies on its back in a ditch. Its blood and guts ripped out of its chest. Perhaps this is what the red kite was after: a sparrowhawk's sloppy seconds. It must be demeaning to feast on the leftovers of a smaller raptor's success. I pass a dumped fridge freezer and a dumped oven, their white skin of paint already blistering with rust.

I walk across the golf course and along the River Ouse to a footbridge that leads to the village of Aldwark. Everything is withering, except a hawthorn bush which is replete with luscious red berries. I stop by St Stephen's Church, with its large round window paned with lead in the shape of a flower and the exposed Jenga of its brickwork arranged at odd angles. The information board in front tells me that the origin of 'Aldwark' may be Anglo-Saxon: 'Ald-Weord', which means 'old fort'. But the Roman fort buildings are now nowhere to be seen. This is what the present sometimes does to the past: obliterates it. Whereas my project is an attempt to reconfigure it.

The River Ure can be glimpsed from this spot. It was used to transport lead in Roman times, and until the previous century it carried farm produce, lime and coal upstream to Ripon, and downstream to York and Hull.

There is a paucity of pathways in this region, the Vale of York. Instead, there are lots of B roads with thick, dense hawthorn hedges either side that hardly let in any light, very few public rights of way, and lots of voluminous farmers' fields, hedged in, barbed-wired and mesh-fenced. This agricultural land would not have been so intensively farmed during the mid nineteenth century, but, even so, it would have been a huge contrast, especially to Branwell, who was a passionate walker, to the Yorkshire moors, with its open spaces that can be roamed in any direction, its bridleways, pathways, pack-horse trails and cart tracks, and its well-established trading routes connecting village to village and market to market, snaking, newting and lizarding across the land.

I walk through the grounds of Low Farm, where there is a galvanised-steel carousel of caged red deer. This is the reality of the venison industry. Not the image of free beasts, hunted nobly by rugged country types, but barred boxes, with a pile of silage in the middle for the animals to feed on and nothing else for them to do, and little room to move. I'm sure in the summer months they get to roam the woods, but that is poor consolation for this lengthy incarceration. As we approach, the deer get a sniff of Wolfie, and they rut and jump as they try to retreat. I wince as I see them bash their bones on the bars. Possession and sale of venison was once tightly regulated under English law, to maintain its status symbol as food for toffs. These days, anyone is allowed to eat the flesh, but it still retains something of its status symbol. And now I imagine the nouveau riche feasting on it until it gives them gout.

We leave the farm and the cages and walk along Ouse Gill Beck, and then through a newly planted wood. We reach the bend in the river where the Ure becomes the Ouse. The same water, the same river, different name. I'm thinking about where Branwell and Lydia Robinson must have done their courting, as secrecy would have been paramount. There would have been plenty of discrete places in this area to find intimate moments together. According to Juliet Barker, they went to a boat house close by, but it has been destroyed. There's an RAF base near Linton on Ouse, and the peace and tranquillity of the vale is regularly interrupted by the flight paths of fighter planes. I come across what is now a holiday cottage that appears to be a log cabin. On closer inspection, it is clear that it is actually plastic made to look like timber. Next to it is an outside sauna in the Scandinavian style. This could well have been the spot where the Robinsons' boat house was, whose walls concealed the illicit pair.

Branwell wrote several poems about Lydia Robinson. There are two called 'Lydia Gisborne' (her maiden name). He used Greek letters to disguise the subject matter. One starts, 'On Ouses grassy banks—last Whitsuntide, / I sat, with fears and pleasures, in my soul'. The fear of being caught; the pleasures of the flesh. It goes on to say 'Where love, methought, should keep, my heart beside / Her, whose own prison home I looked upon'. He must have felt that his love could save her from the clutches of Mr Robinson, who was a much older man and close to death. It concludes by saying that the waters of the river are going far away to the Humber and that his hopes are gliding away too, rolling past 'the shores of Joy's now dim and distant isle'.

I make my way back to Monk's House, where Branwell stayed when he was private tutor to the Robinsons' son Edmund. It is now part of the Thorpe Underwood Estate, which is built on the grounds of the Robinsons' former estate home, which burnt down in 1895. It is expansive and includes the very prestigious Queen Ethelburga's Collegiate, an independent boarding school, where students can bring their own horses. Yes, really. The school is not without its controversies. Brian Martin, the former chair of governors, faced multiple sexual assault charges until cleared in 2018. Monk's House is the only remaining building.

The Thorpe Underwood Estate is very security conscious. There are cameras everywhere and keypads on all the gates and doors. The way the rich secure their property has changed but not the reason why. The walls are sturdy and high. I attempt to climb a tree so I can get a better view of the house, but before I even get to a vantage point, two security men appear, wanting to know what I'm up to. I climb down and tell them I'm writing a book. But this doesn't reassure them.

I make my way back. As I do, I hear a gaggle in the sky and look up to see three Vs of geese above me. They appear to be flying north-west. Thorpe Green Lane is a very unpleasant walking experience. It's just wide enough in some parts for a souped-up SUV to come racing past round blind bends. There are no pavements or passing points or anywhere for a pedestrian to hide, so that each time I hear a car approach, Wolfie and I have to squeeze into the thorny hedge as best we can, in the hope that the driver doesn't Steven King us. Ever since I read his gruesome account of his near-death experience while out walking, I've been more cautious of cars. The hedge seems to go on for ever before I find a gap in it big enough for us to squeeze through, and we walk along the ploughed border of a field parallel to the road. The sun is now a yellow biscuit. There isn't a cloud in sight. I'm anticipating tomorrow's journey to Grafton Hill, to see the view that Branwell would have seen.

I stop outside St Trinity Church, with its ornate rotunda, on the outskirts of Little Ouseburn. I know both Anne and Branwell attended the church, accompanying the Robinsons and their children. I imagine Branwell sitting on a hard, wooden pew, while the vicar or the curate preached about the sins of the flesh. I expect he blushed, or at least shuffled uncomfortably, as the sermon turned to the commandment of 'thou shalt not commit adultery.'

I walk across the river and back into the village of Great Ouseburn. There is a chimney sweep advertising his wares, and I'm sure there is a lot of demand for him in these parts. It's the sort of place where everyone has reverted to burning coal and seasoned hardwood. I pass the boarded-up Crown Inn. It looks bedraggled and neglected. The middle classes don't make a habit of session drinking, and most of the pubs round here that have survived have done so by turning themselves into restaurants that look like pubs. You know they're not pubs because when you go to the bar and order a pint and ask, 'How much?' they say, 'Don't worry, sir, we'll put it on your tab.'

I have to drive more than four miles to Boroughbridge to find any signs of life. Here there are three or four pubs, a chip shop, a hardware shop, a shoe shop and an olde worlde sweet shop. There's a gym full of high-tech equipment, set in the grounds of a medieval hall, two curry houses, a betting shop and a wine shop. I park up in a pub car park. I'll sleep here in my van tonight.

The next morning, stretching my legs and filling my lungs with good clean air, I stand by the bridge where a famous battle took place in 1322 between a band of rebellious barons and King Edward II. The battle included the death of the Earl of Hereford. As he crossed the bridge, he was attacked by a pikeman hiding beneath who thrust his spear up through Hereford's anus.

I drive back to Thorpe Green, stopping on the way to cook a breakfast of spinach, tomatoes and hash browns in my van. I didn't like being fobbed off by the two goons last night, so I return to Queen Ethelburga's Collegiate. It's an open day, and as soon as I drive my van into the car park, I'm approached by two different security guards. They want to know what I'm doing here. I explain that I just want to look around. Have I been invited? Not as such. Is my name on the list? No. I look at all the 4x4 Porsches and Land and Range Rovers. All new models. Mercedes Benz, BMW, Jaguar. The mothers are glamorous, in that quilted jacket and tweed kind of way, and considerably younger than the fathers, who are in smart casual and well fed. Their tans are from holidays in Tuscany rather than the high-street sunbed shop. Their children look scrubbed and prosperous. I'm surrounded by sizeable sculptures and top-of-the-range sporting facilities. I drive back out onto the road.

I park up and set off from Great Ouseburn on foot, on a circular trip that is going to take me to Grafton Hill. But unlike yesterday, which was characterised by blue skies, the weather today is very misty. There is a milky haze over everything, and visibility is about three hundred yards. I'll not see much from the top of the hill if it stays like this. Hopefully, the sun will burn through and the mist will lift.

I cross over the footbridge towards St Trinity Church that we know both Anne and Branwell attended. It's not as idiosyncratic as the church at Aldwark but a very nice design nevertheless. A castellated tower and a wooden Tudor porch entrance.

I pass Little Ouseburn village hall. There is an advertising bill pinned to the board: a quiz-and-supper evening this Friday, with hot-pork rolls and stuffing. I walk through Little Ouseburn and turn right at the boarded-up Green Tree pub. The path goes up towards Brunsell Field, and another path takes me to Brunsell Hill, which at fifty-eight metres above sea level is hardly fitting of the description. A dozen rooks, witches on broomsticks, flap and cackle above me. The path cuts through two ploughed fields that slope down like hip bones as Wolfie and I approach a wooded area called The Dale.

The woods are scarved in mist. They have a haunted, Hansel-and-Gretel feel to them. A few leaves cling to the sycamores like sleeping bats. The rest of the branches are bare. In the middle of the wood is a clearing and a little wooden footbridge over a dried-up beck. It would be a great place to wild camp. Or to enact a pagan sacrifice.

I hear the squawking warble of a pheasant as Wolfie gives chase. It takes refuge in a tree. Pheasants have the flight capacity to reach the top of the trees, but they don't seem to like doing it for some reason. They much prefer low-lying branches. Or, even better, scooting around on the ground. It must just be down to the amount of energy it takes to achieve flight for these elegantly heavy birds.

This area is intensively farmed. Industrialised agriculture has made much of England a green and unpleasant land, a monoculture, but these scraps of wooded areas, often left because of a geographical dip in the Earth's surface, make it hard work for industrial machines. They are an oasis in an arable desert, providing welcome areas of seclusion and biodiversity. But there needs to be more incentive and more encouragement to reforest places like this. Flatness invites plough and tractor. Steepness and wetness are nature's only defence against man and machine. But lakes can be drained, rivers dammed. So, these geographical corrugations offer essential refuge. I am struck, whenever I venture from the Yorkshire Moors that surround my home to gentler contours, how much we rely on glacial folds and river-worn ravines to experience anything approaching wildness. The natural world is vanishing.

I quickly leave the brief oasis and meet ploughed paths again. The mist has cushioned and muffled the land, so there is an eerie quiet, like my ears are stuffed with cotton wool. A path goes over to Grassgills. I call it a path, but it's really non-existent. Marked clearly on the map, the farmer has blatantly ploughed across it, reclaiming it by planting crops right along its length. Green shoots, about two or three inches in length, poke out of freshly turned earth that is claggy and soft and sticks to the soles of my boots. Without the OS map, there would be no indication of this public right of way. That's not to say that the Brontës' beloved moors were a free pass either. Getting access to rural spaces was then, and is now, an ongoing battle. At the end of the field is another wooded area with feeders for pheasants. It is obviously a shooting spot. There are dozens and dozens of pheasants, and the noise is deafening as they take to the skies.

I walk through the grounds of Park House Farm, coated in animal effluence and odious silage. Again, there are no waymarkers and no way of knowing where the path is meant to be. I stop to ask the farmer. He tells me to walk straight across his field towards an ash tree. Once again, the path has been ploughed over, and the farmer's theft is blatant. My feet sink into the claggy ploughed trenches, trampling on the fresh green shoots. I have to guess where the ash tree is, as visibility is not more than two hundred yards now.

Next, I make my way through a field of sheep that look like mist on legs to Gallaber Lane, which I cross, and head towards Marton village via Reas Lane. Marton village is typically picturesque, full of little cottages called things like Orchard Cottage or Plum Tree House, and with wisteria, and other climbing plants, growing up the side, rich with orange-yellow berries.

There is a church like something from a Constable painting with latticed windows. There are two bell towers – the main one has space to house two bells, but one is missing. The entrance to the church is at the side. Inside, there are two rows of pews, exposed brickwork and a fine Roman arch. There are homemade jams for sale and an honesty box. There's a brass-cleaning rota, and this month, November, is the turn of Zoe Hartley-Metcalfe. I notice the brass work is sparkling. Good work, Zoe.

I buy a Styrofoam cup of tea from the post office and sit outside the Punch Bowl Inn. It's a good-looking pub, but a quick glance through the window reveals the tell-tale signs: clothed tables with upturned wine glasses. It looks like a pub but is really a restaurant.

A path takes me across some playing fields. Steep steps lead up to the trig point of Grafton Hill. And here we are, at the top of the hill, standing next to the white triangular pillar that tells us we are seventy-five metres above sea level. It is called Grafton Hills on the OS map, which seems rather optimistic. The hill is really the biggest of a series of hillocks, like upturned pudding bowls. Although Grafton Hill is the highest point in the area, perhaps Juliet Barker is right to call it not a hill but an 'eminence' between Thorpe Green Hall and Boroughbridge.

Visibility now is down to one hundred yards. I can just make out the children's play area directly below me: swings, a slide and a climbing frame. There's a bench close to the swings, and a huddled figure drinks from a tin of Oranjeboom. I can't even make out the trees that line the field.

I've picked probably the worst day of the year to take in the view. But I imagine Branwell standing here, on a good clear day, overlooking the Vale of York, taking in the spires of York Minster and Ripon, and thinking impure thoughts about Lydia Robinson. Full of lust, or love, or both. He didn't really have much luck that way. He'd just come from Broughton-in-Furness, where he'd possibly sired an illegitimate child, and now here he was in the arms of a paramour some years his senior.

They're a funny lot, these vicars' sons, caught between three worlds: they have the status of the middle class and the income of the working class but hang around with gentry. They don't easily fit into any social group and are expected to carry on the tradition of piety and virtue that their fathers have trained them in.

Branwell's untitled poem begins 'O'er Grafton Hill the blue heaven smiled serene, / On Grafton Hill the grass waved bright and green'. It goes on to talk about the Vale of York as 'England's noblest vale' and eulogises about 'summer's sun and balmy gale'. It's very much a poem that a young man in lust and love would write.

I watch the huddled figure below glug from his blue-and-silver can of extra-strength lager. He takes in a lungful of smoke from a vaping device and lets it escape from his mouth like steam from a kettle. I'm not feeling the love today. The air is damp and heavy, fretted and webbed with an ominous quiet. I think about Branwell and Lydia wrapped in one another's arms, using hope to ward off a creeping despair, not quite at that point in their doomed relationship where possibility is smothered by reality.

After heading down from the top of the hill, the path cuts across Gallaber Farm and down Gallaber Lane towards a Roman road. The grass is still limp and sopping wet, and it soon soaks through my Gore-Tex-lined boots. I walk briefly along the Roman road. These dead straight ways must have been a lot of trouble to make, but in the long run they would have saved miles of footfall. It's a decision against nature. The paths and roadways that follow the curves and undulations of the land not only feel more a part of the landscape, but provide a more varied experience for the walker, the view ever changing as the path twists and turns.

Wolfie and I jump over a stile and try to find a path that goes across the field that is clearly marked on the OS map, but, once again, the farmer has thieved it: ploughed and planted it. Dead straight lines as far as the eye can see. I join the road with no walker's path. And although it is clearly marked with thirty-miles-an-hour signs, locals tear arse around in their souped-up Beamers, and pumped-up 4x4s, doing seventy-odd and I again hug the hedge trying not to get Stephen Kinged. I'm in a rather deflated mood, the opposite of the one Branwell would have been in as he meandered back to Monk's House, thinking about his next illicit meeting with Lydia and the pleasures of the flesh.

I wonder about extramarital affairs at a time when women could not grant a divorce – not until the Matrimonial Causes Act 1857 – and were often married for consanguinity or financial stability. Were affairs as common then as they are now? Or perhaps even more common? Affairs these days are the bread and butter of soap operas. *Emmerdale*, *EastEnders* and *Coronation Street* are all exercises in dramatising extramarital intimacies. No other narrative form has taken to this storyline with such zeal.

I kick fallen leaves as I walk, but really what I'm doing as I march back to Great Ouseburn is kicking myself. I'm kicking myself for not taking the opportunity yesterday, when the sky was so clear, of going up to Grafton Hill then. I'm angry. I'm angry with Great Ouseburn for attaching the epithet 'great'. I'm angry with farmers for stealing footpaths hundreds of years old. I'm angry with the drivers who tear up country roads. But I save my greatest anger for myself for being such an idiot to pick the foggiest day of the year to walk to Grafton Hill. Never rely on the English weather.

Post Scriptum

No one really knows what happened between Branwell and Lydia. We have only the poems and a few scraps of biographical information. We don't even know how the couple were discovered. But Juliet Barker thinks it must have been through the Robinsons' gardener Robert Pottage. For some reason, he accompanied the Robinsons to Scarborough. We know this because a payment to Pottage is recorded as an expense for the journey. Barker thinks that this payment was a gratuity for information given. Pottage, if he did know the lovers' secret, was between a rock and a hard place. To tell Mr Robinson would be to betray Mrs Robinson. But surely his loyalty was to his employer.

Mr Robinson's reaction to the news was immediate and unequivocal. He did sack Branwell, but there is no evidence that he said he would shoot him if he returned, as Branwell claimed. Mrs Robinson was never to see her young amour again, although she did send him a large payment. Patrick called Lydia Robinson a 'diabolical seducer'. The end of the affair was certainly the undoing of Branwell. It was his last attempt at paid employment, and the start of his downward spiral into addiction and dissipation.

9

LOOKING FOR THE SLAVES' GRAVEYARD

Dent is the only village in Dentdale, which is possibly the most intriguing and remote of all the Cumbrian Dales. Historically, Dent has comprised a community of maverick farmers and demon knitters, with some marble mining on the outskirts. These days it also contains a few arty 'offcumdens' (the term for out of towners seems to vary from region to region), including Pip Hall, the fine art letter carver who cut the letters into the Brontë Stones. Its streets are paved with higgledy-piggledy cobbles that poke out like pike fins – the walk between the two village pubs can feel like stepping on razors. The town is connected to the outside world by two B roads, neither of which allow you to get out of third gear, and is positioned in the fault line between Yorkshire, Lancashire and Cumbria. People from Dent have triple heritage.

I'm here to explore another *Wuthering Heights* origin myth. I begin at the Dent Village Heritage Centre and Museum, a small, volunteer-run place with plenty of idiosyncratic charm. Inside is a display that celebrates life and work in the region. There's a foreboding gin trap, which was used for snaring poachers by the ankle. I wince as I imagine the iron teeth cutting through skin and meat to the bone beneath. Its use was outlawed in 1827. There is also a lot of specialised farming equipment. I am drawn to one implement in particular: the probang, a length of leather tubing that was used to dislodge chunks of turnips and potatoes stuck in the guts of cattle, or, prior to this, in their rumen – the fore-stomach where the grass is fermented. There's also a trochar and cannula. The trochar is a sharp, pointed steel rod that fits into the shorter steel cannula. This would be plunged through the cow's flank behind the ribs if the beast's stomach was distended. The trochar would then be pulled out, leaving the hollow cannula in place to allow the gas to escape. I read about the practice of lighting the methane gas to create a flamethrower, which came to an end after a barn was burnt down.

There's also an account of the 'Dent Vampire', George Hodgeson, who died in Dent in 1715 at the age of ninety-four. His longevity was attributed to devil-dealing. He had fang-like canine teeth and drank sheep's blood every day. The rumour in the village was that George was one of the undead who slaked their thirst through sucking on human jugular veins. He was interred in a far corner of St Andrew's graveyard, but after he was seen walking in the moonlight, and following some mysterious deaths in the area, a town meeting was held and his body exhumed. A brass stake was driven through his heart, and he was reburied at the church door. Dent folk don't take chances.

I get talking to the woman on reception. I ask her about the Sills, a family of farmers at the centre of a documentary called *A Regular Black: The Hidden Wuthering Heights* by Lone Star that asserts another possible origin for Emily Brontë's novel. 'We sell the DVD here,' she says. 'Sold quite a few.'

'Where did they live?' I ask.

'Whernside Manor.'

'Is that nearby?'

'About a mile and a half away. Turn right at the George and Dragon. When you get to the sign for Ingleton, go the other way. You'll see it next to the old Methodist chapel.'

The film tells the story of the Sills, slave traders based in Dent. They had a plantation in Jamaica called Providence, and they brought back slaves to Liverpool and to their farm at the base of Whernside, where they were put to work. One of these slaves escaped and a bill of notice offered a £5 reward for his capture. There's a reproduction of it in the heritage centre.

During a visit to see his agents in Liverpool, Edmund Sill, the father of the family, brought back an orphan child, Richard Sutton, who was badly treated and beaten by the family. It was also said that he fell in love with Sill's daughter Anne. A historian in the film says that Richard Sutton was 'probably a black man' but doesn't cite any evidence. He apparently inherited the business. Another historian says that Emily Brontë probably heard the story when she was at Cowan Bridge. This is unlikely. She was only six years old at the time, and Cowan Bridge is nearly twenty miles away from Whernside Manor. But Emily may well have read about the story in *Howitt's Rural Life of England*, which was published in 1838 while she was working at Law Hill School.

This short film is interesting, but it does perhaps overstate its case. For instance, Caryl Phillips, a novelist I much admire, says that during Heathcliff's missing years he must have been involved in the slave trade. But, again, there is no real reason why this should be the case. There were plenty of criminal avenues that might explain his fortune. The film also fails to mention the story of Jack Sharp, or

Hugh Brunty, or Rob Roy, or any of the other likely sources. Having said all that, it's an enjoyable half hour, and it makes a good case for Heathcliff's ethnic origins, providing ample food for thought. In fact, it draws many of the same conclusions about Heathcliff's origins as my novel *Ill Will*. At a recent screening, the film very much divided its audience. The same could be said about my book.

It is rather odd that up until 2011 and the casting of Solomon Glave as the younger and James Howson as the elder Heathcliff in Andrea Arnold's adaptation of *Wuthering Heights*, previous films have all cast white actors to play the character: Milton Rosmer in A.V. Bramble's 1920 adaptation, Laurence Olivier in William Wyler's 1939 version, Kieron Moore in 1948, Richard Todd in 1953, Timothy Dalton in 1970, Ken Hutchinson in 1978, Ralph Fiennes in 1992, Robert Cavanah in 1998 and Tom Hardy in 2009. Let's not even think about Cliff Richard. But perhaps it isn't so strange if we consider that white actors have continued to take the role of Othello until very recently. For example, Anthony Hopkins in the BBC Shakespeare television production in 1981, and Michael Gambon in a stage production at Scarborough in 1990.

It is true to say that Heathcliff's ethnicity in the book is ambiguous. He is called 'black as the devil', but this could be a judgement on his morality rather than his ethnicity. He is called a 'dirty lascar'. But lascar itself is an ambiguous term, referring to a sailor from India, Arabia, China or North Africa. He is also called a gypsy several times in the book, which, again, is ambiguous. But for me the clues have always led to one place. The title of the film refers to something that Nelly says as she washes Heathcliff's face and combs his hair: 'if you were a regular black', a sentence she never completes. There is also the fact that he is brought from Liverpool when it was the biggest slave port in Europe, that he is referred to as 'it' and that a little later we are told that Mr Earnshaw tried to establish 'its owner'. He is also found talking 'gibberish'; i.e., another language.

'Are you a writer?' the woman behind the counter asks.

'Er … I'm interested in finding the slaves' graveyard.'

'It's said that I'm descended from one of the slaves,' she says.

'Really? You should do a DNA test.'

'That's the rumour.'

'About this slaves' graveyard—'

'No one knows where they were buried.'

'But you must have some idea?'

'Most likely place is a field behind the old Methodist chapel. There's a ring of trees. There's nowhere else that looks likely.'

I thank her and leave. Outside, the rain is hammering down like silver bullets and brass stakes. Wolfie is waiting by the door, already soaked to the skin. I pull my hood up and call him to follow. I make my way through the centre of the village, past the Sun Inn pub, the pink granite fountain and the memorial stone to Adam Sedgwick, one of the greatest field geologists of his time, and turn right at the George and Dragon.

I traipse up the high road that sits above the River Dee, past Conder Farm, until I come to the crossroads at Howgill Bridge. I go left here past a disused quarry and over Mill Bridge. I soon come to the old Methodist chapel and, next to it, Whernside Manor. Its entrance is grand, and the gates are flanked by two square, no-nonsense pillars of stone. I ignore the 'Private, Keep Out' sign and wander along the path. The house stands back a few hundred yards and is elevated by a walled terrace. It is a solid, rugged structure, with large door-shaped windows and a massive white front door that is studded with black, heavy-headed doornails. The gardens are full of sculptural follies and ornate features. But it is the building behind which catches my eye.

I wander further on. This is the farm's outbuilding, a functional storage space, and yet it has a number of decorative features, including round windows fitted with cut stone and a lovely arched vent. It is claimed in the film that it was modelled on a sugar factory that was part of the Sills' plantation in Jamaica. This building was there to remind them of that place. I have no reason to doubt this. Why waste money on cut stone if the building is merely functional? I imagine the manor as it was during the Sills' tenure, with black Africans doing most of the labour. I wonder how this was received by the rest of the village. It must surely have been a talking point? Were people curious to know more about their origins?

I wander back down the drive and turn up the lane towards Rigg End, which was the house the Sills lived in before the move to Whernside Manor. As I climb upwards, the brow of Whernside looms. It is the least distinctive of the three peaks of Yorkshire. Walkers who take the twenty-three-mile three-peak challenge normally start in the village of Horton in Ribblesdale, where you can check in and out at the local café. From here they climb up to Ingleborough, with its flat top above rugged shoulders, before dropping down then climbing up the comparatively conventional shape of Whernside and finishing the challenge with an ascent of Pen-y-Ghent, which looks like a monstrous flat iron. I've done the walk twice, the first time in my twenties, the second in my mid forties. The mid-forties me was pleased to beat the time set by my twenty-something self.

Just behind Whernside Manor, along Dyke Hall Lane, is the ring of trees in a field that the woman at the heritage centre suggested as the most likely spot for the slaves' graveyard. It is easy to see why she would come to this conclusion. It seems odd to have so many trees lined up in this way. There were said to be at least thirty house slaves at any one time, and they must be buried in unconsecrated land somewhere. It makes sense that you would inter them as close to their place of death as possible. Why waste energy travelling any further?

I stop to ponder the idea of slaves buried beneath this grass, leaning against one of the trees and imagining skeletons underneath my feet. I think back to the facsimile of the newspaper notice that hangs in the museum. On 8 September 1758, an advertisement appeared in the *Williamson's Liverpool Advertiser* for runaway slave Thomas Anson. It read: 'THOMAS ANSON, a Negro Man, about five Feet six Inches High, aged 20 Years or upwards, and broad set. Whoever will bring the said Man back to Dent, or give any Information that he may be had again, shall receive a handsome Reward from Mr. Edmund Sill of Dent, or Mr. David Kenyon, Merchant in Liverpool.'

Thomas wasn't recaptured and never returned to the Sill family. Instead, one 'Anson, Thomas' appeared in military records as having joined the army as a bugler, being barracked first in Edinburgh and then Aldershot before retiring with a pension and his freedom some nine years later. I think about what must have led him to run away. Things must have got pretty bad to flee a place of shelter for these barren dales.

I picture the Sills, or more likely their servants and slaves, lugging the bodies of dead West Africans up the hill to this spot. Digging holes deep in the stony ground to bury them would have been backbreaking work, and planting trees might have been a way of marking the graves that otherwise would have gone unmarked. I think about my own ancestors, indentured servants. Landowners considered them to be their personal property. If you were a commoner in the eighteenth century, you were subjected to servitude of one sort or another. Heathcliff is flogged and beaten with an iron weight.

A little further on, the path leaves Dyke Hall Lane and snakes left towards Rigg End, in a very remote spot in the shadow of the fell. It's extraordinary to think that anyone would choose to live in such an inaccessible spot, as the Sills did before they moved to Whernside Manor. It is a small farmer's cottage, tiny in comparison to the manor. And it is obvious from the comparison that the Sills made a great deal of money from slavery

John Sill, the second eldest son of Edmund, went to sea to seek his fortune. It was John who set up the plantation called Providence. It's a rather grand title for such a dirty business. But it is perhaps understandable that a man with the blood of black slaves on his hands might want to fool himself that his actions were not only condoned by God, but that God was offering him care and guidance along the way.

In the documentary, historian Cassandra Pybus states unequivocally that it was the landscape of this dale that inspired *Wuthering Heights*, not Haworth Moor. It's an odd claim. The landscape here is very distinctive, characterised by white limestone that pokes out from the hills and brows like fractured bones, such that the tops of these dales resemble a giants' boneyard, a piecemeal scattering of clavicles, scapula, ribs, femur, fibula and tibia – white bones, picked clean by some giant corvid. The moors of West Yorkshire are characterised by less porous millstone grit. In West Yorkshire, the water runs off the moors and down into the valley. Here, it finds its way through holes in the limestone. Underneath my feet is a labyrinth of watery potholes and dank caves. You can spend all day exploring these subterranean chambers and tunnels. Nothing Emily Brontë describes in her novel exactly resembles this landscape.

I climb further up to more remote farmhouses, Blake Rigg and Hingabank. I then circumscribe Whernside before climbing to the top of High Pike. Up here the air is clean and still. The sky is bruised with dark clouds, but the rain has thinned to fine mizzle. I come across the corpse of a ram. Its flesh has turned to liquid and all that is left is a white fleece rug with a skull and horns on top, stained red with blood and viscera. The black holes of the eye sockets stare into the abyss. It resembles a satanic offering, and I half expect to find an inverse pentagram inscribed in the chalky stone.

I make my way along the dale tops, before dropping down along Flinter Gill and returning back to Dent village. The rain has stopped, and there is even a window of blue in the distance. I call in to the Sun Inn and think some more about the documentary, and about Richard Sutton. Just how badly treated and beaten was he? Despite all this, it appears it was Sutton who inherited the manor and became the richest man in Dentdale. I'm wondering why the historian in the documentary thinks that he was a black man. There are early photographs in the museum that show that black people were living in the village, but this is not evidence that Sutton was. I wonder where he was buried. There is no sign of him in the local graveyard. Perhaps he too is interred in unconsecrated ground, with the sinners, the suicides, the vampires and the unbaptised.

I think about the last paragraph of *Wuthering Heights* and take out a battered copy of the book to reread it:

> *I sought, and soon discovered, the three headstones on the slope next the moor: the middle one grey, and half buried in heath; Edgar Linton's only harmonized by the turf, and moss creeping up its foot; Heathcliff's still bare. I lingered round them, under the benign sky: watched the moths fluttering among the heath and hare-bells; listened to the soft wind breathing through the grass; and wondered how any one could ever imagine unquiet slumbers for the sleepers in that quiet earth.*

I've read this passage countless times, but each time I reread it something new jumps out. This time it's the moths. Why moths and not butterflies, the obvious choice? But I see why Emily chose moths over butterflies. And it's not just that 'moths' assonate with 'watched' and 'soft'. It's more the sense of night and death, and of formication, that creeping feeling across one's skin. It is moths that come out at night to pollinate, not butterflies. It is moths that are drawn to the naked flame, where they immolate their bodies, not butterflies. Many moths go without food and die of starvation, as it is suggested Heathcliff does. Sharing so many traits, surely it is moths that are Heathcliff's familiars.

THE DEVILISH FACE - HATHERSAGE AND NORTH LEES HALL

In 1845, Charlotte Brontë visited her best friend Ellen Nussey at the vicarage in Hathersage in the Peak District. She stayed for three weeks, and this visit was to greatly influence the writing of *Jane Eyre*. North Lees Hall, a short walk from the vicarage, is probably the main inspiration for Mr Rochester's Thornfield Hall. Moorseats Hall became the Rivers family's 'Moor House', and the small town of Morton is based on Hathersage.

The village, positioned where the Hood Brook meets the River Derwent, has an ancient history. By the late 1700s, brass-button making thrived in the mills nearby. By the early 1800s, the industry had changed to pins and needles. Needle grinding was a lethal trade, and many men, women and children died from the grinding dust. Needles were a rather niche product and weren't made anywhere else in the area, which also connects with the description of Morton in the book, where it is characterised as a manufacturing village where many work in the needle factory. It would have been a bustling manufacturing centre when Charlotte visited. In addition to needles, other items made in the area included buttons, hackle and gill pins, fish hooks, wire for pianos and harps, umbrella ribs, and steel hoops for ladies' crinoline underskirts. The quarrying of millstones was another local industry. It is still a bustling centre, but the people who come here these days do so to climb Stanage Edge, yomp the moors, cycle the winding country lanes or hang-glide over Hope Valley.

It's 24 July 2019. I'm here to meet the writer and academic Dr Claire O'Callaghan, who has written extensively about the Brontës. It's the hottest day of the year so far. The Met Office have issued severe-weather warnings for most of England. All-time temperature records have been set across Europe, and the thermometer as I park my car in the village car park reads 35°C. And it's only mid-morning. I'm a bit early. I decide to have a walk around the village, but as I step out the heat is sweltering. It hits me immediately and clings to my skin. I can already feel a bead of sweat trickle down my back and tickle my spine. I decide to conserve my energy instead. I stand beneath the shade of a sycamore where it is cool. And wait.

I can just make out the huge gritstone escarpment above Hathersage known as Stanage Edge, which is our destination. I think about Charlotte, who also arrived in midsummer. She visited the vicarage from 24 June to 19 July 1845. Was it as hot as this, I wonder? She had probably walked to Keighley, travelled by coach to Leeds, then by rail to Sheffield and completed the final leg by horse-drawn omnibus. She was coming to help Ellen Nussey prepare the vicarage for her brother Henry's bride, who had succeeded Charlotte in his affections. Henry Nussey had proposed to Charlotte on 28 February 1839, and she had rejected his offer ten days later.

When Claire drives up in her red Volkswagen Polo, the temperature has risen another degree. I go over to her car to greet her. She opens the door and climbs out.

'I'm boiling.'

I feel a waft of hot air as it escapes from her car, like getting hit with a hairdryer. It turns out that the air conditioning in her VW isn't working, and she's driven all the way from Loughborough with her hands clinging to a melting steering wheel.

I've worked with Claire before. We did an event together at last year's Emily Brontë conference in York. We were in conversation about the film *A Regular Black*, discussing racial depictions of Heathcliff, both in the documentary and in my novel *Ill Will*. We chat for a bit in the shade, putting off the inevitable trek. We look at the map of the area and work out a route. We walk from Hathersage village up School Lane Road. The sky is a blanket of azure blue with just a few wispy clouds and the sun a golden disk of fire burning its heat into our skin. It makes the grass look greener and the cow parsley radiate whiteness, like wedding confetti. Nectar-heavy bees and butterflies buzz and flutter around low-hanging boughs of frothy lilac blossom that in its indigo glow resemble bunches of luscious grapes. Foxgloves bloom pink and blue. Their proper name is *Digitalis*, Latin for 'finger', which is perhaps a reference to the shape and size of the flower, which resemble a thimble.

'Patrick Brontë had an interest in foxgloves,' Claire says.

'Oh, really. They're poisonous, aren't they?'

'Yes, but they're used in medicine as well. To treat heart conditions. He annotated his copy of *Graham's Modern Medicine*, though you'd struggle to read his annotations.'

We stop at St Michael's Church, the church where Ellen Nussey's elder brother Henry was curate, and where the supposed grave of Little John is placed, but also the graves of the Eyre family, who lived at North Lees Hall. Inside the church are several notable brasses on the tombs of members of the Eyre family. Behind St Michael's is the old vicarage where Ellen Nussey invited Charlotte Brontë to stay in 1845. There is no plaque to mark the occasion.

'It's weird, isn't it,' I say, 'how little Hathersage does to mark its Charlotte Brontë connection.'

'They probably don't need the extra tourism.'

Claire has a point. The village isn't short of visitors.

As we talk about Ellen Nussey and Charlotte Brontë, a car pulls up at the vicarage and an elderly couple get out.

'Is this where Ellen Nussey used to live?' I ask as a conversational opening.

'It's where my daughter lives. Before that it was owned by ...' the woman says – I don't catch the name.

'No, I meant in 1845.' I explain why we have made the journey. She introduces herself to us as Julie.

'Why don't you come inside,' Julie says. 'I'll show you around.'

We weren't expecting this, and I look at Claire, who is smiling. We jump at the chance to have a nosey.

Inside there is a welcome coolness. Julie leads us through a grand hallway and into a front room with a large open fireplace. There's a Mikhail Gorbachev Russian doll on the mantelpiece and some abstract-art paintings hanging on the wall. We walk into the kitchen and interrupt the cleaner, who is mopping the floor. There is a bright-red Aga in one corner and a rustic stone floor. By no means original features, but perhaps not all that different to what was here in the mid nineteenth century. We walk through the main living room, which has patio doors that open into a spacious back garden with a wooden summer house. Huge creepers climb up the outside of the house and the surrounding wall. The garden is filled with lavender and lupins. Wisteria hangs in clumps over a stone archway. The view of Stanage Edge and the surrounding moorland from here is framed by the leafed branches of the trees that line the garden, and the effect is cinematic. The church spire looms over us. In its configuration and layout, this parsonage is very similar to the Haworth parsonage. It too stands on the edge of moorland and is in the shadow of the church and graveyard. It too is a detached stone building of ample size. I wonder if Charlotte felt at home here. We imagine her sitting in the garden with Ellen, having breakfast or taking tea on the lawn.

'What do they do?' I ask the woman.

'Who?'

'Your daughter and son-in-law?'

'She runs a museum in Manchester. He's a barrister. They came up here because he's a keen climber.'

She shows us round the rest of the building. Her daughter and son-in-law have restored a lot of the original features, and it's easy to superimpose Ellen and Charlotte as we explore the property. We interrupt a teenage boy who has created a man cave in the cellar. He is sprawled on a bed in front of a fifty-five-inch plasma screen, playing *Fifa19*. Upstairs, we bump into their eldest son, who looks to be about seventeen or eighteen. He's packing to attend a festival.

'I'm just showing these two people around,' Julie explains. 'They're writing about Charlotte Brontë's stay in the village.'

'Not another one.'

'Have there been a lot?' I ask.

'Yeah. Had two here yesterday.'

Claire gives me a look, which I can't quite read.

We go back downstairs and thank the woman for her time. As we leave, we talk about how strange it must have been for Charlotte to be here helping Ellen prepare the house for his bride to be, having turned down Henry's proposal. She told Ellen that although she 'esteemed Henry', she did not have an 'intense attachment which would make me willing to die for him'.

We take a path that goes behind the vicarage, through the edge of Moorseats Wood, below Moorseats Hall, a possible inspiration for Moor Hall, over some fields, along a path parallel with Birchin Wood. The sun shines through the green canopy, and we walk through dappled light.

'This must be the path that they took to the hall,' I say.

'Makes sense. It's the most direct route.'

We walk along Hood Brook, passing Brookfield Manor, which is now a training centre but at the time of Charlotte's visit was the home of Miss Hannah Wright, who owned North Lees Hall, although it was inhabited by the widowed Mary Eyre, her son George and three daughters. Some say Brookfield Manor is the basis for Vale Hall in the novel. The road takes us past Brontë Cottage, one of the few places in the area to recognise the Brontë connection, before making our way up the track to the hall itself. We are almost upon it before we see its castellated tower reaching out above the tree line, and you have to get very close indeed before it reveals itself completely.

There is a real *Jane Eyre* vibe to North Lees Hall. It is a three-storey castle tower with mullion windows and leaded panes, and it fits the description in the novel: 'steps and bannisters were of oak ... windows high and latticed ... it was three storeys high, of proportion, not vast ... battlements round the top gave it a picturesque look ... further off were hills ... like barriers of separation from the living world'.

The top of the tower is turreted with semi-circular embattlements and there is a roof terrace. There is also a three-bedroom farmhouse attached, with an unfeasibly high chimney stack. The farmhouse is empty, although it would have been in use during Charlotte's visit. The tower, which is owned by the Peak District National Park, is occupied by a woman who occasionally opens it to Airbnb customers, and before that it was used as an educational centre. Stone steps lead up to a black painted iron gate. Moss grows over the slated roof of the farmhouse, and weeds sprout from the flagstones of the path, which leads to a studded wooden door, an original feature. We are staring at the same door Charlotte would have seen.

The hall is positioned with gardens all around it, with another farm building further up called Crook Barn. It is surrounded by trees, where rooks roost. An apple tree bends low with still unripe fruit. We find somewhere to sit in the shade close to the hall. The stone step is comparatively cool. We mop our brows and drink copious amounts of water. I'm thinking about Charlotte's visit. Anne and Branwell had just returned from Thorpe Green. I don't think Charlotte was fully aware at that time of what Branwell had done, but she must have picked up on the subtext, that all was not well. I take out my notes.

'The description of Thornfield Hall in *Jane Eyre* matches quite accurately what we are looking at now. Later in the book, she travels to the roof of the hall to take in the view and talks about how in the immediate vicinity it is surrounded by woods and a rookery. It's basically a description of what we can see. There's even a door that suggests the door that leads to Bertha's place of confinement,' I say.

'Yes, and isn't it weird that when we got here and found no one home, we noticed the window on the third floor was wide open. When I saw that, I thought, Bertha's up there,' Claire says.

'I got the same feeling. Charlotte Brontë came here in June or July 1845 with Ellen Nussey – probably just a social visit. What do you think it was about this place then that inspired her? I mean, she was quite well travelled at this point. She'd been to Brussels; she'd visited many estate homes. She'd stayed in Mary Taylor's Red House, which was rather opulent. And visited Oakwell Hall a bit further up the road.'

'It's perhaps the sense of isolation. It is sort of doubly isolated. It is on its own, in the middle of the countryside. It is separated by trees and also by a ridge of rocks behind it.'

'Yeah, and it's not just isolated, is it? It is actually concealed. It is almost as if whoever built it was hiding from something,' I say.

'Yeah. You don't see it at all until you are almost upon it. What is weird, though, is that it's not particularly romantic for the love story that unfolds.'

'But it sort of suits Rochester's personality, don't you think?'

'In what way? I mean, yeah, it's a really queer building,' Claire says.

'Well, he is referred to as "peculiar", isn't he?'

'Yeah, and it is odd. It's kind of subdued for an aristocratic home.'

'The Fyres were Catholics, and there was a chapel in that field over there, the remains of which are still visible. So maybe they had good reason to hide. And we know Charlotte wasn't much of a fan of Catholics, was she?' I say.

'No, and, of course, in the book you have critiques of the different kinds of religious doctrine.'

'What's Rochester's take on religion, do you think?'

'I don't think he refers to it really. He goes to the church to get married, where he is about to sin before God. I can't really recall any other instances. When I've taught different aspects of religion in the book, I've always concentrated on Mr Brocklehurst, Helen Burns and St John Rivers. Those are the main critiques of religion going on in the book. Rochester is removed from that. And maybe that's reflected in the building. That idea of being removed. When I look at the tower now, for some reason I think of Rapunzel,' Claire says.

'Yeah, another confined woman. There's a fairy-tale look to it.'

'But not in a particularly conventional way,' Claire says.

'And it's not a very practical space. I've walked round the interior.'

'You know the scenes in the book with Jane waking up at night and hearing noises around corridors and Bertha is running around? The descriptions in the text give much more an impression of space and expansiveness. Looking at the size of the building now, this feels like you would just hear everything.'

'Yeah, and that bit when she describes a long corridor with many closed doors. That doesn't fit at all.'

Of course, the world of *Jane Eyre* is a product of Charlotte's imagination, but it is interesting to consider to what extent her vision of it was invented and to what extent there are comparisons with real places. As we sit in the shade, we watch rooks flap their ragged black wings as they circle the rookery. One perches on a branch and bobs its head, making that raspy sound that resembles a football rattle.

'In my Penguin Classics edition from 1996,' Claire says, 'the notes at the back say that the descriptions of Thornfield draw on her experience of two Yorkshire houses: Rydings in Birstall, home of Ellen Nussey till 1837, and Norton Conyers near Ripon. These contribute to the grounds and the external appearance of Thornfield.'

'So, they've completely missed the North Lees Hall connection. That's so interesting. The hall was owned by a family called Eyre, and when Charlotte visited, Mary Eyre was living there with her children. The first mistress of North Lees Hall, Agnes Ashurst, it was said, went mad and was confined in a padded room and died in a fire.'

We talk about whether it was these extraordinary stories of North Lees Hall's residents that inspired Charlotte or whether it was the Gothic setting itself. The rook that was making so much noise is joined by its mate, and this seems to silence it for a while. We sit in quiet reflection. It was also here, at North Lees Hall, that Charlotte saw the so-called 'apostles cupboard', a huge walnut and ebony wardrobe, containing twelve panels, each depicting one of the apostles. No one knows who painted the panels, but they were probably copied from Van Dyk. The furniture was here when Charlotte visited but was bought by the Haworth Parsonage Museum in 1935 and is now part of their permanent exhibition. It finds its way into *Jane Eyre*. In chapter twenty, Jane describes waking in the dead of night, her curtains open, to a full moon and hearing a cry that 'rent in twain' the silent night with a 'savage, a sharp, a shrilly sound that ran from end to end of Thornfield Hall'. She says the noise came out of the third storey, from a room above her chamber. She then hears a struggle and a voice shouting 'help!' repeatedly. The cry wakes the other inhabitants, including Mr Rochester, who tries to downplay the event, saying it is just a servant's bad dream. We learn later that this scream was uttered by Bertha, Mr Rochester's wife, who is imprisoned in the hall and whose very existence he denies. Jane cannot sleep and spends a long time staring out of the window 'over the silent grounds and silvered fields'. She is later called to assist Mr Rochester, fetching a sponge to nurse Mason, who is 'soaked in blood' – Bertha has bitten him and 'sucked his blood', vampire-style.

Rochester locks Jane in the room with Mason while he fetches a surgeon. It is during this confinement that her eyes turn to a 'great cabinet … whose front, divided into twelve panels, bore, in grim design, the heads of the twelve apostles, each enclosed in its separate panel as in a frame'. The flickering candlelight animates the figures so that Luke 'bent his brow' and 'St John's long hair waved' and the 'devilish face of Judas' gathered life.

We stare at the exterior again. I've visited both of the halls mentioned in Claire's Penguin edition, and I didn't get the same feeling as I do now, staring at this hall, of being immersed in the book.

I ask Claire about her essay in a recent edition of *Brontë Studies* called '"He is rather peculiar, perhaps": Reading Mr Rochester's Coarseness Queerly'. It's a brilliant essay that made me revisit *Jane Eyre* and think differently about Charlotte Brontë. In it, Claire talks about how one reviewer (Elizabeth Rigby from 1848) condemned *Jane Eyre*, calling it an 'anti-Christian composition'. This may seem like an odd thing to accuse a clergyman's daughter of, but Rigby would not have known that at the time, as Charlotte was writing under the nom de plume of Currer Bell. I'm wondering whether Rigby's accusation refers to the bigamy in the book, or whether there are other anti-Christian elements. Claire explains that in the full review a lot of the anti-Christian criticism is also aimed at Jane, not just Rochester. Rigby goes on to accuse Charlotte of making an 'unworthy character interesting'. A strange accusation to a modern reader. These days, that's the job description of a novelist. Her sister Emily is similarly accused for her portrayal of Heathcliff. Rigby then goes on to say that Rochester is 'made to be as coarse and as brutal as can in all conscience be required to keep our sympathies at a distance'. This coarseness, then, is a combination of elements. Rigby is talking about coarse as in vulgar, but also base and even obscene. We often overlook underlying aspects of violence around Rochester's character. The fact that he has a woman locked up. The fact that he does threaten Jane with violence.

'And how do you feel about this character that is happy to lock his wife up?' I ask Claire.

'Well, what he was doing was legal then.'

'Was it?'

'Yeah.'

'I didn't know that. So, a husband could lock his wife up?'

'Yeah, private incarceration was permitted. You could be locked up in an asylum or locked up at home.'

'Didn't it require a doctor's certificate or some legal process?'

'Only if you wanted to certify them as insane.'

'But you wouldn't need to do that to legally incarcerate them?'

Claire explains that Bertha was Rochester's legal property at that point. And therefore she was his in every way, and he could do what he wanted to her. It is one of the interesting aspects of the book, that we only ever get his account. Claire talks about Rochester's long monologue where he explains who and what Bertha is.

'When I've taught that in the past, I get students to look at it critically and ask, how reliable is this? We only have his word, and he wants Jane to pity him.'

'And it works.'

'Yeah. But to what extent do we believe that Bertha is mad in a way that warrants his treatment, such that his actions have a bizarre kindness to them by not putting her into an asylum? Or to what extent do we think she has been driven mad by the circumstances of their life together, having been removed from her home and brought to England from abroad?'

'Because if you were incarcerated in that way, and you weren't mad to begin with, you would, understandably, start to exhibit signs of mental illness.'

We stare up at the tower. It's quite hard on a beautiful summer's day like today, when the lattice windows reflect the cerulean sky above, and the sun makes everything shine, to imagine the hall as a place of incarceration, but on a cold winter's day the isolation of the tower would be haunting.

In her review, Rigby wrote that 'the popularity of *Jane Eyre* is a proof how deeply the love for illegitimate romance is implanted in our nature'. I ask Claire if she thinks that there is something transgressive in the very act of love. She shrugs.

'I mean in the sense that it disrupts the status quo. It is a force of disorder. If you like, the ordered, rational Apollonian world is competing with this darker side of desire and passion and irrationality. It's a dark force in a way, isn't it?'

'I guess it is. But I'm not sure I'd characterise Jane and Rochester's love for each other in that way. I mean, she's not obsessing about him all the time. She's fond and respectful of him.'

'And her feelings grow over time. It's a gradual process.'

'And it's also to do with the fact that she speaks freely to him in a way that she doesn't with other people. There is a mutual respect.'

'Yeah, he respects her and in fact is influenced by her.'

'I guess the other thing about illegitimate love here, and what Rigby is gesturing towards, is the idea of the class difference between them. This overstepping of boundaries. Not only does she fall in love with her employer, but they are from very different classes. They should not be together – that crossing of class parameters – and that unsettles Victorian boundaries.'

'But unlike Cathy, Rochester doesn't feel like it would degrade him to marry Jane.'

'I think Rochester is playfully deviant. He is part of an aristocratic world but doesn't have the same airs and graces. Also, part of his narrative is that he loves Jane and that trumps the issues of class.'

I met Claire at the Emily Brontë conference the previous year when she presented a paper that discussed queer theory, and it was interesting to see quite a few people misunderstand it, thinking it meant specifically theory related to queer sexuality.

'Which was weird because I said at the time, I'm not saying that.'

'As a theory, it's intentionally provocative isn't it?'

'Yes, and I'm being provocative with it. And I'm addressing a section of Brontë fans and scholars who see Rochester in very straight heterosexual terms.'

In the essay, Claire says that the book includes 'narratives of homosexual and the homoerotic, tourist masculinities, expressions of feminine fatherhood, tender expressions of manliness and male nursing, queer heterosexual courtship and feminine masculinities'. Which is quite a list. It made me wonder to what extent this was Charlotte's intention? When I first started reading the essay, I was rather sceptical, but by the end of it I was completely convinced. One of the things that really persuaded me was Byron and the obvious connections between Rochester and Byron, and Charlotte's fandom and interest in Byron. Which makes, perhaps, Charlotte a much more radical thinker than what we often give her credit for. If her interest in Byron goes beyond the texts to the cult of Byron, then she is attracted to someone who is a political radical and who supported the Luddites, who is openly bisexual, and who deliberately defies the conventions of his day.

'It's all there in the text. He does dress up as a woman, he does identify as a bachelor, he does nurse Mason, he is doing all of those things, but I didn't come to those ideas thinking about Charlotte and her love of Bryon. Byron came later, when I was working up my ideas writing it.'

Claire goes on to say that 'Rochester's "identity crisis" is evident through the complex gender and sexual politics at play: here is an aristocratic, patriarchal man misrepresenting himself as a bachelor and dressed in women's clothes, passing himself off as an older woman in an attempt to seduce a younger female'. And when you put it like that, the strangeness of what's going on in the book really comes across.

'Have you looked back at that scene when he is dressed as a gypsy?' Claire says.

'Yes, very recently in fact. Jane is seduced by the performance, isn't she?'

'Yeah, she's completely seduced. There is something uncanny going on there.'

'It's like she's under a spell. Because he doesn't speak like a gypsy. He speaks like Mr Rochester,' I say.

'Exactly.'

'And what's interesting about that performance is that he is dressed like a gypsy but not acting like a gypsy. Why do you think he does that? Why doesn't he attempt to complete the performance?'

'I think he's being playful,' Claire says.

'Does he want her to know it is him?'

'I think he does ultimately. I think he's trying to get information off her. He is testing the water. He is seducing her, but it is a very unconventional approach.'

'Is it fair to say that it is one of the most unconventional seduction scenes in Victorian literature?' I say.

'I think so, yes. And with one or two exceptions, it is always missed out. And if you look at the way Rochester is portrayed in those adaptations, he has a bigger house, and they make him more conventional and traditional, a romantic hero.'

'If you leave that cross-dressing scene out, you lose some of the peculiarity.'

'Yes, and then you locate the seduction scenes in more conventional places,' Claire says.

It's interesting to think how film and TV adaptations perhaps change how we approach a literary text. How our original conception of it may be altered by what we see on the screen.

In the scene that immediately follows the cross-dressing gypsy one, Mason is attacked by Bertha. Rochester describes Mason as an 'intimate' friend. And Jane concludes that theirs must have been a 'curious friendship'. The scene where Rochester nurses Mason and attends to his wounds is very intimate and homoerotically charged. He unbuttons his shirt and tends to him, taking on a conventionally feminine role, and Claire talks about how nursing was an intensely eroticised practice. Which is an idea that is still around today, albeit confined to amateur porn sites.

The other thing to note is that all this takes place in Mr Rochester's bedroom, and one of the most taboo things that Charlotte does is put her governess in the master's bedroom very early on. They are both there in their nighties. Bedrooms have a permissive, suggestive element. At this point, Rochester stops attending to Mason's wounds and goes off to fetch the doctor. Jane then takes on Rochester's role. She immediately becomes his surrogate, almost like they are functioning in the same way. Claire goes on to say that 'his compassionate actions are healing and the physical attentiveness creates a homoerotic effect that deepens the bonds between the men, something gestured to when Rochester opens Mason's shirt'.

'Once I read that, it became impossible for me not to think of that scene as homoerotic.'

'I've totally queered it for you,' Claire says.

'You have.'

We sit and drink more water. I suggest, despite the sweltering heat, that we carry on with our journey. We walk up through the woods where North Lees campsite is situated, and then climb the moors below the escarpment. We pass boulders, some of which have been carved for grindstones and millstones but abandoned half-finished. We reach the trig point at High Neb, which marks the highest point in the area, and walk along the edge. The ridge sweeps and curves across the moor, forming a rugged edge of granite that acts as a step and barrier between lower and upper moor.

The sky is watercoloured with a few pillowy clouds that the sun is burning through, but most of it is clear. Loose rocks sit on top of the edge, like leftovers, tossed-up flotsam. Little pools of water glisten in the undulations of the stones. Claire bends down and scoops up some of the water in her open palm, dousing her back and head in an attempt to cool down. Rock stacks lean improbably, threatening to tumble over. If they fell, the weight of any one of these stones would pulverise a passer-by. Verdant fern and moss fret the edges of the rocks. This is the Hope Valley. The air is blustery but peaceful, which we are grateful for as we stand in its flow, enjoying the feeling of the breeze as it cools and soothes.

I did a similar walk a few months before with another Victorian scholar, Dr Merrick Burrow, who specialises in the late Victorian era, only in the opposite direction, walking along Fiddler's Elbow, joining a path that goes past the Cowper Stone and a trig point before arriving at the impressive ridge of Stanage Edge proper. And on that day, it was a Sunday, there were climbers everywhere, dressed in red and blue and yellow. Hang-gliders gyred in the air above us, soaring like buzzards, their legs and bodies cocooned in pods so that they looked like maggots glued to the underside of butterflies. But today there are hardly any other walkers here, and we have the edge to ourselves. It is uncannily quiet, the escarpment creating a soundproof ridge between us and post-industrial Sheffield. We find a cool rock to perch on and take in the scene.

We can see for miles around. The view, of green moorland and darker wooded areas lower down in the valley, encompasses Mam Tor and Kinder Scout, overlooking Derwent, Moscar and Strines Moors. We can see Win Hill and Lose Hill, supposedly named after a seventh-century battle for which there isn't any historical basis. Sheffield is only a few miles to our east, but there is no indication of it up here. The rock tops are white-grey and sparkle with quartz crystals in the blazing sun.

It feels almost rude to break the silence, but I say, 'You talk about the way Rochester is with Adele.' Adele is a French child to whom Jane is a governess at Thornfield Hall. Mr Rochester refuses to accept that he is Adele's biological father but adopts her anyway.

'Because, again, it is so unconventional. Particularly when he says that she's not my child.'

'And if that's true, that she's not his child, and his only evidence is that she doesn't look like him, which isn't necessarily proof, that he would voluntarily take on this role …'

'It's incredibly compassionate, isn't it? He's a man of feeling.'

'You say, "*Jane Eyre* gestures to a range of queer masculinities in varied forms and guises, ranging from the overt (Rochester's feminine masculinity when cross-dressing or his adoptive parenting) to the indirect and suggestive (his touristic masculinity and homosocial friendships)." All of those things … I mean, that's a list of positive attributes.'

'And that's what I was trying to do. I think they are, and we should see them in that way. They are all positive, and this book is far more radical than previously acknowledged.'

We sit in silence for a little longer, before continuing on our way. As we approach Higger Tor, we disturb lapwing and curlew. A stack of rocks is piled up like loaves of fresh baked bread. Further on, another stack resembles a turtle as it climbs out of the water, its head resting on a rock pillow. The stones are striped with layers of sediment, accumulated over geological time, and patched with grey-green badges of lichen. The sun silvers the cloud edges.

'Do you think Charlotte and Ellen would have walked up here?' I ask Claire.

'Why wouldn't they? We know that Charlotte was here for three weeks. And that she loved walking. I'd be surprised if they didn't.'

I agree. Certainly, from the description in chapter twenty-eight, it does appear as if Charlotte walked Stanage Edge: 'dusk with moorland, ridged with mountain … there are great moors behind and … waves of mountains far beyond that deep valley at my feet'. She also describes a stone feature that resembles nearby Moscar

Cross, a stone pillar that acts as a waymarker. In fact, chapters twenty-eight to thirty-five offer accurate descriptions of the Peak District: 'A north-midland shire, dusk with moorland, ridged with mountain: this I see. There are great moors behind and on each hand of me; there are waves of mountains far beyond that deep valley at my feet.' And much of this landscape is unchanged. The ashen and russet-coloured rocks we walk on, the drab crags that cast black shadows and hide the bones of dead sheep, the blooming heather, the thick carpets of fern, and the rolling moors in the distance. The dense wooded areas that patch the landscape, some of which the Eyres owned, right up to the ridge of Stanage itself, would perhaps have been more extensive. A lizard crosses our path, and I think of the lizard that Jane sees running over a crag.

As we make our way down, we encounter more of the grindstones carved in situ and cut from these rocks that were abandoned when the labour was outsourced to cheaper suppliers. There is something poignant about their appearance here, scattered among the fern and tussock grass, like they are growing out of the earth.

As the path leads us back down to the village, Claire turns to me and says, 'If there was a lake here, I'd jump straight in it.' I nod my head. The idea is suddenly compelling. I look for a lake, but there isn't even a puddle. There is no escape from the blazing sun, and all I can think about is the ice-cold lager that waits for us at the end of our journey. I feel like John Mills in *Ice Cold in Alex*. My forehead prickles with sweat, and I imagine the glass on the bar, all steamed up, a condensing drop of liquid trickling down it. I'm almost certain that Charlotte Brontë never craved an ice-cold glass of lager.

As we walk, I realise I've been a bit down on Charlotte for some time, ever since I learnt the extent of her posthumous meddling with both Anne and Emily's writing and literary legacies. I'd written her off as the more conservative, conventional sister, with a bit of a chip on her shoulder. Talking to Claire, I've repositioned Charlotte again and now believe that in her own, very different, way, she was just as radical as Emily and Anne.

11

BOILED MILK - ANNE'S FINAL JOURNEY

In Scarborough on Friday, 25 May 1849, some time in the afternoon, a train pulled up at the station. It had come from York. The doors opened and Anne Brontë alighted. Beside her were her eldest and only surviving sister Charlotte and their friend Ellen Nussey. In three days' time, Anne would be dead, and Charlotte would be the only remaining Brontë sibling.

Charlotte had fought hard to stop Anne's plan of returning to Scarborough, a holiday resort Anne had visited many times with the Robinsons, but in the end she had lost the fight. It was their father Patrick who had intervened and insisted that she go. Charlotte had only recently seen first her brother Branwell, on 24 September 1848, then her sister Emily, on 19 December 1848, taken to their graves.

They made their way to Wood's Lodgings at No. 2 The Cliff, where Anne had previously stayed with Lydia and the rest of the Robinson family. The view overlooked the sea. The lodgings are no longer here. They were replaced by the Grand Hotel in 1867, the 'largest and most handsomest hotel in Europe'. Anne's ghost is said to haunt its corridors.

The Scarborough they saw as they walked from the station to their lodgings would have been much smaller than the town that exists today. Anne would have seen the Town Hall in St Nicholas Street and the Borough Gaol at the top of St Thomas Street, which was opposite the Seaman's Hospital. There was also the theatre close by, 'the only place of amusement in town', according to a general directory published at the time. The Customs House was situated between the piers. Scarborough exported corn, butter, hams, bacon and saltfish. It imported coal from Newcastle and Sunderland; timber, deal, hemp and flax from the Baltic; and groceries from London. There were fifteen beer houses, one billiard room and sixty-six public houses; twenty dressmakers, seven hatters, five stay and corset makers, and one gunmaker. Three boat builders, two fossil dealers and one bone crusher.

I'm trying to picture all this as I wait for poet and playwright Wendy Pratt, who was born and bred in Scarborough but now lives in Filey, down the road. She has written five books of poetry. She has also just completed a play about Anne's last days. She wants to show me around Anne's Scarborough and take me to the key places. We meet in Greensmiths & Thackwrays, which is now a coffee shop but was once a 'colonial outfitters', as the writing above the window still attests.

Wendy introduces herself. She is wearing a bright-yellow cardigan and carries a capacious satchel. We sit and chat before agreeing on our route. The forecast of light cloud and gentle breeze has so far held up, but as we walk down St Nicholas Street to the Grand Hotel the air turns icy. We're passing my van, so I nip in and get a warmer coat.

'Will you be warm enough?' I ask her.

'Yeah,' she says. 'I'm a proper Yorkshire lass.'

I wonder if Anne and Charlotte felt the same way about the breeze.

We dodge kittiwake shit, which falls from the windowsills above us. Kittiwakes are protected seabirds, and they have made a welcome home in the nooks and crannies of Scarborough's buildings. We stand underneath the blue plaques on the wall of the hotel, the highest of which is to mark Anne Brontë's stay here, and her death. Juliet Barker talks about how, on the Saturday, Anne went to the bathhouse nearby but collapsed at the garden gate on the way back. I want to know where this was.

'I think the bathhouse must have been there.' Wendy points to the buildings opposite the Grand Hotel, which are now hotels and town houses, with a Masonic lodge in the middle. She shows me a sketch from *Theakston's Guide to Scarborough* from 1841. It is of Travis's Baths. The baths were made of wood and marble and were adapted for either 'plunging, sitting, or the recumbent position'. Every tide, the baths were supplied with pure sea water. There were four other bathhouses in addition to Travis's.

'The garden gate must have been here,' says Wendy, pointing to the communal garden that still stands between these buildings and the hotel. It is still gated, perhaps even with the same gate, and I imagine Anne clinging on to it, using it to pull herself upright again with arms 'no thicker than a little child's', as Charlotte described them in a letter to Ellen when she wrote to warn her of Anne's decline. She was carried indoors by the hired servant, Jane Jefferson.

'Didn't she take a donkey-cart ride in the afternoon?' I ask.

'Yes, she took the reins herself. She didn't like the cruel way the boy was treating the animal.'

Anne always stood up to the abuse of animals. It's in her poems and her novels. Barker recounts how Ellen Nussey came to meet

Anne at the point that she was giving the boy a lecture, although the conversation was not recorded, so we can only guess in what way she scolded him. There's a drawing of these cart rides in the archives of Scarborough Library, but most of the carts are being pulled by horses not donkeys.

As we talk, we are passed by people dressed as cartoon characters: a Hulk, a Thor and a Black Widow. There has been a comic convention, and it must have just finished. To our left is Spa Bridge, which Anne walked across with Charlotte and Ellen, and would then have been a toll bridge. A day ticket was one shilling. Below is the sandy beach where Anne strolled.

The reason Anne gave for wanting to visit Scarborough again was that she hoped the sea air, thought to be a cure for TB, would revive her. She wrote to Ellen that 'the doctor says that a change of air or removal to a better climate would hardly ever fail of success in consumptive cases'.

But Wendy thinks that the real reason for her visit was very different: 'She knew she was dying. She was thinking about her father, and what he'd been through.'

'Yeah, you think about the close succession of those deaths and how he must have felt.'

However, Ann Dinsdale and other Brontë experts I have spoken to feel strongly that Anne didn't know she was dying and was holding out for a miracle cure. Maybe she was hedging her bets. In the same letter to Ellen, she also wrote, 'I have no horror of death: if I thought it inevitable I think I could quietly resign myself to the prospect.' Scarborough perhaps held both possibilities for Anne: potential remedy and final resting place.

The three women had stayed in York on the way to Scarborough, at the George Hotel in Coney Street, the site of which is now a Waterstones bookshop. We know from Ellen's detailed record of the journey that they bought bonnets and ribbons there so that they could look their best in Scarborough. For me, this is evidence that can be used to bolster either case. Would she have wasted money on expensive garments if she knew she was dying? But if she knew she was dying, why would she care about money?

We can see St Mary's Church from where we are standing. This was Anne's final destination, and we are heading in that direction. In Anne's day, Scarborough was an up-and-coming spa town of great prestige. Like Bath, people came here to rest and restore their health. These days, Scarborough is down on its luck, with one of the highest mortality rates from opioid overdoses in the country. On the seafront, between the candied confectioneries, rainbow slush and pink candyfloss, are shops selling Day-Glo bongs, skunkweed grinding machines and poppers disguised as 'room odorisers'. There's an edge to the town, and it is no longer the holiday destination of the middle classes. It is April, outside of the holiday season, and there isn't much work for the locals, unless you work at the McCain's food factory up the road or at the local hospital. The bars are already starting to fill with hardened drinkers.

Wendy explains the reason for this: 'We just don't get the sort of money coming into the town that we did, so it contributes to the poverty in a way. People who are lost and broken, people who are living in poverty often come to live in Scarborough because of nostalgic memories from the good times they've had on holidays here, which means we tend to get a higher number of impoverished people coming to the area and no jobs to support them if they are able to work. The town then revolves around squeezing money out of these impoverished people by offering many opportunities to gamble. So many betting shops.'

'And pubs selling cheap alcohol?'

'Yeah. We are basically offering them the dream that will never come true, and then anaesthetising them when they realise their life is just endless trauma. There's a reason the town is the way it is.'

We stand outside the Grand Hotel, reflecting on this contrast. I stayed here a few years ago, when I was invited to run a workshop for the National Student Drama Festival. It was more like an old people's home than a holiday resort. I came back late one night and rang for room service, but the only thing they could offer me was a cream-cheese sandwich on milk-loaf bread. Going down for breakfast the next day, it was clear that the menu had been devised to be denture friendly. Porridge and mashed fruit for breakfast, soup and stew for lunch, and a dinner of shepherd's pie. You could eat anything you wanted as long as it was pre-digested and didn't require chewing. It seems as though people still come to the town to see out their last days, albeit with less hope of a remedy for their ailments.

One day, I took the lift to the top floor, even though there was a sign saying that it was out of bounds. There was mould growing over the flock wallpaper and various receptacles were laid out on the mildewed carpet to capture fallen drops of rainwater as it leaked through the roof. There was even a plant growing out of a crack in one of the walls. The management, unable to afford the upkeep, and not needing the extra rooms, had abandoned it to the elements.

Barker writes that in the evening Anne sat and watched 'a particularly splendid sunset', but Wendy points out that this wouldn't have been possible as the view was over the east, over the sea, not the west. It's a minor quibble in what is an otherwise assiduously researched tome.

We walk up Vernon Road to where Christ Church used to stand, the church where Anne's funeral took place, attended by only Charlotte, Ellen and Charlotte's friend Margaret Wooler, who had come to offer her support. She had taught Anne at Roe Head School. Where the church used to be is now a fish restaurant called Wackers.

'Everyone worked at Wackers when I was growing up. You got a Saturday job,' Wendy says.

'It doesn't sound very appetising. When was the church knocked down?'

'I think in 1979. My mum remembers it.'

We look at old photos of the church. It was a grand building with a four-cornered tower and Gothic windows. During Anne's time here, the church would have stood apart from any other buildings, surrounded by trees.

'Why did they knock it down?'

'To build Wackers.'

We walk up Westborough towards the train station. It's a small terminus with five platforms and three rails.

'At one point we had a train to Whitby, but they took it away.'

'Why did they do that?'

'We are historically unlistened to in the town, over everything. The residents are always put second to the need to keep tourist numbers up and to save money for tourism. Apparently, the line was very steep and became very slippery in the frequent sea frets, leading to trains stalling a lot, which caused massive backlogs and delays, so they closed it, despite Scarborough residents petitioning against the closure.'

The skeleton of the station is mostly unchanged. Its ribs are wrought iron, painted austere black.

'They say you are thirty-seven miles from civilisation if you live in Scarborough,' Wendy says.

'And that's the distance to York?'

'It's on a limb.'

We look at the map in front of us, of Scarborough and the surrounding coastland. Scarborough sticks out like an epidermal cyst or a swollen knuckle. We walk through the station. It's a generic space with a Pumpkin café, a chain that specialises in train stations and hospitals: places where journeys start and end. We pass a young mother with her son. She drinks from a foamy paper cup as he forks huge pieces of chocolate cake into his mouth. I don't think dandelion coffee will be on the menu, a beverage that the three women purchased shortly after leaving the train. I wonder why dandelion coffee, a coffee substitute made from roasting the root and not real coffee. Perhaps they were attracted to the novelty of it, or to its comparative cheapness?

Outside we are confronted by the Stephen Joseph Theatre, the first theatre in the round in Britain and home to the plays of Alan Ayckbourn. Its red-and-white curved corner and jutting brick sections are still an impressive example of art-deco design, but it wasn't built as a theatre. Wendy explains: 'The actual first theatre in the round wasn't at the SJT as it is now. The original was in the basement of the library on Vernon Road, next to where Christ Church was. This was originally an Odeon cinema.'

The sign above the door tells us that the latest show is called *Martha, Josie and the Chinese Elvis*. I once drove the actor Richard Wilson here, famous for portraying grumpy pensioner Victor

Meldrew, with his catchphrase 'I don't believe it!' We were late, and I'd forgotten to tell him that the seatbelt was faulty. As I pulled up, he was exasperated to learn that he was belted to the seat and couldn't get out. I had to pull the belt loose so he could slip underneath it. Only he got caught up in the loose webbing. As he pulled and yanked the black strap, becoming more entangled, he went red in the face. He was very close to using his catchphrase.

'It would be great if my play was produced here,' Wendy says.

'Yeah, that would be cool. Aren't they doing a scene study of it soon?'

'I'm really excited.'

'You should be. It's a really good play.'

It tells the story of Anne's last days and is structured around three interwoven monologues: Anne's, Charlotte's and Ellen's. It's funny in places, with Ellen providing most of the comedy, but ultimately it is a heartrending tale.

We walk down Westborough and turn up St Thomas Street towards Castle Road. The terraced houses that line Castle Road are early Victorian. Anne's coffin would have been carried along here on a cart.

'Whenever I walk up this part of town, I feel like I'm following Anne's wake. Especially since working on the play, where I was immersing myself completely in this part of her life and imagining it over and over. It's like I can map out, in my head, what was and wasn't there, what the view was like, what the sounds must have been like, what the smells must have been like, to the point that this part of the town is overlaid with Anne's death.'

'There's a different feel to the town here, isn't there?'

'It's almost immediately quieter, the hustle and bustle of modern

Scarborough drops away. The sounds are muffled. It feels different. It's reflective.'

We walk past Wilson's Mariners Home, a charity that once provided almshouses for 'poor aged persons of good character being ship owners, shipmates' and other nautical folk. Built in 1836, it would have been a comparatively new building. It's an impressive design. The window surrounds are elaborately carved. The gulls screech above us. The route to Anne's grave is well signposted.

'It's a big draw for tourism,' Wendy says.

As we approach St Mary's, we see a group of Japanese tourists coming down the hill. I assume they have been to see Anne's grave, as it's hard to believe they have come all this way just to sample the £2-a-pint lager bars. The church stands above the town and overlooks South Bay. The remains of the earlier chapel are still within its grounds, giving the place an eerie feel.

'Do you think Scarborough fully capitalises on the Anne Brontë link?'

'We don't embrace this part of our story here, and it's always something of a surprise when you see the constant stream of tourists who may well have deliberately come to Scarborough for the specific purpose of visiting Anne's grave. We could have a link to the parsonage. We could easily have a small museum to show the Scarborough of Anne's time here on the east coast.'

We reach the grave. There isn't much left of the original headstone. The salt in the sea air eats into the soft sandstone, and many of the monuments are pockmarked or whittled away by the weather. In 2011, the Brontë Society placed a monument at the foot of the grave, recording the original inscription, which apparently contained five errors. It was refaced three years later when Charlotte returned and discovered the mistakes. And yet the most egregious error – the inscription gave her age as twenty-eight when in fact she was twenty-nine – was not corrected. It isn't recorded anywhere what the others were.

'You've written poems about both Sylvia Plath's grave [in Heptonstall, West Yorkshire] and Anne Brontë's. Sylvia Plath's grave is full of pens and poems, little notes and letters that obsessive fans have left. But you don't get that here. Why is that? They were both poets and novelists. They both died tragically young.'

'It's partly because of the location. You have to deliberately set out to come to Scarborough – it's not on the road or a short diversion away from anywhere else. But I also think that there is a bit of a cult around Sylvia's death. Suicide and mental health and the relationship problems – these are all things that people can relate to. They feel a deep sense of connection with Sylvia and want to give these little votive offerings to her to say thank you. Also, she died within living memory for a lot of people – she's still fresh, we can see pictures of her, we know her life in miniscule detail. Anne died a long time ago, and to be fair she is the lesser known Brontë, unfairly seen as quite pious and prim. Her books are not tearing themselves inside out with passion. She is not romanticised in the same way that Charlotte and Emily have been. Anne seems boring, difficult to connect to, so perhaps the votives, that connection between reader, pilgrim, writer, isn't quite as strong here. What you do get is people quietly tending her grave. There are people in Scarborough who visit every day, who make sure she is remembered as a part of our town story, our heritage.'

I notice that the daffodils at the foot of the grave are blooming. The bench we are sitting on is dedicated to a lost loved one.

'In memory of, and in loving memory of, that's a Victorian tradition,' I say. 'It didn't exist before. So, you can date headstones by that.'

'I didn't know that.'

'I had to research it for my last book.'

We stare out at the sea and listen to the gulls scream.

'She was five years with the Robinsons, wasn't she?' I say. 'And this was their holiday home.'

'Yeah, and she bloody loved it here.'

'It was also her most sustained period of employment.'

'Yeah, and I wonder with Anne, whether being apart from that family, and away from the claustrophobic parsonage, away from the dictated roles of the family, if that was something she was seeking. You know, it was a little house, crammed with people, tiny rooms and everyone on top of each other, all that life, all that death, all that creativity. I wonder whether coming here, all this space, a different sort of wildness to the moors she'd left behind, but something familiar too – distance, big skies, a sense of freedom. It was just so entirely different. It must have had a profound effect on her.'

'She would have written some of both *Agnes Grey* and *The Tenant of Wildfell Hall* while she was here.'

'I think there's mention of this in one of her diary pages.'

We talk about a poem Wendy has written about Scarborough that describes 'hat stealing wind'. It's a very exposed peninsula. There's also a good line about the funicular railway.

'I like the word "funicular",' I say.

'Yeah. I think in Latin it means something like rope.'

'So, the idea is a vertical method of being pulled up or down?'

'I think so. It comes up in pub quizzes round here all the time. In the summer, when you pass the tramway you always overhear someone saying, "You do know it's called funicular, don't you?" It's just one of those things. Everyone thinks of it as a unique piece of knowledge.'

'In the poem, you mention the suicides over Valley Bridge. What's been done about that?'

'They've put up these spiked railings that curve round. You can't climb over them. It used to be a very regular occurrence, to have people jump there. People still do, determined people. My dad was a bus driver, and he was driving under the bridge one day. Someone dropped a guy off it, right in front of him. At first, he thought it was a person. But it was a Guy Fawkes effigy.'

'Well, we all did it,' I joke.

'I never did it.'

'Maybe it was just me. The poem mentions a statue of Richard III.'

'Richard III was the last king to occupy the castle. They poked a cannon through the church tower and fired at the castle.'

'Who did?'

'This was much later. During the Civil War. The bombardment was so intense it destroyed half the building.'

We look at the church tower and imagine the cannons firing up and over to the castle, which stands above us on a massive promontory of rock that rises above the sea. It's not hard to see why it was a favoured location for a fortress.

'There was a statue outside the Richard III restaurant. On the foreshore, a very old statue. But it got stolen,' Wendy says.

'Isn't that a difficult thing to do? I mean, didn't anyone notice?'

'That's Scarborough. At the spa there used to be a massive golden lion's head sculpture, where the spa waters themselves would come out of the lion's mouth, and someone pinched that as well.'

'And that's what the empty cage in the poem refers to then? Where the statue of Richard III was?'

'We keep thinking in Scarborough that we've got something. Like we own our own history, but history in seaside towns is transient, it gets whisked away, it gets replaced with something supposedly better. Like the Futurist Theatre, which has just been demolished to build a roller coaster. It was a beautiful building, a hugely historical building, and now it's gone. It's difficult to have an identity when the identity you think you have is changed so easily. We don't have an identity here. We have nostalgia. We need to write new stories, and we need to honour our old stories.'

She explains that she has just finished writing a poem that deals with Anne Brontë in a more direct way, a tribute to her time here in Scarborough. She fishes into her bag and pulls out a piece of paper: 'You can have it if you like.' I thank her and tell her I will read it later. I fold it up and put it in my coat pocket.

We head back into town to meet Wendy's husband Chris for a drink. Just at the bottom of the slope below Anne's grave Wendy points to a sign: 'Paradise'. It's the name of the street. Next to it is a brick wall with a gap in it. We look through the gap and see the whole of the bay, and it's beautiful. Wendy points out that Anne's grave is on Paradise Hill.

We pass a pub with a Shirley Bassey tribute act and a sign outside saying 'Dogs Welcome. Sorry, No Children'. It's the day of the Grand National, and all the pubs are packed with punters. We start at the Merchant, opposite the Golden Last, a notorious drinking hole that is the headquarters to the Scarborough branch of the English

Defence League and known locally as the Stabbers' Arms. Outside there are six St George flags and two Loyalist flags flapping in the breeze. The landlord was arrested a few years ago on suspicion of supporting a banned paramilitary organisation. The white-and-black exterior is badly in need of a lick of paint. I want to go inside to get a better look, but I'm told this would not be wise.

We have a few drinks in the Merchant, then we move on to the Turks Head followed by the Waterhouse. Huge plasma screens show the race, and people stand and watch, cheering on the horses. A horse called Up For Review falls at the first hurdle. It writhes in pain. It is taken away and shot. As I watch, I think about what Anne would make of it. She wouldn't be a fan. We go to another bar with men dressed as nuns. We encounter those drinking their winnings and others who are sinking that losing feeling with vodka shots.

We end up in the Sub-Aqua Club. We are surrounded by the flotsam and jetsam of wreck salvage: old bells, brass lamps and ship wheels. We're all a bit worse for wear. The night gets ragged round the edges. I'm standing at the bar, surrounded by Sub-Aqua Club members doing a pub quiz. There are wreck divers, underwater photographers and marine biologists. I think the drink in front of me is mine. The quizmaster says, 'Question three: what does the word "funicular" mean?' I smile. I look around for Wendy and Chris, but they've gone. I can't remember saying goodbye to them. I see that a group of women have kidnapped my dog, and I go over to rescue him.

❦

I'm woken early the next morning by the shrieking gulls and crash-ing waves. Wolfie is still fast asleep. My van is parked close to the coast beneath a sign that says 'no campervans to be parked here over night'. I get up, make some breakfast and brew a big mug of tea. I sit by the sea, watching the sun rise through the fret and the tide go out, wave by wave. I think about what Wendy said, about Anne not being able to see the sunset from her window. Did she instead sit and watch it rise over the waves?

Once the tide has subsided and the remnants of tea have gone cold, I take Wolfie onto the beach. It's more or less deserted, just two women clad in neoprene wet suits, attempting a bit of wild swimming. I think about the 'solitary ramble' Agnes takes in *Agnes Grey*, breathing in the 'freshness of the air'. It is here, towards the end of the book, that Agnes and Weston are reunited. Weston is a country parson who Agnes falls in love with, but she believes he loves someone else. In the end, he and Agnes marry.

There's a sci-fi conference at the Spa, and people dressed as their favourite characters are parking up and congregating in the café. They seem a slightly older audience to the comic convention the day before. A Spock lookalike tumbles out of a Mitsubishi Mirage. A Darth Vader fiddles with his mask as he attempts to draw smoke from his vaping machine. A Princess Leia fastens her cinnamon-bun hairstyle with clips, a lightsaber lies to the side of her steaming cappuccino. The sea fret covers everything like a milky shroud.

I walk back into town, dodging the puddles of last night's vomit. I climb up by the funicular tram to the Royal Hotel where a statue of Queen Victoria overlooks the bay. She would have still been a young queen in Anne's day. Born just eight months before Anne, they were more or less the same age. Outside the Grand Hotel a coach pulls up, and I watch as hotel staff help the elderly clients onto the coach. Some shuffle, others hobble using sticks and Zimmer frames – mostly old women, but a few old men too. A disfigured pigeon pecks at a squished chip.

I wander around town. Above the bookies and the pawn shops, with signs outside saying '£10 per gram of gold', there are still remnants of Victorian grandeur: splendid carved edifices and high bay windows. But the general atmosphere is heavy. As I walk up Castle Road again, towards Anne's grave, I think, it's not just the sea fret that makes this place oppressive; it's more pervasive than that. It goes beyond the weather. It comes from the bricks and the concrete. It spills out onto the street from the £2-a-pint lager bars. It comes dressed in a J.D. Sports tracksuit, coughing up phlegm.

I want to take in Anne's grave without the tourists and the Brontë fans. I just want a moment alone with her. But when I get there the bells of St Mary's are pealing. It's only nine in the morning, but the clanging cacophony is deafening. I imagine they are no comfort to those sleeping off a hangover.

Last night, I walked from the more popular South Bay to the North Bay. There isn't much between the two bays, and not much at North Bay when you arrive – just one bar and one shop. Boy racers were congregating in souped-up coupés, their one-litre cars modified with body kits and noisy exhausts, imitation alloy wheels, spoilers, and bonnet scoops. They bounced from the bass coming from the woofers taking up their entire boots. Girls in their teens gathered at street corners sipping from brightly coloured bottles of alcoholic pop.

Scarborough now is no different to so many English towns: inward looking, dejected, unsure of its own identity. The town still wears the edifices of a once opulent and prosperous society, but it is crumbling into the ocean, turning into sand and dust, leaving a lurid scene of poverty and desperation. Plastic bottles and plastic bags are all that will remain of us. We are all like the gulls on high sills, huddled up against the oncoming storm.

I sit on the bench staring at Anne's grave, but there is no peace for the dead. I climb up to the castle where the air is clean. The branches of the trees are alive with green buds. I put my ear to a trunk and listen to the sap rise. It's a great vantage point, and looking back at the town all the rude features that were brought into close range yesterday have now shrunken back, and the effect, along with the sea fret that still clings to the edges of buildings and softens them, is to make Scarborough look beautiful. Scarborough is beautiful. And I can feel for the first time that elevation of spirit that Anne must have felt as she stood here, looking over the bay at the grey seals and lobster pots. White-washed walls and terracotta roofs. The sun rising over golden sands and silver waves. The little houses clustered together, kittiwakes cutting into a gusty breeze.

I sit at the edge of the promontory and feel in my coat pocket for Wendy's poem 'For Anne, a Stone's Throw from Paradise'. I take it out and begin to read:

At Paradise I saw the way
the treadle-footed tourists came,
how they'd worn the words to nothing
on the faces of the other stones. Yet still,
no votive offerings; no pens, no letters
for this girl of sea frets and horizons.
We've both been here before.
Sometimes we up and leave,

I drag you with me; bones and silk
and boots, and walk you back to Wood's.
I leave you underneath your plaque
and you fall down and down again
among the OAPs and cigarettes.
I puppet you along your death, add details
and embellishments. But it can't last.
You're mute; a doll thing, thin as air.
We breathe your mizzle-ghost and pray
to know you. The obsession's there,
we search for likenesses in photographs
and diagnose your mental health, we scour
the *Antiques Roadshow* for a locket of your hair.
On Castle Road I walk your coffin path
to sit beside the other beloveds, to see you fed
into the ground. And I'm surprised each time:
you're peaceful here, above the sounds
of paradise: the seagulls, kittiwakes,
the penny slots and Kiss-Me-Quicks.

On the Monday morning, not physically capable of descending the stairs herself, Ellen carried Anne in her arms to the room downstairs. She had a breakfast of boiled milk. She died at about 2 p.m. on 28 May 1849. Shortly after, dinner was announced. The last words she said were, 'Take courage, Charlotte, take courage.' A week later, Charlotte wrote to William Smith Williams, her literary adviser, 'Papa has now me only – the weakest, puniest, least promising of his six children. Consumption has taken the whole five.'

12

PATRICK'S PISTOLS - WALKING HOME

Walking the Invisible is, in some ways, about recording an absence. It's about what happens when you attempt to walk in the footsteps of literary figures. To strike the same earth, to trudge the same mud. Except it isn't the same earth, or the same mud. The earth that the Brontës walked has eroded. The mud has been washed away. Or else, earth has accumulated, built up from rain silt and falling vegetation, so that it isn't possible to walk exactly in their wake, only above or beneath.

I'm at Oakwell Hall, the start of the Brontë Way, but I'm not joined by other writers today, just a dog. It's the last day of May, and although the sky is blotched with inky clouds, the forecast is favourable. I walk round the park first to get a feel for the place. Cow parsley blooms in the meadows, and hawthorn trees are frothy with white blossom. The woods are spiced with the smell of wild garlic. It's spring half-term, and the park is full of families with prams and toddlers on leashes. The circular walk around the park is about two miles. I encounter lots of dog walkers with French bulldogs and other toy dogs that seem to be the current fashion. The French bulldog, through no fault of its own, has permanent respiratory problems. Bred to be a freak. Bred to have all its strength, speed and agility taken away from it.

I leave Wolfie, a healthy mongrel with no congenital problems, outside the hall while I enter to have a look around. The hall was built in 1583 for John Batt. The coat of arms that decorates the wall contains four bats, and I can only think this is a reference to the surname. The hall itself has been well preserved. The inside is oak panelled, and the great parlour is painted using a technique called 'scumbling'. It gives a three-dimensional effect. When Charlotte Brontë visited, she said the walls were 'a delicate pinky white'. By then it had become a girls' school run by the Cockill family.

The hall was to inspire her creation of Fieldhead in her second novel, *Shirley*. And much of the descriptions of Fieldhead match those of Oakwell: 'the old latticed windows, the stone porch, the walls, the roof, the chimney-stacks, were rich in crayon touches and sepia light and shades'. A silent film of *Shirley* was made here in 1921, but no copies of it have ever been found. The house has been a film location several times since. It was used for the 'Henry's Wives' episode of the TV series *Horrible Histories* and as the location for Wuthering Heights in the 2009 ITV adaptation of the book starring Charlotte Riley as Cathy and Tom Hardy as Heathcliff. Most recently, it was used as a set in the BBC's *Jonathan Strange and Mr Norrell*, adapted from Susanna Clarke's debut novel.

When Charlotte wrote *Shirley*, the name Shirley was most associated with male characters, and the novelty of calling a female character by that name is lost on a modern audience. Now, Shirley is most associated with female characters but only because of the popularity of Charlotte's novel. The only male Shirley in my living memory is Shirley Crabtree, a professional wrestler from Halifax, better known as Big Daddy. Perhaps he entered the profession of wrestling precisely because he was named Shirley. In fact, the idea of a man being called Shirley was made into a famous joke in the 1980 satirical film *Airplane!* Robert Hays, playing pilot Ted Striker, turns to Leslie Nielsen, who is playing Dr Rumack, and says, 'Surely you cannot be serious?' To which Dr Rumack replies, 'I am serious, and don't call me Shirley.'

I leave the main entrance and turn left and then immediately right down a dirt track by the side of fields. I pass a field of shire horses. At one time bred for dragging ploughs or barges by the side of the canals, or for pulling carts and brewer's drays along roads, they are no longer working animals and have been repurposed as pets. Birstall is cloth and coal country – a mining town and a manufacturing town. The forebears of these horses would have pulled carts of coal and cloth. There's a Shetland pony in the field as well, a breed chosen for pit work, due to its reduced size. They are low set, heavy-bodied beasts. In shaft mines, pit ponies were stabled underground, only seeing the light of day on colliery holidays.

Carrion crows pace and turn like funeral directors with their hands behind their backs, before stabbing the earth for worms. The path leads me onto the main road, and I make a slight diversion, turning left to go to St Peter's Church, a heavily turreted structure with quite a low, squat clock tower. The church is closed. Two dog-headed gargoyles guard the entrance. This is where Joseph Priestley is buried, the man who discovered oxygen. It is also where Charlotte's closest friend Ellen Nussey is buried, and Miss Wooler, who first taught and then employed Charlotte at nearby Roe Head School. The church is fictionalised as Briarfield Church in *Shirley*.

I head back the way I came, turning up Monk Ings towards Friary Court through a modern housing estate. I follow a gravel path past the back of some houses. The posters in the window all say 'Vote

Labour', with a photo of Tracy Brabin, the local labour MP. Best known as a television actor, she played the part of Tricia Armstrong for three years in *Coronation Street*. It was a colourful three years that included shoplifting, offering sex for rent and a brief dalliance with the street rake, Terry Duckworth. She is now elected in the seat previously occupied by Jo Cox, who was murdered by Thomas Mair in 2016. Cox was shot and stabbed multiple times outside Birstall Library, where I'd given a talk a few weeks before. Mair, who had links with neo-Nazi groups and shouted 'Britain First' as he stabbed her, was given a whole-life tariff and will never be released from prison. The memorial service took place at St Peter's. Cox was a campaigner for social justice, as Patrick Brontë was.

It was during his stay in this area that Patrick encountered the West Riding Luddites for the first time. They were part of a larger Luddite movement, a secret oath-based organisation of textile workers that had originated in Nottingham, where lace makers had protested against mechanisation by destroying machinery. Among these Luddites were a high number of croppers whose skilled labour was under threat.

I left school at sixteen to become an apprentice winder. Like the croppers of the West Riding Luddites, my trade no longer exists. The machines the men were replaced with were shearing frames, driven by belts powered either by waterwheel or steam engine, that mechanically cropped the nap off rolls of cloth, doing the same work as seven croppers using handheld shears. The end product was inferior to that produced by human labour. The men were not just fighting for their livelihoods. They were also fighting to maintain the quality of the cloth. Their jobs were highly skilled and well paid. They used huge cutting shears that weighed between fifty and sixty pounds (about the weight of an eight-year-old boy) and were four feet long. You could spot an experienced cropper by the hoof of skin on his wrist caused by the handle (or nog) of the shears rubbing against it.

In fact, the machines that replaced them were not new. The technology had been around for hundreds of years. Gig mills were outlawed under Charles I to protect the livelihoods of workers, but the government repealed all the protective legislation in 1809, and everything that seemed to secure the position of the shearsmen was swept away.

Now, the term Luddite often unfairly refers to someone who is opposed to new technology, rather than men who in desperation fought for their livelihoods. Before reaching the point of attack, the workers had written letters to the mill owners, signing them 'yours faithfully, General Ludd'. The idea was to strike fear into them. These men were caught in a trap of poor harvests, high food prices and economic depression caused by the Napoleonic Wars. How desperate does a man have to get before he is willing to risk his neck?

I cut through a meadow of buttercup and ragged-robin. The path meanders through the wild flowers before opening out into a new housing estate of topiary hedges, neatly mowed lawns, polished cars and freshly swept block-paved driveways. At the main road, I approach the Red House Museum, situated next to Gomersal Public Hall. The Red House is famous because it also appears in *Shirley*. It was home to Charlotte's friend Mary Taylor and was renamed 'Briarmains' in the novel, although curiously there is also a house called the Red House in the book. Charlotte and Mary were school friends together at Roe Head, along with Ellen Nussey. Charlotte visited both Oakwell Hall and the Red

House in the 1830s. She spent a good deal of time here and became friendly with the family. Mary's father, Joshua Taylor, was the owner of Hunsworth Mill. He could speak fluent French. He was also a radical, and Charlotte's establishment values would sometimes lead to heated discussions between the pair. Joshua Taylor was the inspiration for Hiram Yorke in *Shirley,* a cloth manufacturer who lives in Briarmains with his family and who also speaks fluent French. In fact, Joshua, his wife Anne and some of their six children found their way into the book.

Until a few years ago, the house was a museum, restored carefully to how it was in the 1830s. Despite numerous attempts to save the place, it is now closed up, and Kirklees Council are selling the building and the grounds. All the Georgian furniture and interior features have been stripped, repurposed or sold off. Its open gardens attract local stoners.

I follow a walkway behind the house and turn right at the main road to St Mary's Church, where Mary Taylor is buried. From the church, I walk down Shirley Road, past Shirley Walk, past another street called Shirley Square. Kirklees Council, who built this estate, seem keen to capitalise on the connection to Charlotte's novel. The path crosses a recreational field, past Gomersal Lodge. Here the view opens out over fields and hedges. I can see Emley Mast to the south, and to the west, the edges of the moors. Rooks strut through freshly cropped yellow-green grass. I walk down a dirt track and across a field full of cows, their udders so full of milk they almost touch the ground. The one nearest to me drags the bag of her udder along the grass like a sack of coal.

I walk down New Street to the main road, through Liversedge and the outskirts of the area known locally as Rawfolds. I cross the

River Spen, stopping to look at the area where William Cartwright's mill once stood. There's a half-demolished building and gypsy caravans close by. Three men standing around a bonfire of pallet wood and joists chat and smoke roll-ups. Dogs play fight. I can feel the heat of the fire from where I'm standing close to the river, which powered the mill.

It was here on the night of Saturday, 11 April 1812, that an organised paramilitary force of between 150 and 300 men met in a field beneath the Dumb Steeple about three miles south, near Cooper Bridge on the edges of Brighouse and Mirfield, not far from The Three Nuns pub. These men were the West Riding Luddites, and they had gathered to attack Cartwright's mill. They probably met there because it was an easy access point for various towns that the men were travelling from, but it is also a stone's throw from Robin Hood's grave in the Kirklees Park Estate, where he was supposed to have been bled to death by the prioress, and I like to think that this would have been another factor in choosing this meeting place.

By 11 p.m., all the men had gathered. They had decided on this night because it was a new moon, and the sky was black. They wore dark clothing and covered their faces with rags and masks, and they were divided by the tools they packed: hammers, hatchets, pistols, muskets. The Enoch hammers some of them carried were so named after the smith who had invented them, Enoch Taylor. Along with his brother James, Enoch also built the cropping machines that had replaced the men's labour. The hammers were huge tools, bigger even than sledgehammers. A couple of months earlier, in February, the Luddites had ambushed a cart bringing these cropping frames to Cartwright's mill, smashing them to smithereens using Enoch hammers. I'm sure the irony would not have been lost on the Taylor brothers. The drivers were blindfolded and tied up. This scene from real life is accurately fictionalised in *Shirley*.

They had been training for this mill attack for weeks, perhaps even months. The men glugged from bottles of rum. April evenings can be cold, and records show that this particular night was especially chilly, but no doubt the rum was also to strengthen their mettle. Then, under the moonless sky, they marched across Hartshead Moor to Hightown. You can recreate this walk today – it's clearly marked up with signs saying 'The Luddite Trail'. However, when I attempted it in the middle of October, after three weeks of unrelenting rain, it was almost impossible to do. The trail took a left past a steak house and over several farmers' fields that had been ploughed up and the path turned into mud, so that I was wading through a soggy quagmire.

As the masked men marched over the moor, Cartwright was getting ready for them. He'd received a warning two weeks before from Abraham Pule, a cropper and former worker, and had assembled his own army: employees of the mill. But out of hundreds, only six men actually showed up. He had also asked the Cumberland Militia for help. They brought five soldiers. Despite the lack of numbers, the mill was well positioned to be defended, high up on a hill and surrounded on one side by the moat-like Spen Beck. Cartwright had replaced the main door with one studded with iron and had fitted, at great expense, an alarm bell to the roof. Men were positioned strategically on the first floor, ready to fire muskets, and the mill owner had also fitted secret weapons. The staircase was modified with sixteen-inch spiked rollers to impale any intruders, and at the top there were huge carboy jars full of sulphuric acid to tip on the head of anyone who got too close.

By midnight, Cartwright decided it was a no-show and time to retire to bed, but the Luddites were now close by. Then, the sentries heard gunshot, and out of the pitch-black night the army of masked men made their attack. They quickly overpowered Cartwright's guards outside. The windows of the mill were smashed. Men with Enochs pounded the main door. Men with pistols fired shots. Cartwright's men retaliated. One man tried to raise the alarm, but as he yanked on the bell rope it snapped. Another man climbed onto the roof and rang the bell by hand. Cartwright's men took aim behind raised flagstones. Bullets flew back and forth. Some Luddites were wounded, lying on the floor in pain. Despite their best efforts, the men failed to batter the door down. And seeing many men shot at, the Luddite leaders decided to retreat.

It is estimated that 140 rounds were fired during a twenty-minute attack. The Luddites left two men behind, Sam Hartley and John Booth. They were tortured by Cartwright and later died, according to social historian Robert Reid. Thousands attended Sam's funeral to show solidarity with the cause. Because of this support, John was buried in secret. In the light of the following day, the yard was strewn with discarded weapons, masks, pools of blood and even a finger. Fifty panes of glass had been smashed either by hammer, axe, pistol or musket. In fact, the Luddites had almost got through the main door, and it was so damaged that it had to be replaced rather than repaired. Having successfully smashed machines, this was the first defeat of the West Riding Luddites. By 1820, the job of cropping by hand was no more.

Patrick, a single man at the time, was lodging at Lousey Thorn Farm, close to his place of work, when the West Riding Luddites struck. On the night of the attack, he was likely woken by the sound of the men's hobnailed boots as they marched past. And if not by that, then by the alarm bell rung shortly after. Surely Patrick, from humble stock, and someone who fought for workers' rights, would have had some sympathy for their plight? Unlike his friend Reverend Hammond Roberson, he did not answer Cartwright's alarm call with a sword in hand. Roberson is said to be the model for Matthew Helstone in Charlotte's novel. She only met Roberson once, but his anti-Luddite stance was well known.

Despite any sympathy he might have felt for the men's cause, he felt so threatened by them that he bought a pair of pistols. At a later date, Patrick must have also bought another pair of pistols. One of these was sold in 2004 to a private collector. It was a flintlock boxlock pistol by Aston Manchester, with Birmingham proof marks dated c. 1815–1820, a bayonet attachment underneath and Branwell's initials engraved on it. Patrick must have given this pistol to his son. It is not known where he purchased the original pistols, but it must have been around the same time as the attack on the mill. They were a different make and model with no spring bayonets. One of them was part of the Parsonage Museum's collection, but it was stolen in the sixties.

Patrick was clearly fascinated by guns, and he even wrote to Lord Wellington on one occasion, offering a great deal of technical advice – suggestions for developing firearms for the military. We don't have a record of that letter, but we do have Wellington's response: 'much time would be saved if others in power would follow the Duke's example and avoid to interfere in matters over which they have no control'. Which basically meant, mind your own business. So that was Patrick told.

According to Lock and Dixon, Patrick's biographers, he was

approached at this time by members of his congregation who informed him that 'threats against his person had been overheard locally'. As a result, Patrick kept a pistol with him for the rest of his life, firing it each morning to discharge the bullets, but presumably to also practise his aim. Emily also fired Patrick's pistols and was a good shot according to John Greenwood, the Haworth stationer from whom the Brontës obtained their writing paper.

I walk down Primrose Lane, the opposite way from which the men came, and I imagine passing the tooled-up army of masked militia on a crisp pitch-black Saturday evening. It must have been a fearsome sight. It would have been kicking-out time that night, and I imagine those returning home after an evening in the pub, now half-cut, would have done a double take as they passed. Returning home, they would have told a tale hardly believed by their wives.

The lane meanders until it reaches Halifax Road and the Shears Inn. There is a black plaque on the wall, informing the reader that the pub was owned by the Jackson family, whose cropping shop was further up Halifax Road. It became an ale house in 1803 and was popular with croppers. It was here where much of the West Riding Luddites' planning was done. The inn is a rather grim-looking building now, with a grey slate roof, whitewashed walls that have turned a dirty shade and patches of plaster that have crumbled to reveal the stone layer beneath. It stands on its own, apart from the other buildings. I think about the conversations the Luddites must have had within the four walls of this inn, discussing all the possible alternatives before concluding that their only hope was to attack the mill itself. It was an act of self-sabotage. But this was a time when a number of laws restricted public assembly and labour unions. I want to go inside to see where the secret meetings took place, but the pub is closed, and the doors are locked. I peer through the mullioned windows, but it's too dark to see anything.

Next to the pub, a planning notice has been attached to a lamp-post: demolition of existing public house and erection of four dwellings. It looks like that's the end of the Shears. Despite the grim appearance of this building, I feel sad about its imminent destruction. It is a vital piece of history. The National Trust should extend its remit to protect not just stately homes and other places of interest, but also historic inns like this that have such an important story to tell.

It is clear from Charlotte's writing where her sympathies lay: not with the workers, but with Robert Moore, the fictional mill owner in *Shirley*. The Luddites in Charlotte's book are called 'vermin', 'scoundrels', 'ruffians' and 'hyenas' – an animal associated with coarse and cowardly behaviour. Conversely, Moore is called a 'lion' – an animal associated with strength and courage. Cartwright, like the fictional Moore, was dark skinned, with 'foreign blood'. However, Cartwright was not liked by his workers, and his actions do not fit the description of Moore: 'a gentleman: his blood is pure and ancient'. Robert Moore would not be the kind of man who would callously leave two men mortally wounded without water or medicine in order to extract a confession of their accomplices' whereabouts, as Cartwright did in real life.

I carry on down Halifax Road until I come to Clough House. The plaque above the door states that this is the home to which

Patrick brought his bride Maria after their marriage, and it was here that Maria and Elizabeth were born. They must have moved here shortly after the attack. It's a three-storey terrace house of a decent size, at least as big as the parsonage at Thornton. Perhaps he felt that it was a more secure place to raise a family. From here, I turn down Clough Lane, which Clough House overlooks. Patrick would have walked this lane every day as he travelled to and from work. I follow a footpath to my right, through the grounds of a farm, close to the one where Patrick was lodged before his move to Clough House. A little further on and I arrive at Patrick's church. It's a low, dumpy building, its squatness necessitated by its exposed spot here on Hartshead Common, overlooking Hartshead Moor.

The main entrance gate has been bricked up, and the church only seems to be open one Saturday every month. The windows are covered with grills and flexiglass. I look around the graveyard, but there is no sign of the unmarked Luddite graves of the men who were executed for their crimes and who Patrick reputedly buried here.

In *Shirley*, Cartwright's mill finds its fictional match in Hollows Mill. The book opens with the mill owner, Robert Moore, waiting for delivery of labour-saving machines, which will enable him to lay off some of his employees. Robert's cousin Caroline Helstone was modelled on Charlotte's sister Anne and Ellen Nussey. Shirley, who Caroline befriends, was partly based on Emily. Writing the novel so soon after the death of her sisters, it is easy to see why she would want to immortalise them in the pages of a book. In the early part of the novel, Caroline and Shirley overhear some Luddites as they debate whether to murder Robert Moore's friend the Reverend Helstone. This mimics real events. Again, according to Lock and Dixon in their biography of Patrick Brontë, Patrick was told by members of his congregation that they had overheard men threatening to attack him. In the novel, Caroline and Shirley also hear of a planned attack on some new shearing machines that are being delivered and go to warn Robert. But they are too late. They witness the battle from a concealed place. This also accurately records a real-life incident.

What's missing from Charlotte's account is the wider social context of abject poverty caused in part by the Napoleonic Wars, poor harvests, and the already mentioned high food prices, but also by the government's efforts to repress working-class dissent. There's a good argument to make that the phenomenon of Luddism helped provide a template of solidarity and mass action that led to successful social campaigns, such as that to reduce factory hours for children to ten hours a day and the one to repeal the punitive new Poor Laws. Lenin called the Luddites 'the first broad truly mass and politically organised proletarian revolutionary movement'. And the Chartists who followed in the Luddites' wake, and who were actively campaigning while Charlotte was writing *Shirley*, changed for the good a number of conditions for the working classes. Trade unions were fully legalised in 1871, and the Representation of the People Act 1884 allowed suffrage for some working-class men for the first time, although all women and 40 per cent of adult males would have to wait until 1918 to be able to vote.

There were a number of arms thefts reported at this time, carried out in this area, but they didn't start until after the military were deployed. They were not part of the original Luddite strategy, but rather a reaction to the deployment of soldiers, an act of defence rather than attack. Charlotte reverses this in *Shirley*. The Reverend Helstone visits a group of curates who are having a social gathering, in order to enlist their help in defending the mill. Helstone asks one of the curates, Malone, if he has 'any arms?' Malone comically replies that he does, as well as legs. Here it is the mill owners who need weapons to defend themselves, not the other way around. Helstone informs the curates that fellow mill owners Pearson and Armitage have been shot, one in his own house and the other on the moor. He then goes on to explain that he thinks Moore will be assassinated.

This 'trouble at t'mill' scenario is a thrilling start to the novel, and one of the most accomplished scenes Charlotte ever wrote. There is, however, something very strange about Helstone turning to curates for armed help. They are not the obvious choice. We do not assume parsons pack pistols, although Patrick was to do precisely this. Surely her father's love of firearms must be one of the inspirations for this scene?

In any case, in reversing the order of cause and effect, Charlotte is guilty of the same distortion the BBC carried out in 1984 when reporting the 'Battle of Orgreave', the famous violent confrontation between pickets and officers of the South Yorkshire Police at a British steel-coking plant. When they broadcast footage of the conflict, it was edited out of chronological sequence, so that it looked like the mounted police charge was a reaction to stone throwing by the miners. In fact, the miners only threw the stones in response to the unprovoked attack.

Charlotte would have known about the Luddites both from her father and her school teacher Miss Wooler. And, according to Elizabeth Gaskell, Charlotte also researched the Luddite attacks by reading copies of the *Leeds Mercury* newspaper. The interests of the media and the mill owners were aligned. Those who owned the means of production and those who owned the method of disseminating new events shared the same class, ate at the same table, drank at the same clubs.

The leader of the Luddites in *Shirley* is Moses Barraclough, and he is described as having 'cat-like trustless eyes'. But George Mellor, the real-life inspiration for Moses, who led the attack on the mill, was not an illiterate yob; he was well travelled and self-educated, with socially progressive views. Born in 1789, the same year as the French Revolution began, he was a proficient cropper by 1812, but he soon saw the value of his trade drop from more than £12 million to around £1 million per annum. At the same time, he witnessed a series of disastrous harvests. Mellor saw Luddism as a vehicle to improve the lot of his people.

The failed attack on Cartwright's mill and the death of two workers set off riots all over the country. And it was following the death of his close friend John Booth that Mellor was probably tipped over the edge. Shortly afterwards, he took the disastrous decision to escalate the campaign, not through the destruction of machines but through the destruction of men: first, a successful assassination of neighbouring mill owner William Horsfall, who had called the Luddites 'cowards', then the failed assassination of William Cartwright, who managed to dodge bullets from two assassins. Mellor was hanged at York for his crimes, along with sixteen other Luddites.

William Horsfall's catchphrase was 'I'll ride up to my saddle girth in Luddite blood'. He was shot four times on Black Moor Foot Lane. The assassins shot his balls off, but he didn't die immediately. He made it to the pub down the road, where he bled to death a few hours later. How different the legacy of the Luddites would be had they remained confined to attacks on property instead of people.

As I walk away from the church, I can hear the roar of the M62 motorway in the distance. My journey now takes me over the footbridge of the motorway, through Bailiff Bridge and Norwood Green, leading me home to Thornton. I reckon I've done close to twenty miles, and my feet are aching. I've worn the wrong boots. My regular walking boots were still wet from the day before, so I donned the emergency boots that I'd bought from a cheap camping shop. Up to this point, I've never gone more than six or seven miles in them. I have learnt that they are not meant for long distances.

As I pass the Old Bell Chapel, I see Marje Wilson, the woman who wrote *The Brontë Way* guidebook. She volunteers here once a week and helps with the upkeep of the space. I stop to introduce myself and ask her about her project.

'I know who you are and where you live,' she says, rather ominously. 'Your house is haunted. Isabel. That's the name of the ghost.'

'I've not met her yet,' I say. I tell her about my book and ask her how she came to write the guidebook. She tells me that it came about because of a chance encounter with another writer at a youth hostel in Donegal, who advised her to self-publish. She wrote her guide, then got back in touch with this writer, who asked her to send it to him.

'He had it six months. Sent it back by post. He said, "Sorry, Marje, I haven't been very well and haven't been able to do anything with this."'

She tells me that she then approached the Ramblers' Association to see if they would publish it. The association liked her book but when they had their next meeting, the writer she had originally approached was there.

'He was the first person to speak, and he said, "I'm thinking of publishing a book called *The Brontë Way*." And this bloke from the Ramblers' Association said, "That's strange because we've just accepted some material from Marje Wilson." Two and a half years later, I was in Haworth and I saw *Brontë Way* by this writer in a bookshop.

'I made no money from my book. All the profits went to the Right to Roam campaign. We won a lot of access and opened up the land for walkers.'

'You did a good thing,' I say, and leave her to weed the graves.

❧

As I sit at my kitchen table, drinking black tea and soaking my feet in a bowl of hot water, I reflect back on the past few years and this project that has obsessed me. How long? Four, five, six years? Maybe as long as ten years. Before I began, the act of writing and the act of walking were two very different activities in my mind. But somehow, over the course of this project, they have become the same thing. Taking a line of carbon over the page, treading feet across the land, the same rhythm, the same head space, the same solitary place.

In *Common People,* Anita Sethi writes about how the English countryside excludes people from certain class and cultural backgrounds. I feel very much the same about England's rural spaces. They are political. There is still a class divide between town and country. In 1932, a group of about four hundred walkers organised a mass trespass of Kinder Scout in Derbyshire. The walkers were made up of mill workers and miners, and there were violent scuffles with gamekeepers. The event began a campaign for access to rural spaces that culminated in the Countryside and Rights of Way (CRoW) Act in 2000.

The act, which gives walkers the right to travel through common land and open country, is a great triumph. But still, many so-called custodians of our rural spaces deliberately neglect their legal duties to manage and maintain access: allowing pathways to become overgrown; letting cattle tramp up rights of way, turning them into impassable swamps; blocking stiles with barbed wire; ploughing up footpaths. And so much of our moorland is still taken up with grouse shooting and is restricted, dogs forced to be put on leads, birds of prey shot, heather burnt, weasels and stoats trapped.

Emily found a merlin out on her moors, and it became a pet. She would not find a merlin on the moors today. Nor would she find a hen harrier, a bird that should be commonplace but is now threatened with extinction. England has sufficient habitat to support three hundred hen harrier pairs, yet in 2019 it hosted only twelve successful nests. What should be a diverse space is a monoculture. Some of the moors around Haworth are policed by gamekeepers riding 4x4 jeeps, carrying rifles, patrolling the land like soldiers not rural workers. I've had several run-ins with gamekeepers who operate more like goons, one of them pointing his rifle in my face and threatening me.

In his book *Inglorious*, Mark Avery outlines this conflict on our uplands. He writes about how Walshaw Moor, close to Haworth, was bought by millionaire businessman and grouse shooter Richard Bannister in 2002. It became a scene of dispute between Natural England and his estate. Natural England thought the estate was acting illegally and in conflict with the conservation of nature. They wrote to explain that the estate had breached their agreement and charged it with forty-five offences, including thirty incidences of moor gripping (installing draining channels), the construction of five tracks and five car parks, the creation of two ponds by peat extraction, and the installation of shooting butts. They were also accused of damaging the moor and unnecessary burning, which could contribute to the destruction of two-thirds of heather moorland in England. The criminal court case was scheduled for the summer of 2012. It was set to be a landmark trial that would have massive implications for other grouse-shooting sites. But, surprisingly, Natural England reached a settlement with the Walshaw Moor Estate, and the criminal case was dropped. Why was this agreement reached? The details have never been released to the public.

Shortly afterwards, in October 2012, the RSPB sent a complaint to the European Commission over the case and its wider implications. This complaint is still running. Richard Benyon, the Department for Environment, Food and Rural Affairs minister involved in sorting out the dispute, is himself the owner of a grouse moor. So far, the case has cost the taxpayer more than a million pounds. The valleys below the moor, and the towns there, have been victims of severe flooding caused in great part by the way the estate has managed the land. Hebden Bridge, Mytholmroyd and Todmorden have all suffered floods that have caused millions of pounds' worth of damage. We are still a long way from a rural space that is as diverse as it should be or as accessible to those who pay for its upkeep as we have a right to demand.

I top up my cup and swirl my feet in the now tepid water. I've tramped the north of England in search of the landscapes that inspired the Brontës. I've traipsed through mud, clambered up steep cloughs, endured unrelenting rain. My journey has taken me to places that have been drastically transformed from how they would have appeared to the siblings, but also to places that are largely unchanged. Modern Scarborough would not be to Anne's tastes, but Branwell would find much of Broughton the same.

As I stare down at my bruised and battered feet, I ask myself, to what extent are we products of the places we live? Would Charlotte, Branwell, Emily and Anne have written the same poems and stories had they lived in London, let's say, or even been writers at all? The peculiar conditions of their upbringing combined with the landscape that surrounded them must have shaped them just as surely as a potter shapes clay. They are, as far as I know, unique in world literature: four siblings who all became published writers, three world acclaimed. When we launched the Brontë Stones project at the Bradford Literature Festival in July 2018, people came from all four corners of the globe to see the stones in situ and walk in the footsteps of the Brontës. It is hard to imagine another literary equivalent.

Every day, I see literary tourists standing on the same steps they would have played on as children or leaning against the fireplace near where they were born to have their photographs taken, having made a pilgrimage that, to them, is as important as a visit to Mecca. I can only take inspiration from this and be awed afresh by their legacy. When Charlotte wrote 'what author would be without the advantage of being able to walk invisible?', she was still unknown to the world, writing under the pseudonym Currer Bell. She is now, after William Shakespeare, Jane Austen and Charles Dickens, probably the best-known English writer of all time. Her other sisters are not far behind her. Branwell is still waiting for his day in the sun.

I pass the place of their birth every day, walking my dog or making a trip to the shops, and it has become just another part of the scenery. Another house in a street full of houses. But some days, it stops me in my tracks. I look up at the plaque outside and think, Wow, what you all did, that was really something else.

MAPS

Maps drawn and designed by Christopher Goddard:
www.christophergoddard.net

THE CHARLOTTE BRONTË WALK

A straight-forward short loop across the hills around Thornton. The route starts in the village at St James' Church, opposite the site of the old Bell Chapel where Patrick Brontë worked. The route takes in Thornton Hall, Hanging Fall, the Brontë Birthplace and Thornton Viaduct, and has some great views over the valley. The walk is on good paths that are generally dry.

'I am no bird; and no net ensnares me.'

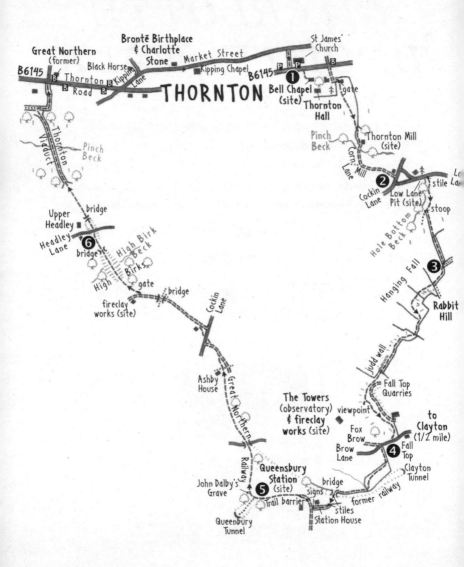

Great Northern
(former)

Brontë Birthplace
& Charlotte
Stone

Black Horse

St James'
Church

Market Street

Kipping Chapel

B6145

B6145

Thornton
Road

Kipping
Lane

THORNTON

Bell Chapel
(site)

Thornton
Hall

gate

Thornton Mill
(site)

Pinch
Beck

Thornton
Viaduct

Pinch
Beck

Corn Mill
Lane

Cockin
Lane

Low Lane
Pit (site)

stile Lane

stoop

Upper
Headley

bridge

Hole Bottom
Beck

Headley
Lane

bridge

High Birk
Beck

Hanging Fall

Rabbit
Hill

Birks

High

gate

bridge

Cockin
Lane

Judd wall

fireclay
works (site)

Fall Top
Quarries

Ashby
House

Great Northern

The Towers
(observatory)
& fireclay
works (site)

viewpoint

to
Clayton
(1/2 mile)

Fox
Brow

Fall
Top

Railway

Queensbury
Station
(site)

Brow
Lane

Clayton
Tunnel

John Dalby's
Grave

signs

bridge

former railway

Trail barrier

stiles

Queenbury
Tunnel

Station House

210

Distance: 4 miles (6.3km)
Ascent: 175m
Difficulty: Easy

Public Transport: Thornton is served by the 607 bus from Bradford and 67 between Bradford and Keighley.

Parking: Free parking along B145 by St James' Church in Thornton.

Refreshments: Refreshments: There are various pubs and cafés in Thornton, including the dog-friendly New Inn, the Plenty at the Square café at South Square, and of course Emily's at the Brontë Birthplace itself.

Charlotte Brontë was born in an unassuming house in the middle of Thornton. **No 74 Market Street** was built in 1802, when Thornton was still a small village with just over twenty buildings, but it quickly grew during the early nineteenth century. The house had four bedrooms and three staircases and served as the parsonage for the village's church, located out near Thornton Hall. At the time, Market Street was the main road to Bradford and there were no buildings on the opposite side of the street, just open fields leading down into the valley. Patrick and Maria Brontë moved to Thornton in 1815 with their two young daughters, one year old Maria and three month old Elizabeth. Over the course of the next five years, Maria gave birth to Charlotte, Branwell, Emily and Anne. In a letter written in 1835, Patrick Brontë said, 'I've never quite been well since I left Thornton. My happiest days were spent there'.

❶ The route starts on the B6145 by **St James' Church** at the east end of **Thornton** village. A gate opposite leads into the old graveyard and the site of the **Bell Chapel** where Patrick Brontë preached 1815-1820. Rejoin the road heading east and turn right down the next track. By the gates to **Thornton Hall**, bear left through a small gate and follow the clear path down the field to Pinch Beck. Join a walled lane by the site of the old corn mill at **Thornton Mill** and follow Corn Mill Lane to its end.

milling wheel at
Thornton Corn Mill

Thornton Hall is a medieval hall that is thought to be a possible inspiration for Thornfield Hall, home of Mr Rochester, in Charlotte Brontë's Jane Eyre. In the 16th century the hall was owned by Sir Richard Tempest, a knight of Henry VIII. There would have been a view of the hall from the parsonage at that time. The fireplace was rebuilt in the 19th century and designed by William Morris. A set of stocks dated 1638 are in the grounds.

2 Turn right on **Cockin Lane**, but be careful of the traffic coming quickly round the blind bend here. Almost immediately turn left into Low Lane where a pavement leads past the site of **Low Lane Pit** (now Hole Bottom Beck Yard). Turn right at an unsigned footpath beyond, where a path leads along the edge of the field from a rough stile. Reaching a stone stoop, turn left up the line of an old wall onto the hillside of **Hanging Fall**, where there are great views back across towards Thornton.

3 At the top of **Hanging Fall**, turn right along the wall then skirt round the foot of **Rabbit Hill**, which is peppered with myriad rabbit holes. Beyond, climb steeply back to the wall at the top of the slope and follow a clear path along the crest, soon walking along the top of a judd wall built from the spoil of **Fall Top Quarries.** At the end do not join the quarry's vehicle track, but stay on a path to the right past another fine viewpoint overlooking **The Towers** observatory and chimney of the adjacent fireclay works. This eventually bears right down some steps to reach **Brow Lane** on the edge of Clayton.

4 Turn right briefly down **Brow Lane** only as far as a narrow gate on the left opposite the drive to Fox Brow. A path leads down the fields and then along the wall beside the former railway line, before crossing it at a broad stone bridge. Head straight across the rough track beyond to reach a stile in the wall behind **Station House**. Follow the narrow path to the end, then turn right on a track that soon becomes the Great Northern Railway Trail by the site of the former **Queensbury Station**.

Queensbury Station was oddly located at the junction of three railway lines and had separate platforms on each side of the large triangle of lines. There was also a three-arch viaduct at the north end that was pulled down in 1990. Though distant from the hilltop village of Queensbury, local mill owners successfully petitioned for a station here to transport their goods. The adjacent 1.5 mile **Queensbury Tunnel** was constructed in the 1870s and linked the station through to Holmesfield and Halifax. Though closed in the 1950s, there are ongoing plans to re-open the tunnel as part of the cycle network.

❺ **The Great Northern Railway Trail** follows the line of the old railway between Queensbury and Thornton stations. At **Queensbury Station** another branch forks off through the Queensbury Tunnel towards Holmesfield and Halifax. The entrance can be seen via a brief diversion off to the left, but the main route bends right past **John Dalby's Grave**. Beyond Ashby House, head straight across Cockin Lane. Soon after passing under a high bridge, bear right through a gate. The trail continues above **High Birk Beck**.

The headstone of **John Dalby** that stands by the Great Northern Railway Trail near the site of the former Queensbury Station is something of a mystery. John Dalby worked for the rival Midland Railway for over 50 years, first as a clerk and later a canvasser espousing the virtues of his company over its rival, so its location here is more the product

John Dalby's headstone

of accident than intent. John was born in Clayton in 1817 and was working as a porter when he married a local farmer's daughter, Ann Greenwood, in 1848. He died three years after her, in 1893, and was buried in St John's Church in Clayton, but some of the gravestones were dumped here subsequently. Most were disposed of, but perhaps John's lay hidden under the brambles until it was rescued and resurrected more recently. A contemporary of the Brontë children, his ordinary life is ultimately commemorated in an unlikely fashion.

6 Continue straight across Headley Lane, following the railway onto **Thornton Viaduct**, a vast structure crossing the broad valley of Pinch Beck. At the end, turn right around the school to emerge on the B6145 at the west end of **Thornton**. Follow the road right for 300m, then bear left up Kipping Lane into the old heart of the village. Market Street continues past the **Brontë Birthplace**, where the **Charlotte Stone** is engraved in the side of the wall of the café. Continue along the road for another 500m, then turn right down a signed path beside **St James' Church** to return to your starting point.

Thornton Viaduct is an impressive twenty-arch structure carrying the Great Northern Railway 120 feet above Pinch Beck. It was a part of a very expensive line built between Queensbury Station and Keighley whose construction was delayed; its hilly nature earned it the nickname the Alpine Route. The viaduct was completed in the 1870s and incorporates a rare S-shape into its design. The last train crossed it on November 8th 1963, but it has more recently been opened as part of the Great Northern Railway Trail.

Thornton Viaduct

The **Black Horse** is the only surviving pub from the time of the Brontës' residence in Thornton.

During the time of the Brontës, **Kipping House** was occupied by The Firths, who were close friends of the family. Elizabeth Firth was a godmother to both Charlotte and Anne. The original eighteenth-century **Kipping Independent Chapel** was replaced by today's grand edifice in 1843.

The Bell Chapel was the local nickname for the original St James' Church, whose ruins are seen in the lee of Thornton Hall on the opposite side of the road from the current late nineteenth-century building. The Bell Chapel was built in 1612, though it stood on the site of earlier chapels that may have been here as early as the twelfth century. Revd **Patrick Brontë** was curate here from 1815 to 1820 and the Bell Chapel was partially rebuilt under his direction in 1818 – probably the third time the chapel was altered. The striking cupola that still stands on the site and was the building's defining feature was only added at this time, along with a series of new windows. The evocative ruins of the Bell Chapel are now grade II listed. Inside the current church, there is a permanent exhibition of the Brontës in Thornton, as well as the bell and stone font from the old chapel, which would have been used to christen all of the Brontë children except Maria.

The cupola of the old Bell Chapel

Elizabeth Gaskell published her biography of **Charlotte Brontë** in 1857, just two years after her death, and is responsible for many of the myths about the Brontës that were perpetuated for years. One such myth was that Patrick was an eccentric patriarch who remained aloof and distant from his motherless children. Another was that Haworth was some remote, primitive, rural village, which completely ignores the Industrial Revolution and the impact it had on life in the township, as it did on Thornton. Finally she created the downtrodden and frail spinster image of Charlotte Brontë that persists to this day.

The Brontë Birthplace was bought and restored by Yorkshire novelist Barbara Whitehead in 1997, who remained there until 2007. Today it is home to Emily's café and restaurant. The **Charlotte Stone** is built into the wall of the twentieth-century extension that houses the café and is carved with a poem by Poet Laureate Carol Ann Duffy.

The bright **jay** has the equally colourful scientific name garrulus glandarius. This shy pinkish-brown crow has a white throat and rump and bright blue feathers on its wings. It is common across the UK and most likely found in search of acorns, beech mast or hazelnuts. **Jays** play a hugely important role in the distribution of oak trees due to their penchant for burying large numbers of acorns in the autumn.

THE BRONTË STONES WALK

A beautiful linear route over the moor from Thornton to Haworth that passes each of the four Brontë Stones. The route also takes in Ogden Kirk, Denholme Beck, Nan Scar and Oxenhope, following the Brontë Way in places but elsewhere offering interesting alternatives to this well-trodden trail.

'The idea of being authors was as natural to us as walking '

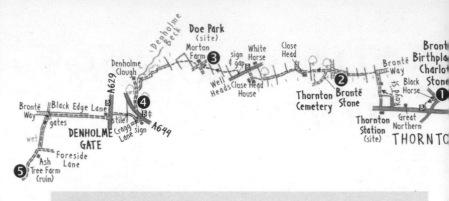

Distance: 9 miles (14.3km)
Ascent: 365m
Difficulty: Moderate

Public Transport: To get back from Haworth to Oxenhope, take the B1/B3 bus (Brontë Bus, towards Keighley) from one of the stops at the bottom of Main Street or by Haworth Station. Get off at Cross Roads and cross the A629 to catch the 67/68 bus (Keighley Bus Company, towards Bradford) to Thornton.

Parking: Pay car parks in Haworth. Free car parking near Oxenhope Station and street parking in Thornton.

Refreshments: There are various pubs and cafés in Haworth and Thornton. In between, there are pubs in Oxenhope and a cafe at Oxenhope Station, and Asa Nicholson's Tea Room is a 1/4 mile off the route on the A644 at Keelham.

The Brontë family's closest friends in Thornton were the Firths who lived at **Kipping House**. Members of the two families met often, took tea and dined together and sometimes went for walks in the surrounding countryside. Patrick enjoyed the 'sweet counsel' of the head of the household, Dr John Scholefield Firth. After moving to the parsonage in Haworth, Patrick remained in touch and often made the walk back over the hills to Thornton. Sadly, he soon found himself returning to comfort a dying man and, on 2nd January 1821, he conducted the funeral service of his friend. Later that month, Patrick's wife Maria fell gravely ill and Dr Firth's only daughter, Elizabeth, and her stepmother provided practical help. Elizabeth took the two youngest Brontë children to Kipping for a month to look after them and after Mrs Brontë's death, Patrick corresponded with Elizabeth. It has been conjectured that Patrick made a marriage proposal to Elizabeth before she married Revd James Clarke Franks, but whatever the exact truth, their friendship remained for many years.

❶ From the **Brontë Birthplace**, follow Market Street west to the junction with West Lane and head straight on across the open ground to the left of the Black Horse. Continue down through the small park, then turn right on the main road. Beyond the Great Northern, turn second right up Royd Street, shortly before the site of Thornton Station. At the top, turn left along a grassy bank below a small playground to reach a vehicle track heading right up the hill. At the top, turn left through a gap and join the Brontë Way as it crosses several small fields across the hillside.

Though only a small village when the Brontës lived there, **Thornton** had six pubs at the time. The Black Bull stood in the middle of the junction of Market Street and West Lane by the Black Horse, the heart of the village before Thornton Road (the B6145) was built in 1826.

It was while living in **Thornton** that Patrick Brontë published two books: *The Cottage in the Woods* in 1815; and *The Maid of Killarney* (or *Albion and Flora*) in 1818. It may have been these publications which inspired the Brontë children to write.

Thornton Station opened in 1878 as the terminus of a rural branch line out of Bradford, part of the Great Northern Railway. It stood near the end of the impressive Thornton Viaduct and had an island platform reached by an iron bridge from the road. The line was extended to Keighley in 1884, the so-called 'Alpine route' across the hills via Cullingworth. The station was used primarily for goods – wool, coal and livestock – and the goods platform can still be seen from the retaining wall alongside Thornton Road. The primary school grounds have been built around what remains.

❷ The now-fenced path soon enters **Thornton Cemetery**, where you'll find the **Brontë Stone**, carved with a poem by Jeanette Winterson. Bear left on the lower path to pass the stone on the left under some trees. Continue to some steps, following these back up to the higher path and a gate at the far end. Follow the path above **Close Head** and climb to a bend, where you bear left through the gate. Follow the edge of the fields through a series of gates to reach **Close Head House,** where a track leads up to the road near the White Horse. Follow the road left for 100m through **Well Heads**, then turn right at a sign. The path bends left to cut a defined line across a series of fields towards **Morton Farm**.

❸ Keep to the left of the farm buildings at **Morton**, heading straight across the track and through a field gate. Descend diagonally across further fields with a good view down **Denholme Beck** to Doe Park Reservoir, then follow a wall across the hillside towards the building at **Denholme Clough**. Cut left through a gate just before the stream and soon after join the drive leading up to the **A644**. There is a teashop less than a 1/4 mile along this road in Keelham if refreshments are needed before heading out onto the moor.

❹ Follow the road left briefly, then turn right up Cragg Lane. Almost immediately turn right at a sign, following a path behind the houses that soon pulls up to the A629 through **Denholme Gate.** Bear left across the road and follow Black Edge Lane up onto the enclosed wastes above. After half a mile, turn left through a gate at an obvious junction, then drop down to join Foreside Lane leading right past the ruins of **Ash Tree Farm**.

Doe Park was the lower part of a fifteenth-century deer park enclosed by the Tempest family as a hunting chase for red deer. It was surrounded by an earth bank and wooden palisade fence and covered most of the valley around the Denholme Beck between Denholme and Cullingworth. The name **Denholme Gate** refers to one of the entrances to the deer park. Eventually deer hunting fell out of fashion and the land was divided up when the Tempest family fortune was gambled away in the early seventeenth century.

5 Continue along Foreside Lane, heading straight on through a gate where the track bends left near a ruined barn. Beyond the next gate near the site of **Moscow Farm**, fork right as the path gets wetter to soon reach the dramatic crest of **Ogden Kirk**, near the far end of which you'll find the **Emily Stone**. Turn right here along the main path up the side of **Ogden Clough**, then fork right again soon after another gate. This well-defined path leads over the shoulder of **Thornton Moor** and there are great views from the top over Bradford and Rombalds Moor.

Moscow Farm, like many remote dwellings was given a name befitting its far-off location.

Ogden Kirk, site of the Emily Stone

6 Continue down **Hambleton Lane,** soon joining a fence line to descend steeply to **Thornton Moor Conduit.** Head straight on past the gate, then fork left at a sign to descend past the remains of a metal hut to an old wall line. After a stone stoop, the path bears left before descending straight down the hillside to reach a bridge over **Stubden Conduit**. However, part-way down, near a waymark post lost in the reeds, you can head right through the reeds (not as wet as they look) to the abandoned farm of The Hays in the lee of a solitary sycamore tree. **The Book Stones** are a bonus carving that take in this beautiful vista over Oxenhope.

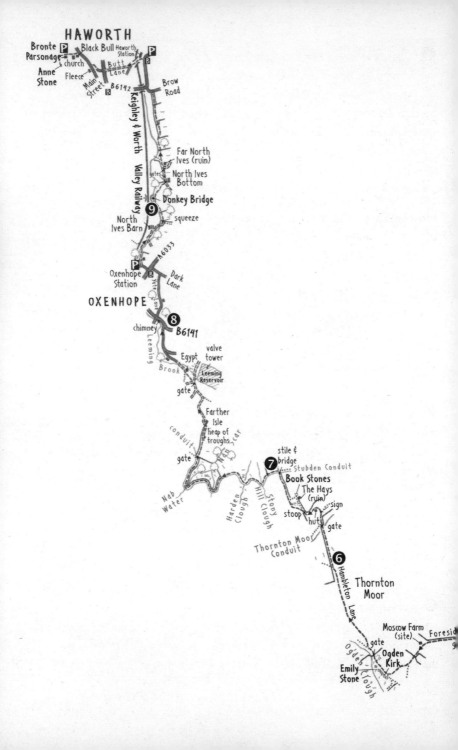

7 Turn left along **Stubden Conduit** and follow its beautiful meandering line around several steep cloughs. After the wooded hollow of **Nan Scar,** where twite may be seen if you're lucky, the path reaches a gate for the first time. Leave the conduit and follow the top of the field down past a heap of old stone troughs to **Farther Isle**. Follow the track left of the farm and wind steadily down to a gate near the corner of **Leeming Reservoir**. Head straight across the track beyond, following a signed path steeply down into the valley. Turn right past Egypt Cottages and join the road as it crosses **Leeming Brook** and continues through Back Leeming all the way to the B6141.

In the 1880s there was a rifle range at the bottom of the wooded beck of **Nan Scar**. Its name comes from the Welsh word nant for a small river. Further up the stream, there is a local nature reserve, where rare birds like twite and honey buzzards may be seen.

Thornton Moor and **Stubden Reservoirs** were built in the 1880s by the Bradford Corporation, the former acting as the city's high-level water supply. Their conduits string out across the northern slopes of Nab Hill, the higher feeding straight into Thornton Moor Reservoir, the lower passing through the hillside to Stubden Reservoir – the air shafts across the hill mark its line. The whole hillside was cleared of its population to prevent contamination of the drinking water and the remains of many of the old farms are identifiable by the presence of the lone sycamore trees planted to shelter them.

Leeming Reservoir's ornate valve tower

8 Follow the B641 left into Oxenhope, then turn right at the crossroads just beyond the old chimney of Lowertown Mill. Follow quiet Yate Lane all the way to Dark Lane, then turn left down to the A6033. Bear left across the road to follow Harry Lane towards Oxenhope Station. On the bend, bear right on a path past Wilton House and cross Bridgehouse Beck. Stay alongside the stream to join a track past the water works, then bear right before North Ives Barn and re-cross the stream.

Rather than one village, **Oxenhope** is a conglomeration of several hamlets, including Uppertown, Lowertown, Leeming, Shaw and Marsh. Oxenhope only became the village's name when it was adopted by the station built as the terminus of the Keighley and Worth Valley Railway in 1867.

9 Continue along the right bank of Bridge-house Beck until the path climbs to North Ives Bottom. Turn left through a gate in front of the building and descend past the ruin at **Far North Ives**. Continue straight on to rejoin the stream, then follow a path along the bottom edge of a series of fields towards the edge of **Haworth**. At the end, turn left on Brow Road, then right on the main road. Turn left in front of **Haworth Station** and cross high above the railway before bearing right up Butt Lane. Head straight across the road at the top to cut up to Main Street near the Fleece. Head up the cobbled hill, then turn left up the steps after the Black Bull to pass through the gate by St Michael's Church and reach the **Brontë Parsonage**. The **Anne Stone** stands at the top of Parson's Field and is reached by a gate just beyond the parsonage.

The Reverend Donne in Charlotte Brontë's novel *Shirley* was inspired by Joseph Brett Grant who was Patrick Brontë's curate. He became the first vicar of **Oxenhope** in 1851, when the fine Norman-style church was built there. Previously Oxenhope had been a part of Bradford parish; indeed its name means 'valley of the oxen', referring to a time when it was part of the estate of Bradford Manor.

The **Parsonage** would probably have felt far more austere when the Brontës were children as it was right on the edge of the village with the moors quite literally as its back garden. There were no trees around it and inside there were bare walls, cold stone floors and no curtains. However, the Brontë children fared better than the majority of Haworth's inhabitants. Forty per cent of children born in Haworth didn't reach their sixth birthday and the overall life expectancy was about twenty-five, almost the worst in the country. In 1850 Charles Babbage was sent by the government and wrote a damning report about conditions here and the need for some kind of sewage system. As Patrick suspected, Charles saw the churchyard (with approximately 42,000 bodies packed in it) as contributing to the problems of the village and one of the first recommendations he made was to close the churchyard down. Babbage also suggested that trees were planted in the church yard, to help to break up the bodies and drain the soil.

Donkey Bridge

The **Black Bull** public house was a favourite drinking hole of Branwell Brontë. Branwell was once Secretary to the Freemasons Lodge of the Three Graces. who met at this inn. According to Elizabeth Gaskell, Branwell's great conversational talents 'procured him the undesirable distinction of having his company recommended by the landlord of the Black Bull to any chance traveller who might happen to feel solitary or dull over his liquor.' Branwell was also known on occasion to make his escape through the back door, or by jumping through the kitchen window, when his family came to seek him at the front door of the inn.

THE EMILY BRONTË WALK

A hearty yomp across the wild moorland Emily loved to roam high above Haworth and Oxenhope. The route takes in Top Withins, Alcomden Stones and Ponden Hall, as well as various other beautiful sites. Parts of the route are wet year-round so good footwear is essential and, although most of it is on clear paths, a compass and good navigational skills may be needed in bad weather.

'I'll walk where my own nature would be leading: It vexes me to choose another guide.'

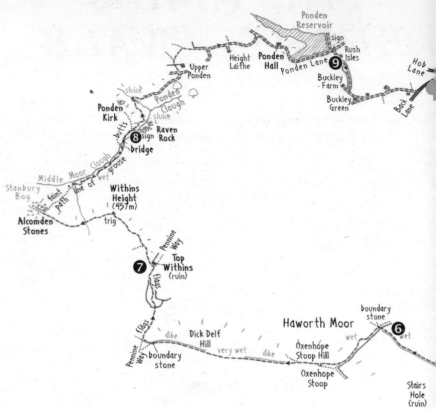

Ponden
Reservoir

sign

Rush
Isles

Hob
Lane

Upper
Ponden

Height
Laithe

Ponden
Hall

Ponden Lane

9

Buckley
Farm

Buckley
Green

Back
Lane

sluice

Ponden
Kirk

Ponden Clough

sluice

butts

8 sign

Raven
Rock

bridge

Middle Moor Clough

line of wet grouse

Stanbury
Bog

faint path

Withins
Height
(457m)

Alcomden
Stones

trig

Pennine Way

Top
Withins
(ruin)

7

flags

boundary
stone

Haworth Moor

6 wet

flags

dike

Dick Delf
Hill

very wet

dike

Oxenhope
Stoop Hill

wet

Pennine Way

boundary
stone

Oxenhope
Stoop

Stairs
Hole
(ruin)

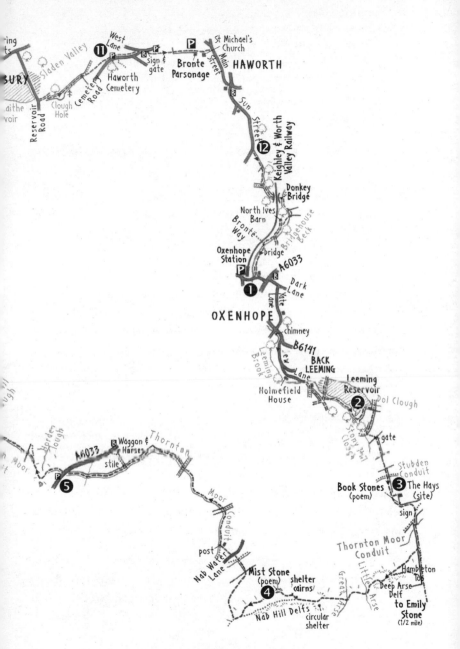

HAWORTH

KEIGHLEY
—ring
—ts
West
Lane
Sladen Valley
11
P
P
St Michael's
Church
B
sign &
gate
Bronte
Parsonage
Haworth
Cemetery
Cemetery Road
—BURY
Main Street
Reservoir Road
—aithe
—oir
Clough
Hole
Sun Street
B
Keighley & Worth
Valley Railway
12
Donkey
Bridge
North Ives
Barn
Bridgehouse Beck
Brontë
Way
bridge
Oxenhope
Station
P
B
bridge
A6033
1
Dark
Lane
Yate Lane
OXENHOPE
chimney
Leeming Brook
B6141
BACK
LEEMING
New Lane
Leeming
Reservoir
Holmefield
House
2
Dol Clough
—lough
Marden Clough
—n Moor
—t
Thornton
A6033
B
Waggon &
Horses
stile
Stony Croft
gate
Stubden
Conduit
P
5
Moor Conduit
Book Stones
(poem)
3
The Hays
(site)
sign
Thornton Moor
Conduit
Hambleton
Top
post
Nab Water Lane
Mist Stone
(poem)
shelter
cairns
Little Arse
Deep Arse
Delf
to Emily
Stone
(1/2 mile)
4
Nab Hill Delfs
circular
shelter

229

Distance: 14½ miles (23.7km)
Ascent: 510m
Difficulty: Strenuous

Public Transport: Oxenhope and Haworth are on the Keighley &
Worth Valley Railway and served by regular buses from Keighley,
Bradford and Hebden Bridge. If struggling, a bus can also be
caught from Stanbury.

Parking: Free street parking in Oxenhope. Car park at Oxenhope
Station may be available by arrangement.

Refreshments: There is little on the remote moorland route
between Oxenhope and Stanbury, other than the Waggon &
Horses pub on the A6033.

Emily Brontë was the most reclusive of the sisters and so she remains
something of a mystery. She suffered extreme homesickness when away
from the Parsonage, and was more than happy to remain at home in the
role of housekeeper after the death of Aunt Branwell. Her great love was
for the solitude of the moors and the company of animals, and she roamed
these heights extensively. She died of tuberculosis on 18 December 1848,
shortly after her brother Branwell's death.

❶   From **Oxenhope Station**, follow Mill Lane past the overflow car park
up to the main road. Head straight across into Dark Lane, then turn right
along quiet Yate Lane. Reaching the B6141, turn left past the **chimney**,
then first right along Jew Lane. Fork right down a dead-end at the bottom
of **Back Leeming**. At the end, continue up past Milton House, then fork
left up the side of the dam wall. Turn left then immediately right at the
top to join a path around the shore of **Leeming Reservoir**.

❷   At the far end of the **Leeming Reservoir**, turn right and, just before
crossing **Stony Hill Clough**, turn sharply left up to a narrow gate. A good
path leads straight up the slope, crossing **Stubden Conduit** before nearing a lone sycamore tree in the ruins of The Hays, by which stands the

Book Stones. Turn left across the rushes near a waymark post to reach this great viewpoint.

shelter cairn on Nab Hill

❸ Return to the main path and climb to a sign on the crest. Bear right here and then head straight on across **Thornton Moor Conduit** and climb up towards Hambleton Top. The **Emily Stone** is carved at Ogden Kirk, three-quarters of a mile on along this track (see Brontë Stones Walk for details), but this route turns right through a gate after 150m, following a faint path angling up one of the old holloways leading to **Deep Arse Delf**. Turn right at the top (joining the route from Hamleton Top) and follow a clear path along the hillside towards the prominent shelter cairns on **Nab Hill**. Fork right to reach these, then continue along the edge to the next prominent cairn, below which is the **Mist Stone**, one of Simon Armitage's Stanza Stones.

> **Deep Arse Delf** has been marked on OS maps as Deep House Delf since the nineteenth century, but its real identity may lie in the folds of land along the northern edge of Nab Hill. From the hill opposite, the cloughs of Great Arse and Little Arse cleave the hill into buttocks, from which the quarry took its name. Early map-makers decided to make it less amusing.

❹ Continue along the edge from the **Mist Stone** and, shortly after rejoining the main path, turn right down the slope. At the bottom, recross the conduit and head straight across the road beyond. Rejoin **Thornton Moor Conduit** at a waymark post and follow it all the way round the hillside to the A6033. A short diversion right at a stile leads down to the whitewashed **Waggon & Horses** pub.

The **Waggon & Horses** was originally on the opposite side of the road, but the licence is thought to have been transferred to new premises around

1850. It remains a traditional moorland pub and serves as the start of the annual Oxenhope Straw Bale Race; every July the locals don fancy dress and run, walk or stumble the three miles into the village and up the opposite hillside while carrying a bale of straw and downing pints in every pub along the way.

5 Head straight across the main road and continue along **Thornton Moor Conduit** around Horden Clough. The drain continues across the hillside to the junction with **Stairs Lane**, the old route between Haworth and Hebden Bridge. Carry straight on through a gate with the conduit until you reach the edge of the moor soon after a very wet section. There are good views throughout over Oxenhope, Haworth and Keighley.

6 Reaching the edge of **Haworth Moor**, turn left at a boundary stone marked H and follow a path parallel to the wall up onto Oxenhope Stoop Hill (bypassing as much as possible a wet hollow). Turn right at the top to pass **Oxenhope Stoop** and continue along the boggy moorland ridge. Fork left soon after to follow the line of a dead-straight dike gently up onto **Dick Delf Hill**. Some stakes are picked up descending the other side and, just beyond another boundary stone, you should fork

Oxenhope Stoop, one of a series of boundary stones marking the extent of Haworth parish

right to reach the flagstones of the Pennine Way. Follow this right down to the prominent ruin of **Top Withins**.

Top Withins

❼ Turn left just before **Top Withins** and follow a faint path bearing right up the slope behind. Keep right along the top of the slope to reach the trig point on **Withins Height**. Turn left here on a good path towards **Alcomden Stones**; a possible inspiration for Penistone Crag, these impressive rocks look out across the wastes of **Stanbury Bog**. From the nearest (easternmost) rocks, head roughly down the heather into **Middle Moor Clough**. There is a very faint path, but you should aim to pick up a line of wooden grouse butts along the right side of the stream. A path follows these all the way, crossing the clough to reach a sign above **Raven Rock**.

Alcomden Stones

Alcomden Stones (also known as Oakenden Stones) stand on the brink of the wilderness. Despite suggestions of druidical sacrifices and the presence of a dolmen, it is now generally thought that these are entirely natural features.

Stanbury Bog is an evocative place, dark and forbidding. In September 1824, though, the silence of the moors was broken by an unlikely explosion as the bog spewed out rock and earth across the surrounding hillside after a heavy storm. It polluted the River Aire such that its water could not be used for a time and created two large depressions. Patrick Brontë witnessed the event and thought it an earthquake.

❽ Head straight on down the steep slope to reach a dam in **Ponden Clough** that marks the start of Ponden Aqueduct, an underground conduit. Follow the path around the head of **Ponden Clough**, joining a vehicle track soon after passing another sluice. Keep straight on at the next junction to stay left of **Upper Ponden**, then fork right down a grassy path. Turn right at the bottom and rejoin the vehicle track to head down towards **Ponden Reservoir**. At a T-junction, turn right, passing **Ponden Hall** (the inspiration for Thrushcross Grange) before joining the reservoir shore.

Ponden Reservoir was built in the 1870s as a compensation reservoir for the mill owners in the valley below, as all the water from Middle Moor Clough and Stanbury Bog is taken via Ponden Aqueduct, an underground conduit, to Watersheddles Reservoir.

Ponden Hall is an Elizabethan farmhouse that is usually cited as the model for Thrushcross Grange in Wuthering Heights. The lower section is thought to have been built around 1634 with the upper half added in 1801. Until 1898 it belonged to the Heaton Family, who owned Ponden Mill and Crow Hill Quarries and were friends of the Brontë family, who regularly visited its extensive library. The adjacent building called the Bunkhouse served as a stopping point on the Pennine Way for a number of years, but was originally built as a peat store and cow shed in 1680. The precipice of **Ponden Kirk** has long been associated with

the plaque at Ponden Hall

Penistone Crag in Wuthering Heights, though it is equally likely Emily was inspired by Alcomden Stones. Beneath it is a small gap in the rock through which it is said a maiden should crawl if she was to be married before the year was out. There were also suggestions of sexual rituals according to Halliwell Sutcliffe: 'This dark kirk of the wilderness, at which Pagan mothers once worshipped lustily'.

9 Just beyond the far end of **Ponden Reservoir**, turn right at a sign and follow a path around Rush Isles. It leads up to join the lane at **Buckley Farm**. Follow this left along the top of the hill and, at its end, turn left along Back Lane, which soon joins the road heading into **Stanbury** village, beautifully perched on a ridge above Lower Laithe Reservoir.

⑩ The road can be followed all the way through **Stanbury**, but a lovely path avoids the narrow road. Turn left at a sign just beyond the school and follow the track round behind the old Sunday school, then fork left along a walled path that runs behind the **Wuthering Heights** pub (which can be reached via a gate from this side). Rejoin the road, then turn right on Reservoir Road, which drops down dramatically to cross **Lower Laithe Reservoir's** dam wall. Turn left at the far end and follow a bridleway up to **Cemetery Road**.

> **Stanbury** is an ancient settlement on a ridge of land that represented an important route across the Pennines, and is likely to pre-date the Norman Conquest. It developed greatly in the nineteenth century and Patrick Brontë was instrumental in establishing a church and Sunday school here in 1846. The **Wuthering Heights** inn was built in 1763 and was previously known as the Cross Inn.

⑪ A path follows the left edge of **Cemetery Road** down to its junction with West Lane. Turn right, then almost immediately go right again through a gate and follow a path across the fields to the edge of **Haworth**. The path continues behind the houses to reach the **Brontë Parsonage** (in the field behind which the **Anne Stone** can be seen). Continue past the church and turn right down the cobbled **Main Street**. At the bottom turn right along Sun Street and follow it all the way out of the village.

⑫ At the end of the houses of **Haworth**, where the road bends right up the hill, turn left along the edge of the fields. The path soon joins an old packhorse route leading down through the trees to **Donkey Bridge**, reached just beyond a tunnel beneath the **Keighley & Worth Valley Railway**. Turn right along the river before recrossing it near North Ives Barn. Briefly join a vehicle track, but bear right to stay on the right bank until a footbridge where the route joins the Brontë Way. The path emerges back on Mill Lane near **Oxenhope Station**.

Oxenhope Church

The ring ouzel is a migratory mountain thrush closely related to the blackbird. The ring refers to the white band around its neck. Not unlike Emily, the ring ouzel prefers its own company and is fond of steep-sided moorland cloughs

THE ANNE BRONTË WALK

This varied route follows the Railway Children Walk along the Worth Valley out of Haworth, before climbing through Oakworth and Holden Park to charming Newsholme Dean. The route returns via Newsholme and Pickles Hill, before following the River Worth back towards Haworth. The walking is on good paths throughout, though some parts may be muddy.

'He that dares not grasp the thorn should never crave the rose.'

Newsholme
Dene Cottage
Fellow Lane
Newsholme
❻ Dean
Dean Bridge
(clam bridge)
gate
bridge
Newsholme
Dene
pond
gate
gate
gate
Carr
Laithe
True
Well Hall
❺
HOLME
HOUSE
Cat
Clough
gate
Newsholme Beck
Slack
Lane
Baptist
Church
NEWSHOLME
Mackingstone Lane
Slack Lane end
St John's Church
Chapel
Fold
Slaymaker Lane
pond
Gill
Clough
Farm
trough
Green
Lane
Gill
Lane
Gill Clough
Race Moor
Lane
gap
❹
pumping
station
❼
White Lane
Holden
Park
Clough
gate
Tewitt
Hall
B
sign
OAKWORTH
stone
East
Royd
Willgutter
Lane
Hol..
Hous..
PICKLES
HILL
Scholes Lane
❸
pond
railway
B
Lower
Scholes
Low
Wood
Vale Mill
stile
Worth River
stile
Vale
Mytholmes
Lane
waterfall
stile
Lumb Beck
Murgatroyd
Wood
Long Bridge &
Scholes Hippins
(site)
packhorse
bridge
❽
gate
Oldfield
Gate
Ebor
Lane
Lumbfoot
Mill (site)
gates
River Worth
Sladen Beck
ladder
Ebor
Mill
Oldfield
stiles
gate
HAWORTH
railway
stone
plaque
West Lane
Sun Inn
❷
B
Bridgehouse
Beck
Bronte
Parsonage
P
B
❶
Haworth station
Anne
Stone
(in Parson
Field)
Fleece
Inn
Butt Lane
B
Main
St
Central
Park
N

0   200   400   600
METRES

Distance: 7 miles (11.2km)
Ascent: 350m
Difficulty: Moderate

Public Transport: Haworth is served by various buses from Bradford, Halifax and Hebden Bridge. It is also on the Keighley and Worth Valley Railway.

Parking: Various pay car parks in Haworth, including by Brontë Parsonage. Some free street parking further up West Lane.

Refreshments: The Turkey Inn at Laycock is a natural stopping point 1/3 mile off the route near Holme House. There are plenty of options in Haworth, and Sewing Days Café is on the route in Oakworth, where there are also a couple of pubs.

❶ From the **Brontë Parsonage**, follow the cobbled path down the hill past **St Michael's Church**. Turn right down Main Street until the Fleece Inn, opposite which you bear left down a road. Head straight across the B6142 and bear right into **Central Park**. Keep left to return to Butt Lane and follow it to the bottom, where a path leads left over the Keighley & Worth Valley railway to **Haworth Station.**

The **Keighley & Worth Valley Railway** is a single track branch line that didn't reach Haworth until 1867 and was subsequently extended to Oxenhope due to persistence from local mill owners. Thus the Brontës had to walk an eight mile round trip to Keighley over steep hills to pick up and return library books, and to attend lectures and other events, sometimes returning in the dark. They also took these moorland tracks and field paths to catch the regular coach from Keighley to Bradford or Leeds. The line was closed in 1962 after the Beeching Report, but re-opened in 1968 as a volunteer-operated heritage railway specialising in the serving of real ale on-board. Its sale to the local preservation society represents the very first privatisation of British Railways, and it thrives to this day. The famous 1970 film of E. Nesbit's **The Railway Children** was extensively filmed on this line, particularly around Oakworth Station, and the route follows part of the Railway Children Walk.

② Turn left along the main road and follow it up the hill, before bearing left into Ebor Lane (on the corner of which there is a **stone plaque** in the wall). Over the stream, turn right on a path alongside the railway and follow **Bridgehouse Beck** all the way to Vale Farm. Turn right here. then left on the road at the end to pass the vast works of **Vale Mill**. At the sharp corner (where drivers are exhorted to hoot), head straight on up the steps and under the railway.

The **stone plaque** at the end of Ebor Lane is a public notice about the private road from here to Mytholmes Lane. It was one of three erected in 1843 by John Craven of Dockroyd in Oakworth. It was only reinstated in 2013 after the wall was damaged. Others were allowed to use the road for certain fees. **Ebor Mill** was built by the Craven family in 1819 on the site of an earlier mill and used for worsted manufacture. Much of the buildings were destroyed by fire in 2010.

Ebor Lane plaque

③ At the top, turn right along a narrow walled path, then fork right through a gate to reach a road. Just up the hill, turn right on **East Royd** and then left at a sign. A path continues across the fields to another road; keep straight on to the main road at the end and follow it left into **Oakworth**. Turn right before the roundabout, following Clough Lane into the woods of **Holden Park**. Cut through a gap in the wall to the left to continue up its left side and, at the top of some steps, cut back right through another gap to emerge on **Race Moor Lane**.

Holden Park was once the grounds of Oakworth House, an Italianate mansion built in the 1860s for Sir Isaac Holden. It lasted only until 1907, when it was demolished following a serious fire. The grounds were given to the people of Oakworth and are worth exploring for the grotto, portico and summerhouse.

the Anne Stone

❹ Turn right around **Race Moor Lane** and, after the bend, turn right up a narrow path. Carry straight on across the fields to reach Slaymaker Lane, which you follow left to its end at **Slack Lane**. Turn right on Mackingstone Lane for nearly half a mile until it drops down to the hamlet of Holme House, where the route turns left on a farm track to **True Well Hall**. If you want to visit the **Turkey Inn** at Laycock, carry straight on for another third of a mile. You can return to the route by following the Millennium Way footpath just before the pub.

Slack Lane Baptist Chapel dates from 1819. It was originally known as Shaw's Chapel after Joseph Shaw, the first Baptist preacher in the area. After building of a larger chapel at the crossroads in 1879, the old church was used as a Sunday school. The new chapel is now a private residence (Chapel Fold) while the old church is still used for services.

❺ Follow the track past **True Well Hall** to Carr Laithe, just before which a narrow, walled path leads right down into the field. After the next gate, bear right across a very soggy patch to a small gate leading down into the trees of **Newsholme Dean**. Across the bridge, keep left along the wall to emerge on Fellow Lane above the farmhouse. Follow the track left back down into the valley, forking left of **Newsholme Dean Cottage**. At the end of the track, keep left along the wall to cross the packhorse pridge adjacent to the ancient **Dean Bridge**.

The delightful wooded glen of **Newsholme Dean** feels very secluded these days, but was a popular post-war picnic spot, with families paddling in the stream and a cafe at one of the farms. Dean Bridge has been a significant crossing point for centuries, though; its beautifully balanced ancient clapper bridge stands alongside a packhorse bridge made to look ordinary. Though it has been modified at some point, it has been suggested that the clapper bridge was originally Roman and part of the same ancient trans-Pennine route as that over the clapper bridge at Wycoller.

Dean Bridge

6 Bear left beyond **Dean Bridge** to a gate into the woods and follow a muddy route up the side of **Cat Clough**. At the top, go through a gate to join a walled path into the hamlet of **Newsholme**. Bear

stoops in Cat Clough

right at the end to join the road and pass the tiny St John's Church, built into the adjacent house. Follow Gill Lane back across **Newsholme Beck** and turn right at the top, cutting up to join Green Lane. Beyond a small pumping station, turn left into **White Lane**.

7 Follow White Lane straight on, passing a turn off for Tewitt Hall Farm and heading straight on across another track (Turnshaw Lane). Turn left soon after and follow Willgutter Lane down to **Pickles Hill**. Head straight across the road and follow Scholes Lane down to **Lower Scholes**. Beyond the buildings, follow waymark discs straight on into a grassy track that soon emerges in the fields. Follow the wall until it bends sharply left,then head down to the far corner of the field where a stile leads into the trees. Keep left down the side of **Lumb Beck** to reach a beautiful packhorse bridge at Lumbfoot

8 Do not cross the bridge, but turn left on the track just beyond. Almost immediately fork right through a gate and follow a lovely path along the **River Worth**. At the next gate, follow the left side of a fence to return to the river at **Long Bridge,** another fine packhorse bridge. Cross the bridge and climb up to a ladder stile at Lower Oldfield via the holloway of **Oldfield Gate**. Keep left of the farm and join a walled path leading along the top of the fields. After a second stile, keep right up the side of the field to a gate and cut through to West Lane on the edge of **Haworth**. Turn left, then immediately right after the Sun Inn and follow the estate road to its end where a path leads up to the route heading left back to the **Brontë Parsonage**. Just before, turn right through a gate into Parson's Field to end the walk at the **Anne Stone**, situated at the top right corner with a poem written by Jackie Kay and a fine view over the town

The **Brontë Parsonage** was built in 1778 from local millstone. It is a classic Georgian house that has been maintained pretty much as it appeared in the time of the Brontës. The family arrived in 1820, but Maria Brontë died in 1821, leaving Patrick a widower with six children. Aunt Branwell stayed on to help, but Patrick only earned £180 a year as curate of Haworth, (probably equivalent to 12-13K salary today) and had to pay for any repairs, or alterations to the house out of his salary. The only significant alterations were made subsequently by Charlotte in 1850 and 1854, and Reverend Wade in 1878. Patrick Brontë lived here for 41 years until his death on 7 June 1861; at age 84, he had outlived all six of his children. When Patrick arrived in 1820, there wasn't a school in Haworth, and given his passion for education, he campaigned to raise funds to build a **Sunday school.** The school opened in 1832, and provided a basic education for the local children, many of whom would be working in local mills during the week. Charlotte, Anne and Branwell all taught here.

the Brontë Parsonage

In May 1849, whilst suffering from tuberculosis, **Anne Brontë** made her final journey to **Scarborough**, where she had spent time with the Robinsons, for whose children she was governess. Anne said goodbye to her family and her faithful spaniel, Flossy, neither of whom would comprehend the finality of this parting. Accompanied by Charlotte and family friend, Ellen Nussey, one likes to think she would have followed our route out of Haworth towards Keighley. Despite hopes the sea air may help her recover, she died on 28 May 1849 and her last words to Charlotte were 'take courage'. Anne was buried at St Mary's Church in Scarborough but this memorial stone, with a poem written by Jackie Kay, acknowledges the return she had hoped for. This stone lies close to where the rest of her siblings are buried

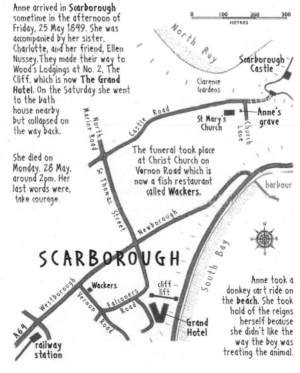

ANNE BRONTË'S SCARBOROUGH

Anne arrived in **Scarborough** sometime in the afternoon of Friday, 25 May 1849. She was accompanied by her sister, Charlotte, and her friend, Ellen Nussey. They made their way to Wood's Lodgings at No. 2, The Cliff, which is now **The Grand Hotel**. On the Saturday she went to the bath house nearby but collapsed on the way back.

She died on Monday, 28 May, around 2pm. Her last words were, take courage.

0   100   200   300
METRES

North Bay

Scarborough Castle

Clarence Gardens

Castle Road

St Mary's Church

Church Lane

Anne's grave

North Marine Road

St Thomas Street

The funeral took place at Christ Church on Vernon Road which is now a fish restaurant called **Wackers**.

harbour

Newborough

SCARBOROUGH

South Bay

Westborough

Vernon Road

Wackers

Falconers Road

cliff lift

Grand Hotel

Anne took a donkey cart ride on the **beach**. She took hold of the reigns herself because she didn't like the way the boy was treating the animal.

A64

railway station

THE WANDERING BARD WALK

A wonderfully varied trek from the Calder Valley, where Branwell Brontë worked at Luddenden Foot Station, over the tops to his family home in Haworth. The route takes in rich woodlands, open moors, lively brooks and of course many pubs.

'Amid the worlds wide din around I hear from far a solemn Sound That says "Remember Me!"'
(taken from Branwell's Luddenden Foot notebook)

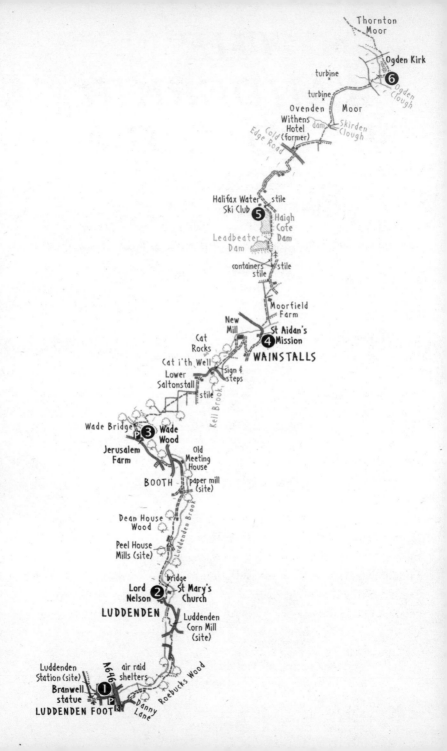

Thornton
Moor

Ogden Kirk

6 Ogden Clough

turbine

turbine

Ovenden Moor

Withens
Hotel
(former)

dam

Skirden Clough

Cold Edge Road

Halifax Water
Ski Club   stile

5

Haigh
Cote
Dam

Leadbeater
Dam

containers
stile   stile

Moorfield
Farm

New
Mill   St Aidan's
Mission

Cat
Rocks

4

WAINSTALLS

Cat i'th Well   sign &
steps

Lower
Saltonstall

stile

Kell Brook

Wade Bridge

3 Wade
Wood

Jerusalem
Farm

Old
Meeting
House

BOOTH

paper mill
(site)

Dean House
Wood

Luddenden Brook

Peel House
Mills (site)

bridge

Lord
Nelson

2 St Mary's
Church

LUDDENDEN

Luddenden
Corn Mill
(site)

Luddenden
Station (site)

air raid
shelters

A646

Branwell
statue

1

LUDDENDEN FOOT

Danny
Lane

Roebucks Wood

Distance: 10½ miles (17km)
Ascent: 520

Public Transport: Bus 500 runs hourly from Haworth to Hebden Bridge. Buses 590 and 592 run regularly from Hebden Bridge to Luddenden Foot.

Parking: Pay car parks in Haworth. Free car park by canal in Luddenden Foot, in Oxenhope and at Jerusalem Farm.

On April 1 1841, Branwell Brontë was promoted from his post in Sowerby Bridge to the position of clerk-in-charge of the railway at Luddenden Foot. He was paid £130 a year and lodged at nearby Brearley Hall. He befriended Francis Grundy, a young railway engineer whose descriptions of Branwell (provided forty years later) are responsible for the belief that this period proved his downfall. In fact, it was a very creative period for him with the first of many of his poems being published in the Halifax Guardian under his favourite pseudonym, Northangerland. He spent a lot of time exploring the countryside of the the the Calder Valley, so much so that in March 1842 he was dismissed for neglecting his duties.

❶ The route starts by the old station in **Luddenden Foot**, of which there is now little sign, but a statue of Branwell Brontë stands alongside Station Road nearby. Return to the main road, following it right for a few yards to some steps cutting up onto Danny Lane. At the next bend turn left down some steps and join a path along an old pipeline through **Roebucks Wood** that passes a series of brick air raid shelters for the mill that used to stand below. Continue along Luddenden Brook to emerge on a quiet road. At the bend, continue ahead on a snicket, then go briefly right to the site of **Luddenden Corn Mill**, where a path cuts left back to follow the stream again. At the road, turn left to reach the **Lord Nelson Inn** at the heart of charming **Luddenden**.

The Lord Nelson was built in 1634 as a private dwelling, then served as the Black Swan until the Battle of Trafalgar. Branwell regularly drank here while working in Luddenden Foot and Branwell enjoyed being caught up in the society of local writers and artists. He and friends, such as poets William Dearden and William Heaton and sculptor Joseph Bentley Leyland, formed a sort of informal society, meeting here as well as the Anchor and Shuttle at Luddenden Foot (now the site of the post office). Luddenden Library was housed in the Lord Nelson's Upper Chamber between 1776 and 1917, though Branwell is not recorded as being a member.

ramsons (or wild garlic) growing in Roebucks Wood

2 Head through the churchyard opposite the **Lord Nelson** and turn left just before a bridge over the stream. A clear path follows the left bank of Luddenden Brook all the way to **Booth**, passing the sites of a number of the valley's old mills before turning into a metalled road. Turn left up the hill at the end, then go right up some steps opposite the old school. Reaching another lane, follow it right to **Jerusalem Farm**, where there are public toilets near the car park.

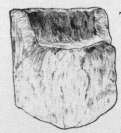

the Boggart's Chair

The Boggart's Chair stands in the far corner of St Mary's Church. It is actually the oldest of four fonts, but was removed to the garden of Ellen Royd House when the church was attacked during the Civil War. It was only recognised in 1902, by which time it had acquired its new folkloric name.

❸ Follow the main track down from the **Jerusalem Farm** car park to cross Wade Bridge, and take the higher of two paths heading right through **Wade Wood**. At the next junction turn left, then go right at a sign, climbing steeply to the top of the wood. Head diagonally across the fields beyond and turn left up to **Lower Saltonstall** after the last stile. Follow the road right past the **Cat i'th Well** pub, then turn left up some steps immediately over Kell Brook. Climb steadily to reach a vehicle track near **New Mill**, following it right as it zigzags up into the village. Looking back in places, you catch sight of the white-painted **Cat Rocks** on the hillside opposite.

Caty Well, a seventeenth-century stone cistern alongside the pub, is thought to be a corruption of St Catherine's Well, named after St Catherine of Alexandria. The painted rocks on the hill above are known as **Cat Rocks** as, from the right angle, they appear rather cat-like. It is said Robin Hood began the custom of painting the rocks when he hid out in a priest hole in the pub and stashed some of his money near the rocks. However, it's more likely they were painted to commemorate the many Liverpudlian orphans who died in the mills of Wainstalls. They lived at **St Aidan's Mission** and some are buried at nearby Dean Chapel.

the white-painted Cat Rocks

Lower Saltonstall was the birthplace of Richard Saltonstall, a sixteenth-century MP and Mayor of London who famously left £100 to the poor of Halifax. The name Saltonstall refers to a 'farmstead near the willows'.

❹ Turn left along the road in **Wainstalls**, passing **St Aidan's Mission** before turning right at a stile beyond the stream. Fork left up the side of the next fenceline, following it past **Moorfield Farm**, then cutting diagonally right across a field. Turn left up a wide track, then go left over the second stile on the left, from which a path leads past some old containers and young plantations. Fork left up the low dam wall of **Leadbeater Dam** and follow it right, crossing the other path again to reach the larger **Haigh Cote Dam**, a fine lunch spot unless it is particularly windy.

Leadbeater and **Haigh Cote Dams** were constructed in 1835 by the Cold Edge Dam Company to supply ten mills in the Wainstalls and Luddenden area, who paid rents for the water. It is topped up by a conduit from Warley Moor Reservoir and the name comes from Leadbeater and Stansfield, the company who constructed the dams.

5 Follow the right-side of **Haigh Cote Dam** to a stile before the water ski club building leading down onto the track below. Turn left along the track, passing a couple of farms before climbing up to **Cold Edge Road**. Head straight across the front of the old **Withens Hotel** and follow the track onto the moor. Turn left by the next fenceline, crossing Skirden Clough and following a fenceline across **Ovenden Moor**. Beyond the huge new wind turbines, drop steeply down into beautiful Ogden Clough.

6 Climb up beside the rocks of **Ogden Kirk** and turn left along the top. Hambleton Lane leads a broad route up onto the top of **Thornton Moor**, from where there are great views over Halifax, Bradford and Keighley.

7 From the top of **Thornton Moor**, continue along the well-defined path as it descends towards Oxenhope and Haworth is glimpsed for the first time. Go through a gate over the conduit at the bottom, then bear left at a sign, following the Brontë Way down the hill towards **Leeming Reservoir**. The sometimes boggy path runs parallel to an old walled track, then goes straight on across another conduit to descend into the trees near the reservoir.

a curlew, whose distinctive trill is commonly heard on Thornton Moor in early summer

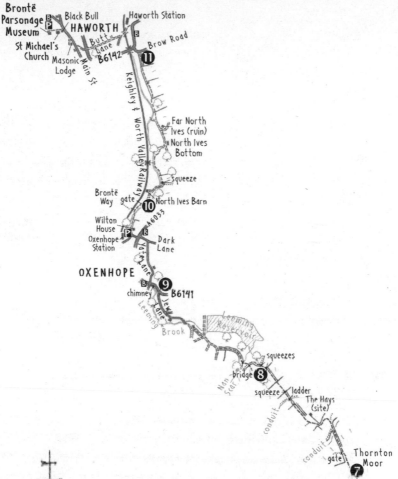

Brontë Parsonage Museum

Black Bull

HAWORTH

Haworth Station

St Michael's Church

Masonic Lodge

Main St

Butt Lane

B6142

Brow Road

11

Keighley & Worth Valley Railway

Far North Ives (ruin)

North Ives Bottom

squeeze

Brontë Way

gate

10

North Ives Barn

Wilton House

Oxenhope Station

B6033

Dark Lane

OXENHOPE

chimney

9

B6141

Jew Lane

Dove Lane

Leeming Brook

Leeming Reservoir

Man Scar

bridge

squeezes

8

squeeze

ladder

conduit

The Hays (site)

conduit

gate

Thornton Moor

7

the bright blue valve tower
at Leeming Reservoir

8 Emerging on a path at the bottom, turn left across the stream. At the next junction, descend right to cross another bridge and join a narrow walled pathway. At the end, follow the track right to the corner of **Leeming Reservoir**, where a signed path leads straight on down the slope. Turn right at the bottom and join Jew Lane running delightfully along **Leeming Brook**.

Jew Lane is thought to come from the Old English ceo (or chew), referring to a hollow.

⑨ **Jew Lane** continues all the way down to the B6141, which you follow left along the stream into **Oxenhope**. Turn right soon after an old chimney, following Yate Lane to its end. Turn left down Dark Lane and head straight across the main road. Turn right on the first bend, passing Wilton House and rejoining the stream, now **Bridgehouse Beck**. Cross the stream, but ignore the Brontë Way as it continues across the **Keighley & Worth Valley Railway**. Instead stay by the stream and soon join a track past the water works.

The Keighley & Worth Valley Railway is a single track branch line that was extended to Oxenhope due to persistence from local mill owners as Haworth was originally planned as the terminus. The line was closed in 1962 after the Beeching Report, but re-opened in 1968 as a volunteer-operated heritage railway specialising in serving real ale on-board and it thrives to this day.

Oxenhope is one of the most unspoilt villages in West Yorkshire, its grey terraces climbing across the hillsides of the Leeming Water. Rather than one village it is really a conglomeration of several hamlets, including Uppertown, Lowertown, Leeming, Shaw and Marsh. The name Oxenhope means 'valley of the oxen', referring to a time when it was part of the estate of Bradford Manor. Oxenhope only became the village's name when it was adopted by the station built as the terminus of the Keighley and Worth Valley Railway in 1867.

⑩ By **North Ives Barn**, bear right and cross Bridgehouse Beck again. Follow a lovely path along its right bank until it climbs up to **North Ives Bottom**. Turn left, passing in front of the farm and descending a narrow path to the ruin of Far North Ives. Carry straight on, rejoining the right bank of the stream. The path leads into fields, which you follow the bottom edge of all the way into **Haworth**.

⑪ Reaching Brow Road, turn left, then follow Station Road right to **Haworth Station**. A path leads left in front of the station and high over the railway. At the end continue straight on up the cobbles of Butt Lane. Carry on across the B6142, joining **Haworth's Main Street** near the Fleece Inn. After 100 yards you can divert left down Lodge Street, a beautiful dead-end square where you'll find the old **Masonic Lodge**. Continue up the hill to the **Black Bull**, one of Branwell's many hangouts, and turn left past the church to reach the end of the route at the **Brontë Parsonage Mueum**.

Branwell was an enthusiastic member of the Masonic Lodge in Haworth in his early twenties, acting as organist, junior warden and secretary before he left town in 1840.

Branwell returned to the **Parsonage** in Haworth in 1842 and by the end of the year had secured a position as tutor at Thorp Green, near York, where his sister Anne worked. He was dismissed in 1845 after an alleged affair with his employer's wife, and sank into a deep alcoholic depression for the last three years of his life. Despite his early precocious talent, Branwell died unrecognised and unfulfilled, but his personality, imagination, and ultimate self-destruction are integral elements in the Brontë story.

the original Parsonage in Haworth

BIBLIOGRAPHY

Throughout my journey, *The Brontës* (Abacus, 2010) by Juliet Barker has been my constant companion, as has *The Oxford Companion to the Brontës* (2018). Early on, I found inspiration in Ann Dinsdale and Mark Davis's *In the Footsteps of the Brontës* (Amberley, 2013). I've read many other books along the way. Here are some of them:

By the Brontës

Novels:

Anne Brontë, *Agnes Grey* (1847), *The Tenant of Wildfell Hall* (1848)

Charlotte Brontë, *The Professor* (posthumously published, 1857), *Jane Eyre* (1847), *Shirley* (1849), *Villette* (1853)

Emily Brontë, *Wuthering Heights* (1847)

Poetry:

Anne, Charlotte, Emily Brontë, *Poems* by Currer, Ellis and Acton Bell (1846)

Branwell Brontë, poems published in the *Bradford Herald*, *Halifax Guardian* and *Leeds Intelligencer* (1841–47)

Patrick Brontë, *Winter Evening Thoughts* (1810), *Cottage Poems* (1811), *The Rural Minstrel* (1813)

The Cottage in the Wood and *The Maid of Killarney* are included in *Brontëana*, ed. Joseph Horsfall Turner (1898)

Collected Poems:

Anne Brontë, *The Poems of Anne Brontë*, ed. Edward Chitham (1979)

Branwell Brontë, *The Poems of Patrick Branwell Brontë*, ed. Victor A. Neufeldt (1990)

Charlotte Brontë, *The Poems of Charlotte Brontë*, ed. Victor A. Neufeldt (1985)

Emily Brontë, *The Poems of Emily Brontë*, ed. Derek Roper with Edward Chitham (1995)

Biographies

Juliet Barker, *The Brontës* (Abacus, 2010)

Edward Chitham, *A Life of Emily Brontë* (Amberley, 1987)

Edward Chitham, *A Life of Anne Brontë* (Blackwell, 1991)

Stevie Davies, *Emily Brontë: Heretic* (The Women's Press, 1998)

Daphne du Maurier, *The Infernal World of Branwell Brontë* (Virago, 1960)

Samantha Ellis, *Take Courage: Anne Brontë and the Art of Life* (Chatto & Windus, 2017)

Sophie Franklin, *Charlotte Brontë Revisited* (Saraband, 2016)

Elizabeth Gaskell, *The Life of Charlotte Brontë* (1857)

Lyndall Gordon, *Charlotte Brontë: A Passionate Life* (Chatto & Windus, 1994)

Claire Harman, *Charlotte Brontë: A Life* (Penguin, 2015)

Adelle Hay, *Anne Brontë Reimagined* (Saraband, 2020)

John Lock and Canon Dixon, *A Man of Sorrow: The Life, Letters and Times of the Revd. Patrick Brontë, 1771–1861* (Nelson, 1965)

Claire O'Callaghan, *Emily Brontë Reappraised* (Saraband, 2018)

William Scruton, *The Brontës* (Arthur Dobson, 1968)

Books about the Luddites

Lionel Munby, *The Luddites: And Other Essays* (1971)

Robert Reid, *Land of Lost Content: The Luddite Revolt, 1812* (Penguin, 1988)

Malcolm Thomis, *The Luddites: Machine-Breaking in Regency England* (David & Charles, 1970)

John Wheatley, *Enoch's Hammer* (2019)

Miscellaneous

Mark Avery, *Inglorious: Conflict in the Uplands* (Bloomsbury, 2015)

Juliet Barker, *The Brontës: A Life in Letters* (Viking, 1997)

W. Greenhalgh, *Broughton-in-Furness and the Duddon Valley: A Guide and History* (1989)

Allan and Andrea Pentecost, *The Brontës in the English Lake District* (Cloudberry, 2016)

Michael Steed, *A Brontë Diary* (Dalesman, 1990)

John Sutherland, *Is Heathcliff a Murderer?: Puzzles in 19th-Century Fiction* (Oxford, 1996)

John Sutherland, *The Brontësaurus: An A–Z of Charlotte, Emily & Anne Brontë (& Branwell)* (Icon, 2016)

Marje Wilson, *The Brontë Way* (Ramblers' Association, 1997)

Steven Wood and Peter Brears, *The Real Wuthering Heights: The Story of the Withins Farm* (Amberley, 2016)

Common People: An Anthology of Working-Class Writers, ed. Kit de Waal (Unbound, 2019)

Theakston's Guide to Scarborough (1840)

Essays

Brontë Studies: The Journal of the Brontë Society, especially the following essays:

Edward Chitham, 'Law Hill and Emily Brontë: Behind Charlotte's Evasion'

Sophie Franklin, '"Ay, ay, divil, all's raight! We've smashed 'em!": Translating Violence and "Yorkshire Roughness" in Charlotte Brontë's *Shirley*'

Claire O'Callaghan, '"He is rather peculiar, perhaps": Reading Mr Rochester's Coarseness Queerly'

ACKNOWLEDGEMENTS

At some point along the journey, a book becomes a collaborative exercise, and perhaps this book more than most. I'd firstly like to thank all those writers and friends who have looked at various drafts of this and given me helpful feedback. They are: Simon Crump, Steve Ely, Jim Greenhalf, Wendy Pratt and Claire O'Callaghan.

I'd like to thank my agent Jemima Forrester at David Higham Associates for all her help and advice. A big thanks to everyone at HarperCollins and HQ Stories, especially to Lisa Milton, Kate Fox, Abigail Le Marquand-Brown and to Paul Murphy.

The maps in this book have been drawn and designed by Christopher Goddard and are reproduced here with his kind permission. The Wandering Bard map was commissioned by the Brontë Society and is reproduced with their permission (©The Brontë Society). The poems in this book by Kate Bush, Carol Ann Duffy, Jackie Kay, Wendy Pratt and Jeanette Winterson have been printed by kind permission of the authors.

I'd like to thank individual contributors who were kind enough to take a walk with me and give me their time, thoughts and ideas: Claire O'Callaghan, Sarah Fanning and Wendy Pratt.

A special thanks goes to everyone at the Brontë Society and

the Brontë Parsonage Museum, who have helped at every stage. In particular, I'd like to thank: Danielle Cadamarteri, Ann Dinsdale, Diane Fare, Harry Jelley, Sarah Laycock, Lauren Livesey, Sue Newby, Kitty Wright and Rebecca Yorke.

The journal *Brontë Studies* has been a great resource and source of expertise and scholarship, and I would like to thank the editorial panel for all their help.

The 'Boiled Milk' chapter first appeared as an ebook through the University of Huddersfield Press. Thanks to everyone at the press and at the university for their support: Monty Adkins, Dawn Cockcroft, Martin Gill, Zoe Johnson, Jessica Malay, Alison McNab and Catherine Parker.

In researching this book, I was allowed access to various archives, and I would like to thank everyone at Chetham's Library in Manchester; the Merseyside Maritime Museum and Central Library in Liverpool; and Scarborough Library, especially the librarian Angela Kale for going out of her way to source texts and images.

The Brontë Stones project was delivered in collaboration with the Bradford Literature Festival. I'd like to thank Stephen May at the Arts Council for brokering this relationship, and the then festival co directors, Syima Aslam and Irna Qureshi, for their support.

Finally, thanks to Donna and Christian Stretton for copious cups of sack. *Alis aquilae.*

ONE PLACE. MANY STORIES

Bold, innovative and
empowering publishing.

FOLLOW US ON:

@HQStories